MORNINGS
with JESUS
2022

DAILY ENCOURAGEMENT *for Your* SOUL

365 DEVOTIONS

SUSANNA FOTH AUGHTMON

JEANNIE BLACKMER

ISABELLA CAMPOLATTARO

PAT BUTLER DYSON

GWEN FORD FAULKENBERRY

GRACE FOX

HEIDI GAUL

SHARON HINCK

PAMELA TOUSSAINT HOWARD

JEANETTE LEVELLIE

DIANNE NEAL MATTHEWS

CYNTHIA RUCHTI

CASSANDRA TIERSMA

BARBRANDA LUMPKINS WALLS

Guideposts
Devotional

ZONDERVAN
BOOKS

ZONDERVAN BOOKS

Mornings with Jesus 2022
Copyright © 2021 by Guideposts. All rights reserved.

Requests for information should be addressed to:
Zondervan, *3900 Sparks Dr. SE, Grand Rapids, Michigan 49546*

Zondervan titles may be purchased in bulk for educational, business, fundraising, or sales promotional use. For information, please email SpecialMarkets@Zondervan.com.

ISBN 978-0-310-36332-3 (softcover)
ISBN 978-0-310-36533-4 (audio)
ISBN 978-0-310-36333-0 (ebook)

Scripture quotations marked (AMP) are taken from *The Amplified Bible* and *The Amplified Bible, Classic Edition*. Copyright © 2015 by The Lockman Foundation, La Habra, CA 90631. All rights reserved. Copyright © 1954, 1958, 1962, 1964, 1965, 1987 by The Lockman Foundation. Used by permission. www.Lockman.org • Scripture quotations marked (CEV) are taken from *Holy Bible: Contemporary English Version*. Copyright © 1995 American Bible Society. • Scripture quotations marked (ERV) are taken from *Easy-to-Read Version Bible*. Copyright © 2006 by Bible League International. • Scripture quotations marked (ESV) are taken from the *Holy Bible, English Standard Version*. Copyright © 2001 by Crossway Bibles, a division of Good News Publishers. Used by permission. All rights reserved. • Scripture quotations marked (GNT) are taken from *Good News Translation*. Copyright © 1992 by American Bible Society. • Scripture quotations marked (GW) are taken from *God's Word Translation*. Copyright © 1995 by God's Word to the Nations. Used by permission of Baker Publishing Group. • Scripture quotations marked (HCSB) are taken from the *Holman Christian Standard Bible*. Copyright © 1999, 2000, 2002, 2003 by Holman Bible Publishers, Nashville, Tennessee. All rights reserved. • Scripture quotations marked (ICB) are taken from *The Holy Bible, International Children's Bible*. Copyright© 1986, 1988, 1999, 2015 by Tommy Nelson, a division of Thomas Nelson. Used by permission. • Scripture quotations marked (ISV) are taken from *The International Standard Version of the Bible*. Copyright © 1995-2014 by ISV Foundation. All rights reserved internationally. Used by permission of Davidson Press, LL. • Scripture quotations marked (KJV) are taken from *The King James Version of the Bible*. • Scripture quotations marked (MSG) are taken from *The Message*. Copyright © 1993, 1994, 1995, 1996, 2000, 2001, 2002 by Eugene H. Peterson. • Scripture quotations marked (NASB) are taken from the *New American Standard Bible*. Copyright © 1960, 1962, 1963, 1968, 1971, 1972, 1973, 1975, 1977, 1995 by the Lockman Foundation. Used by permission. www.Lockman.org • Scripture quotations marked (NCV) are taken from the *New Century Version*. Copyright © 2005 by Thomas Nelson, Inc. Used by permission. All rights reserved. • Scripture quotations marked (NIV) are taken from *The Holy Bible, New International Version*. Copyright © 1973, 1978, 1984, 2011 by Biblica, Inc. Used by permission of Zondervan. All rights reserved worldwide. www.Zondervan.com. • Scripture quotations marked (NKJV) are taken from *The Holy Bible, New King James Version*. Copyright © 1983, 1985, 1990, 1997 by Thomas Nelson, Inc. • Scripture quotations marked (NLT) are taken from the *Holy Bible, New Living Translation*. Copyright © 1996. Used by permission of Tyndale House Publishers, Inc., Wheaton, Illinois 60189. All rights reserved. • Scripture quotations marked (NRSV) are taken from the *New Revised Standard Version Bible*. Copyright © 1989 by the Division of Christian Education of the National Council of the Churches of Christ in the U.S.A. Used by permission. All rights reserved. • Scripture quotations marked (RSV) are taken from the *Revised Standard Version of the Bible*. Copyright © 1946, 1952, and 1971 the Division of Christian Education of the National Council of the Churches of Christ in the United States of America. Used by permission. All rights reserved. • Scripture quotations marked (TLB) are taken from *The Living Bible*. Copyright © 1971 by Tyndale House Foundation. Used by permission of Tyndale House Publishers Inc., Carol Stream, Illinois 60188. All rights reserved. • Scripture quotations marked (TPT) are taken from *The Passion Translation*. Copyright © 2016 by Broadstreet Publishing Group, Savage, Minnesota. All rights reserved.

Any internet addresses (websites, blogs, etc.) and telephone numbers in this book are offered as a resource. They are not intended in any way to be or imply an endorsement by Zondervan, nor does Zondervan vouch for the content of these sites and numbers for the life of this book.

Cover and interior design by Müllerhaus
Cover photo by Shutterstock
Indexed by Indexing Research
Typeset by Aptara, Inc.

Printed in the United States of America

21 22 23 24 25 26 27 28 29 30 31 32 33 /LSC/ 17 16 15 14 13 12 11 10 9 8 7 6 5 4 3 2

Dear Friends,

Welcome to *Mornings with Jesus 2022*! Whether you are a new reader or are already familiar with this devotional, know that each reading, like the voice of a trusted friend, offers inspiration, hope, and the peace that comes from walking with Him.

Our theme this year is, "Courage" as found in Psalm 31:24: *"Be of good courage, and He shall strengthen your heart, all you who hope in the* LORD*"* (NKJV). In 365 new devotions, fourteen women of faith share stories of how Jesus strengthens their hearts as they walk with Him every day. As you read the daily Scripture and narrative and contemplate the "Faith Step," we pray that you will draw closer into fellowship with Jesus.

This year Susanna Foth Aughtmon shares the lessons she learned in a series called "Transitions." Sharon Hinck reflects on the Beatitudes, and Jeanette Levellie meditates on Holy Week. Isabella Yosuico, writing now as Isabella Campolattaro, talks about the grace found after divorce. Heidi Gaul shines a light on Advent and the joy and expectation that lead into Christmas. Returning, too, are veterans Gwen Ford Faulkenberry, Grace Fox, Dianne Neal Matthews, and Cynthia Ruchti. Jeannie Blackmer, Pat Butler Dyson, and Pamela Toussaint Howard are back as well. Two new voices, Cassandra Tiersma and Barbranda Lumpkins Walls, join the chorus, sharing grace notes and wisdom about the presence of Jesus in their daily lives.

It is our hope that *Mornings with Jesus 2022* will put a song in your heart and encourage you to take a daily "Faith Step" that draws you closer to Jesus.

Faithfully yours,
Editors of Guideposts

P.S. We love hearing from you! Let us know what *Mornings with Jesus 2022* means to you by emailing BookEditors@guideposts.org or writing to Guideposts Books & Inspirational Media, 100 Reserve Road, Suite E200, Danbury 06810-5212. You can also keep up with your *Mornings with Jesus* friends on facebook.com/MorningswithJesus.

Especially for You!

Enjoy the daily encouragement of *Mornings with Jesus 2022* wherever you are! Receive each day's devotion on your computer, tablet, or smartphone. Visit MorningswithJesus.org/MWJ2022 and enter this code: courage. Sign up for the online newsletter *Mornings with Jesus* at Guideposts .org/newsletter-sign-up. Each week, you'll receive an inspiring devotion or personal thoughts from one of the writers about her own devotional time and prayer life and how focusing on Jesus influenced her relationship with Him and others!

New Year's Day, Saturday, January 1

Because of the LORD's great love we are not consumed, for his compassions never fail. They are new every morning; great is your faithfulness. Lamentations 3:22–23 (NIV)

OUR DOG, FLASH, HAD A new experience this winter: snow. This Jack Russell-Chihuahua mix seemed tentative about the snow at first. (Or maybe it was just the fact that we dressed him in a gray sweater with a pom-pom on the hood before letting him outside!) It took him all of ten seconds to plunge into the wintry wonder of our snow-covered backyard. He got up to his belly in snow and left tracks circling the entire yard. You could almost sense his pleasure at being the first to leave his mark. He was an adventurer, going where no dog had gone before.

New Year's Day feels to me like a pristine snow-covered yard too. Fresh. Clean. Full of possibilities. It is the grand reboot, a new start. I get to plunge in and forge a new path.

Jesus is all about reboots and fresh starts. The amazing thing is, He doesn't hold my mess-ups against me. Instead, He offers mercy and love and a truckload of forgiveness. He has a new plan for me. He wants me to follow Him on a new adventure this year, one where He leads me with the light of His hope and strengthens me with His power. He intends to use my gifts, dreams, and compassion to leave His mark on the world. —SUSANNA FOTH AUGHTMON

FAITH STEP: *What kind of clean start do you need this year? Take a moment to own up to your mess-ups and ask Jesus to forgive you and empower you, giving you a new start as you head into the new year.*

SUNDAY, JANUARY 2 ✓

Grow in the grace and knowledge of our Lord and Savior Jesus Christ.
To him be the glory both now and to the day of eternity. Amen.
2 Peter 3:18 (ESV)

FOR THE PAST FEW YEARS, I've chosen a word for each year. My word last year was *grow*. I desired growth in all areas of life, but I especially wanted to know Jesus more. I chose this word hesitantly, because often growth comes from pain. But as Jesus said, "In this world you will have trouble. But take heart! I have overcome the world" (John 16:33, NIV). I chose the word *grow* anyway and decided I would try to consider all circumstances (whether good or bad) as opportunities to know and experience Jesus more deeply.

Some unexpected painful events occurred. My husband had a setback with his hip implant, one of my sons lost his job, and I had my own bouts with purposelessness. Yet because I intentionally wanted to grow, I wasn't overcome by my circumstances. I stayed in constant contact with Jesus, asking Him to show me what He wanted me to know about Him. When my husband's hip pain was resolved, Jesus reminded me that He cares about our physical health. My son dealt with his job loss and grew in his trust that Jesus works all things out for good. My need for purpose caused me to think creatively. I discovered new projects and possibilities, which renewed my hope that Jesus cares about my future.

In the past year, day by day, morning by morning, I've grown in my knowledge of Jesus. And knowing Him more intimately has increased my love and dependence on Him, for now and for eternity.
—JEANNIE BLACKMER

FAITH STEP: *Choose a word for the year that you can focus on to help you grow and know Jesus more deeply.*

MONDAY, JANUARY 3 ✓

*A man who has friends must himself be friendly, but there is a friend
who sticks closer than a brother. Proverbs 18:24 (NKJV)*

I DIDN'T LINGER AFTER BIBLE study to chat with my friends as I usually did. I had too much to do. As I zoomed out of my parking spot, I caught sight of my friend Linda frantically waving at me. *Not now, Jesus!* She had a dead battery and needed a jump to get going. This shouldn't take long. Linda got her jumper cables, and we hooked them up. I revved my engine, hoping that would hurry the charge. Linda turned the key. Nothing. We charged some more. When she tried again, all we heard were some discouraging clicks.

"Can you give me a ride home, Pat?" Linda asked. How could I say no? "Oh, and we'll need to stop and pick up my dog from the vet." My heart sank. Now I would never get all my errands done. What would Jesus do? Furthermore, what would Linda do? I had no doubt about the answer in either case.

In 1855, Joseph M. Scriven wrote a poem to comfort his mother, who was living in Ireland while he was in Canada. This poem was set to music in 1868 by Charles C. Converse and has become one of the most beloved Christian hymns of all times: "What a Friend We Have in Jesus." Jesus set a high standard of what a true friend should be. As the hymn goes, "Can we find a friend so faithful, / Who will all our sorrows share?" No one is a better friend than Jesus. Nothing on my to-do list was more important than helping my friend. —PAT BUTLER DYSON

FAITH STEP: *Are you the kind of friend Jesus would want to have?*

TUESDAY, JANUARY 4 ✓

---

*The Lord is not slow in keeping his promise, as some understand
slowness. Instead he is patient with you, not wanting anyone to perish,
but everyone to come to repentance. 2 Peter 3:9 (NIV)*

RECENTLY, I NOTICED THAT MY son, Pierce, was on his computer, flipping between two programs to do his schoolwork. The inefficiency made me both batty and curious, so I asked what he was doing. He explained he was fast-forwarding through a twenty-minute video in one program and searching for the answers to related comprehension questions in another. He was cutting corners by skipping back and forth, and as a result, he was harrumphing with frustration at his method.

I explained not only that what he was doing was more time-consuming than watching the video in its entirety but also that he wasn't really learning anything. His answers were vague, and he was missing the whole point! As I spoke to Pierce and pointed a proverbial finger at him—my three other fingers pointed back at me. Sigh.

Throughout my life, before and after Christ, I've sought shortcuts to get what I wanted, skipped ahead of Jesus's story for me, or worse, created my own. I suspect my shortcuts actually delayed outcomes, prolonged my learning and preparation, undermined the results, and in general, was far more stressful.

I've learned the hard way that slowing way down and being fully present to Jesus's unfolding story is indeed the easier and infinitely more effective way. Even when I feel certain I have an inspired vision of where He's taking me, restfully waiting on God allows me to marvel, with peace and faith, at His creativity and loving provision.
—ISABELLA CAMPOLATTARO

FAITH STEP: *Are you rushing ahead of Jesus to get to a certain place? Confess your haste and ask Him to help you slow down. Set a goal for waiting and then keep pace with His slower pace.*

WEDNESDAY, JANUARY 5 ✓

Remember the LORD in everything you do, and he will show you the right way. Proverbs 3:6 (GNT)

NEVER MIND BAD HAIR DAYS, I have issues with my eyebrows: flying off in different directions, acting bushy and bold when I need them to lay flat, and even—*horrors*—turning gray. How dare they!

Having a lifelong aversion to pain, I'm not one to pluck renegade hairs from my face. I thought about coloring my eyebrows when I do my hair, but then I'd risk dripping color in my eyes. No thanks.

So I decide to shape them. A little snip here, a little eyebrow pencil there. Now I look like I'm shocked on my left side and angry on my right. This is fine if you look at only one side of my face or my profile. Otherwise, it appears I can't make up my mind.

Finally, desperate to end this foolishness, I cry out to Jesus, *Help me, Lord!* It embarrasses me to ask the Master of all creation for help with wonky eyebrows. But I've discovered that *Help me, Lord* is the wisest prayer ever.

True to His word and His nature, Jesus came to my rescue. He gave me the bright idea to let my eyebrows do their own thing. Now I'm free to concentrate on more important issues: relationships, work, creating the next sermon or devotional story.

I sigh in relief and thank Him for His infinite kindness. My requests—or panicky pleas—for help honor Him. He's pleased when I acknowledge that He's smarter than I am. After all, He invented eyebrows. —JEANETTE LEVELLIE

FAITH STEP: *If you, like me, let minor irritations bother you, choose one and pray the wisest prayer ever:* Help me, Jesus! *Now get ready for His creative solution.*

THURSDAY, JANUARY 6 ✓

He said to me, "My grace is sufficient for you, for my power is made perfect in weakness." Therefore I will boast all the more gladly about my weaknesses, so that Christ's power may rest on me. 2 Corinthians 12:9 (NIV)

MY GUIDEPOSTS EDITOR INVITED ME to write about my divorce, both to help others and to explain my name change. I agreed because I knew readers might be curious and I'm always motivated by a desire to comfort and encourage others—but the divorce is still new. Plus, how would I share about it in three hundred words or less?

After taking time to think about what I wanted to say, I can say this with joyous certainty: Jesus's grace is indeed sufficient. When I was weak, He was strong. *He* alone is powerful.

Jesus's grace was sufficient when I insisted on marrying even though God said no. Sufficient to keep me in a marriage that was difficult from the onset. Sufficient to enable me to grow in dry and rocky soil. Sufficient to give me two wonderful children I thought I'd never have. Sufficient for them to continue to flourish despite the divorce. Sufficient to forgive myself and my ex-husband for our considerable failures. Sufficient to know we can all have a good future when we keep Jesus as our focus. Sufficient to have a kind and cooperative relationship with my ex-husband now. Sufficient to see Him pouring out blessing upon blessing, grace upon grace.

Jesus is more than able, more than willing, and more than enough. And none of it depends on my goodness. Hosanna!

—ISABELLA CAMPOLATTARO

FAITH STEP: *Reflect on a difficulty in your life. Invite Jesus to help you see His amazing grace.*

FRIDAY, JANUARY 7 ✓

It is God who works in you to will and to act in order to fulfill his good purpose. Philippians 2:13 (NIV)

I LOVE FLOWERS. DURING THE dark winter months, my husband, Dave, sometimes brings home bouquets. Nothing fancy, just a mixed batch to brighten my day. My husband knows those blooms give me hope for the future. So does Jesus.

One day, my mood was anything but cheery. A dream for which I'd been saving money for years had fallen through, and I couldn't stop crying. Unsettled thoughts left me shaken, wishing for a sign—for some way to know Jesus was watching and listening. As afternoon turned to evening, I busied myself with preparing dinner while awaiting Dave's return home from his work at a nearby store.

He entered the kitchen, two dozen long-stemmed roses overflowing in his arms. I paused before accepting them. *How could we justify buying expensive flowers, especially now?* Dave sensed my hesitation and explained the flowers had been about to be discarded. They'd cost nothing.

I held the delicate buds close. These were much more than simple castoffs. Yes, my caring husband had spotted the roses and rescued them from the trash, acting on Jesus's prompting.

But Jesus had picked them out for me. He'd heard my cry and stepped in to wipe away the tears, as He does for all of us. Some days He sends a friend to visit. Other mornings we might suspect the words of a devotion were written specifically for our needs. And sometimes He shares a loved one's heart and hands to present us with two dozen roses. —HEIDI GAUL

FAITH STEP: *Find ways to be the hands of Jesus for others. A call, a card, or even a smile can be enough to share His much-needed love with others.*

SATURDAY, JANUARY 8

We proclaim to you what we have seen and heard, so that you also may have fellowship with us. And our fellowship is with the Father and with his Son, Jesus Christ. 1 John 1:3 (NIV)

LAST NIGHT, MY YOUNGEST DAUGHTER, who lives in Nashville, organized a family game night over the internet. My older daughter in New York and her boyfriend joined in, and my husband and I participated from our couch in Minnesota. At one point, my younger son, also in New York, popped in to say hello. We played Trivial Pursuit, wheedled for clues, argued the validity of answers, and laughed until we were exhausted. When we signed off, my heart felt warmer than it had in days. Even with geographic distance between us, I felt the glow of fellowship.

There are days when the world feels stark and cold. I sometimes struggle with loneliness even when plenty of people are around. My failings and guilt can make me feel cut off from the Father. Yet the testimony of Jesus's disciples in Scripture breaks through the lie that I am alone.

Because of Jesus, my relationship with God is restored. As a follower of Jesus, I'm invited into a huge family that spans continents, languages, and time. Just as an internet link brought my family together, Jesus connects me with Himself and all who believe in Him. When I lift my voice in worship, I join a mighty chorus. When I grieve, I never grieve alone. And as I wait for His return, I serve with courage side by side with other believers. My work is lighter because I have fellowship in Christ. —SHARON HINCK

FAITH STEP: *Reconnect with an old friend today. Thank Jesus for the gift of fellowship that He provides.*

SUNDAY, JANUARY 9 ✓

Jesus said, "Let the little children come to me, and do not hinder them, for the kingdom of heaven belongs to such as these." Matthew 19:14 (NIV)

I OPENED THE DOOR TO the children's church classroom last Sunday, excited to teach little Marissa, who followed right behind me. I hadn't always felt eager about this way of serving Jesus.

My husband, Kevin, and I pastor a small rural congregation, and Sunday mornings used to exhaust me. I taught a ladies' Sunday school class, led songs and prayer time during the worship service, and then taught children's church. Often there was only one child. Sometimes two. I came home feeling as if I'd put in a full day of work. I sometimes wondered, *Is it worth all this effort?*

One Sunday morning as I entered the kids' classroom, Jesus spoke to my heart. In a voice rich with love, He whispered, "Jeanette, this is the most important thing you do every Sunday."

Really, Lord? These one or two children?

Suddenly I remembered how much Jesus values little ones. How He rebuked His followers for trying to prevent children from coming to Him. How He took the kids in His arms and blessed them. How He told the disciples that we must become like children to enter the kingdom of God.

Children are a priority with Jesus. Each one matters to Him. As only He can, Jesus loves these little ones in a big way. Every minute I spend with either one child or many—teaching, guiding, and modeling Jesus's esteem for them—is never wasted. I am planting seeds for the future and for eternity. —JEANETTE LEVELLIE

FAITH STEP: *Remember what it was like to be a child, when the world was sometimes scary and overwhelming. Do something kind for a child today.*

MONDAY, JANUARY 10 ✓

In the beginning was the Word, and the Word was with God, and the Word was God. John 1:1 (NKJV)

BACK IN COLLEGE, WHEN I first accepted Jesus, I was eager to learn all I could about this Man who forgave me and cleansed me of my sin. I was already an avid reader, so I dug into the Bible and read as much as I could, not understanding everything but enjoying the journey. I discovered different translations that gave me more insight and understanding; some used plainer words while others made stories out of every principle.

After a while, I saw the value of not only reading the Word but also memorizing certain passages. I would get up at dawn, and while everyone was still asleep, I would stand in our little front hallway and repeat Scriptures aloud. I would personalize the verses by inserting *I, me,* or *my.* Doing this made the Word of God come alive in my heart as a declaration of faith, not just rote memorization. Little did I know that I was hiding Jesus's precious promises in my heart so that when trials and troubles came, I could rely on His Word. I built up an arsenal of spiritual weapons to use instantly in those situations when searching for a Bible verse would not have been expedient or even possible. Now as I speak His Word with authority, I know that He is with Me and that His Word will come to pass. —PAMELA TOUSSAINT HOWARD

FAITH STEP: *Choose a Scripture verse that's meaningful to you. Meditate on it and memorize it, and watch His Word come alive in your life.*

TUESDAY, JANUARY 11 ✓

*The LORD takes pleasure in those who fear him, in those who
hope in his steadfast love.* Psalm 147:11 (ESV)

I HAD TO LAUGH WHEN my daughter, Holly, texted a conversation
she'd just had with her four-year-old daughter Lilah: *We were listening
to VeggieTales in the car and Lilah was singing along, and then she
stopped and said, "I think I just heard God speak to me! In my heart!"
And I said, "Yeah, what did He say?" And she said, "I appreciate that."*
When Lilah was three, I'd watched through the window as she
played alone on the patio. Suddenly, she dropped her toy and stood
still as a statue. When I noticed her lips moving, Holly smiled and
assured me that Lilah must be praying. Holly had recently seen Lilah
standing in the yard looking up at the sky, telling God how she loves
Him "so, so, so much." No agenda, no requests. Just a simple response
because of her understanding of who Jesus is and what He means to
her. What a powerful reminder of something I too easily forget.

Many Scriptures command me to honor, worship, and praise
the Lord, not because He needs it but because He deserves it. And
because *I* need it. Whether it's a natural outburst in response to blessings or an act of obedience during tough times, praise sets things in
motion. It changes my attitude and focus, infusing me with joy. It
strengthens my faith and helps me grow closer to Him. Most importantly, it brings Him pleasure. What other reason could I possibly
need to praise Him every single day? —DIANNE NEAL MATTHEWS

FAITH STEP: *Before you bring your requests to Jesus today, take time to tell Him
how much you love Him. Imagine Him smiling as He listens to you.*

WEDNESDAY, JANUARY 12 ✓

Jesus was praying in private and his disciples were with him. Luke 9:18 (NIV)

I READ THE BIBLE THROUGH twenty-first-century lenses, so it's not unusual when some of the terms or wording strikes me as curious. Luke 9:18 is one of those verses for me: "Jesus was praying in private and his disciples were with him."

So which was it? Was Jesus alone or was He with people? Both. He was off at a safe enough distance that the disciples couldn't distract Him or likely even hear what He was saying in prayer. He wasn't praying *so* they could hear. In this instance, He prayed privately to His Father.

Alone yet with others. It's a compelling concept. A widow may be technically alone but have friends and extended family still in "the circle," and even with them around, so much of the widow's journey is a solo walk. A student may arrive on a college campus, not knowing one other person, but that status might not last as long as the trek to the dorm. Though surrounded by soon-to-be friends, at the moment the student's overwhelming feeling is aloneness.

Jesus found a way to be both with people and alone with His Father. It's a challenge for us, isn't it? The family, coworkers, friends, or tasks calling out for my attention can so easily distract me. I'm going to spend some time today watching for creative ways to both be with those I care about and be alone with Jesus. Join me?
—CYNTHIA RUCHTI

FAITH STEP: *What's your chosen way of expressing "Do Not Disturb" when you're spending time alone with Jesus? If you don't have a method, spend creative energy thinking it through today.*

THURSDAY, JANUARY 13

May the God who gives endurance and encouragement give you the same attitude of mind toward each other that Christ Jesus had. Romans 15:5 *(NIV)*

CRUISING ALONG THE HIGHWAY, I saw a giant banner across the back of a semitruck announcing, "Test in Progress." Switching lanes to bypass this, I was struck by this concept of preparing other drivers for possible mistakes by disclosing that the driver wasn't perfect. I wondered, *If I wore a T-shirt emblazoned with "Test in Progress," encouraging people to be understanding if I made mistakes—not just on the road but in life—would people be more patient and accepting of my flaws and imperfections?*

How significant, those three simple words: *test in progress.* They describe the entire human race. Everyone's undergoing some kind of test in progress. We just don't broadcast it with a banner on our backside. When I reflect on various tests in progress among my own family and friends, I recall struggles with addictions, income losses, unpaid bills, eviction threats, terminal illnesses. These tests, and more, are the daily reality for people we pass on the highway of life.

 While I was desiring extra grace for myself, Jesus reminded me to have a heart of compassion for others. I want to have an attitude like Jesus for people enduring personal hardship that's not proclaimed on a banner. —CASSANDRA TIERSMA

FAITH STEP: *Whether at home, at church, at work, or on the highway, consider each person you meet as someone undergoing a test in progress that you may not be aware of. Will you switch lanes to bypass them? Or will you offer a word of encouragement? Ask Jesus to give you the same attitude He has for others. Thank Him for loving and accepting us wherever we are in our test in progress.*

FRIDAY, JANUARY 14 ✓

Set a guard over my mouth, LORD; keep watch over the door of my lips.
Psalm 141:3 (NIV)

I ENJOY WATCHING NBC's *Today* show as part of my morning routine. One day, I heard news anchor Craig Melvin share a story about riding the elevator at work with a colleague. After noticing the woman's round tummy, Melvin cheerfully asked her, "So when are you due?" Much to his dismay, she looked at him and replied, "I'm not pregnant." Mortified by his gaffe, Melvin quickly exited the elevator at the next stop—and it wasn't even his floor!

I chuckled at the story, but I could certainly relate. My mother often told me as a child, "Think before you speak." But I still fall short of always heeding that wise advice. How many times have I said something and immediately wished I could snatch back the words as soon as they left my mouth? An unkind comment about a colleague. Harsh criticism of my husband. Complaints about my life. Words that have hurt others and reflected badly on me as a Christian and, even worse, have not glorified God.

James, the brother of Jesus, does not mince words when he talks about the power of the tongue: "The tongue also is a fire, a world of evil among the parts of the body. It corrupts the whole body, sets the whole course of one's life on fire, and is itself set on fire by hell" (James 3:6, NIV). Even King David asked the Lord to set a guard over his mouth, as we see in Psalm 141:3. And like David, I ask Jesus every day to be a guard over my mouth too.
—BARBRANDA LUMPKINS WALLS

FAITH STEP: *Do some quick thinking before you speak. Before you make a comment, ask yourself,* Is it true? Is it kind? Is it necessary?

SATURDAY, JANUARY 15 ✓

Every good and perfect gift is from above, coming down from the Father of the heavenly lights, who does not change like shifting shadows.
James 1:17 (NIV)

MY HUSBAND, SCOTT, AND I have a family tradition of giving our sons big surprises when they turn sixteen. We choose experiences that encourage their creativity and fill them with joy. When our son Jack turned sixteen, we surprised him with tickets for him and Scott to see *Hamilton*, the acclaimed Broadway show. Jack had memorized the musical's soundtrack months before, and his excitement was palpable. For our son Will's birthday, we promised to buy him a piano once we moved to Idaho. (A used piano on Craigslist. We have our limits!) Hearing Will play for hours on end has been a gift for all of us. Our son Addison has two years before he turns sixteen, but I'm already pondering the perfect gift. I love surprising the people I love with good gifts. It brings me a whole lot of joy.

Jesus feels the same way. He is the giver of good and perfect gifts. He got that trait from His heavenly Father. Jesus knows me inside and out. The hopes and dreams that fill my thoughts. The big and small desires of my heart. And unlike me, He has no limits. He provides amazing, life-altering gifts. He begins by offering forgiveness, mercy, and a new way of living. He delights in us. His love surrounds us. And that's just the beginning. —SUSANNA FOTH AUGHTMON

FAITH STEP: *In the spirit of Jesus, give a loved one a thoughtful gift, like a hand-written note or a gift card. Prepare to feel His joy!*

SUNDAY, JANUARY 16 ✓

Remember the Sabbath day by keeping it holy. Exodus 20:8 *(NIV)*

I TEND TO BE A fairly organized person. Until I am not. The other day I walked into my closet and it looked like a cyclone had hit it. Clothes that needed to go to Goodwill were piled in one corner. Old files and papers were stacked on top of plastic bins of summer clothes. Wrapping paper and tape were leaning against the back wall, along with random workout equipment and a giant foam roller. In the other corner stood an ironing board. The closet felt cluttered and claustrophobic. When things get too cluttered in my life, I feel like I can't breathe. I had to block out a chunk of time the next day to get everything sorted. The process was restorative.

My weekdays are a lot like my closet. They are crowded with work, appointments, cleaning, cooking, and taxiing my children to school and back. The weekends aren't much better. Somehow, the Sabbath tends to get away from me, but I know I need that margin—that day of rest—to be able to connect with Jesus and breathe. Jesus didn't only honor the Sabbath, but He also incorporated margin, extra time in His life, communing with His Father daily. He knew that the crush of life was too much to bear without that sacred time of rest and connection. He invites me to find that same rejuvenation with Him. He knows that I need the restorative process of connecting with Him, hearing His voice, and finding rest in His presence. —SUSANNA FOTH AUGHTMON

FAITH STEP: *Find some sacred margin in your week to spend time with Jesus. Block out time each day to connect in prayer and worship with the One who loves you most of all.*

MARTIN LUTHER KING JR. DAY, MONDAY, JANUARY 17 ✓

For as we have many members in one body, but all the members do not have the same function. Romans 12:4 *(NKJV)*

I SOMETIMES COMPARE MYSELF WITH friends in an unfavorable light. *I wish I had the talent to knit like Marie does. Why don't I enjoy cleaning as much as Betty?* If I'm not careful, I may covet someone else's talents.

And then I consider heroes who inspire me, but I'm not jealous of them: humanitarian Mother Teresa, author and speaker Helen Keller, and civil rights leader Reverend Doctor Martin Luther King Jr., a minister who used his gifts of leadership and speech to lift up the downtrodden.

Dr. King received his bachelor's degree in sociology at age nineteen and his doctorate at age twenty-six. He could've chosen a prestigious career. Instead, he followed God's call to engage the powerful weapons of prayer, words of reconciliation, and peaceful demonstrations. King brought light into the darkness for millions. He changed the world.

I may never implement the changes made by Dr. King. Yet Jesus calls me to make a positive difference with the gifts He's given me. I can use my talent of communication to help change a heart from despair to hope. I can employ my flair for humor to help a timid person feel at ease.

Dr. King said it best himself: "Everybody can be great . . . because anybody can serve. You don't have to have a college degree to serve. You only need a heart full of grace. A soul generated by love."

Like Dr. King, all of us have been given the opportunity to serve in our own unique ways—ways that will change the world.
—JEANETTE LEVELLIE

FAITH STEP: *Ask Jesus to help you utilize your special gifts to make a positive difference in someone's life and the world.*

TUESDAY, JANUARY 18

Work willingly at whatever you do, as though you were working for the Lord rather than for people. Colossians 3:23 (NLT)

I'M THE QUEEN OF PROCRASTINATION. Often, when facing a new project, I have to muster up the courage to start. With a recent writing assignment, I did all sorts of other tasks before I got started. I swept the garage, threw out old stuff from the fridge—I even cleaned the fish tank. I busied myself with a few more distractions until I decided it was too late in the day to start because my creative juices flow best in the morning. Once I did start writing, the words flowed, time flew, and I felt a peaceful satisfaction when done.

So why do I procrastinate? Truthfully, I fear what others will think of me. But allowing that fear to control my actions, or inaction, only leads to more anxiety. It's a vicious cycle. When I find myself stuck in this cycle, I know I have to look to Jesus as my inspiration. He never procrastinated. He was always about His Father's work (John 5:17; Luke 2:49). He never cared what others thought about Him. He did His work for His Father, not to please people. To overcome my fear and to do my work for God rather than people, I now try these three simple steps: first, ask Jesus for help; second, recite Colossians 3:23; and third, start!

When I'm tempted to procrastinate, I take a moment and ask myself, *Am I working for the Lord or for people?* Once I truly believe my work is for Him, I gain the courage to start. —JEANNIE BLACKMER

FAITH STEP: *Write down a task you need to start, pray for Jesus to help, and specify a time for doing it. Then do it wholeheartedly for the Lord.*

WEDNESDAY, JANUARY 19

Now to him who is able to do immeasurably more than all we ask or imagine, according to his power that is at work within us, to him be glory in the church and in Christ Jesus throughout all generations, for ever and ever! Amen.
Ephesians 3:20–21 (NIV)

"DAYS PASS, YEARS VANISH, AND we walk sightless among miracles." Hearing those words from a Jewish friend's Sabbath prayer were a wake-up call. For weeks, I'd lived life as if in a trance, with each day starting and ending the same. It was time to actively live, to open my eyes and ears—and soul—to the miracles taking place around me. How many blessings had I let slip by unnoticed?

Making myself fully aware of God's blessings and miracles wouldn't be easy. I'm a creature of habit. I started with breakfast, switching out my usual meal for a slice of toast slathered with raspberry jam. My mouth watered. Bypassing the kitchen table, I stepped outside on the porch, where the rocker called to me. Soon, I heard the steady buzz of a hummingbird at the feeder, and an instant later it floated in front of me. Its beak inches from my face, it gazed at me intently. That tiny, perfectly formed creature hooked me. Jesus's creation includes all things, seen and unseen (Col. 1:16, John 1:3). When I have eyes to see, ears to hear, and a heart to perceive (Deut. 29:3–4, NKJV), I can acknowledge the miracles and blessings surrounding me, and live life to the fullest (John 10:10). Praise be to Jesus. —HEIDI GAUL

FAITH STEP: *Start a blessings journal, and make note of every blessing, miracle, and wonder that Jesus gifts you with.*

THURSDAY, JANUARY 20

Show me your ways, LORD, teach me your paths. Guide me in your truth and teach me, for you are God my Savior, and my hope is in you all day long.
Psalm 25:4–5 (NIV)

EVERY JANUARY, I ATTEND A retreat that helps ready me for the year's ministry demands. I've developed friendships there, and one of those friends enjoys watercolor painting. She began posting pictures of her art on Facebook. The beauty of her paintings inspired me to try, but I didn't know where to begin. So, one year, I packed a paint palette and a pad of watercolor paper for the retreat. When we had free time in our schedule, I asked my artist friend to teach me some beginner techniques.

Show-and-tell works best for me when I want to learn a new skill. Listening to someone tell me what to do is okay, but combining that with watching a demonstration makes a world of difference for me.

Jesus knew that show-and-tell is an effective way to teach spiritual truths too. On one occasion the disciples asked Him to teach them to pray (Luke 11:1). Using words, He gave them a template to follow. Not only did Jesus use words to instruct them, but He also demonstrated by example. He rose early in the mornings to talk with His Father (Mark 1:35). He prayed before performing miracles and when in distress (Matthew 14:19–21; Luke 22:44).

Jesus knew how best to instruct me for victorious living. He taught me with His words, and then He demonstrated with His life. Now let me do as He did. —GRACE FOX

FAITH STEP: *Jesus taught and lived a holy life. Ask Him to help you follow His example.*

FRIDAY, JANUARY 21 ✓

Be on your guard; stand firm in the faith; be courageous;
be strong. 1 Corinthians 16:13 (NIV)

BEFORE GETTING DRESSED, I PUT on the bracelet my husband, Jeff, had given me for my birthday. I rarely wear jewelry, but I always wore this bracelet when I needed to *feel* the words engraved on it: *Unexpected Strength.*

My friend Wendy, who'd suffered a stroke and couldn't drive, rode with me to our annual mammogram appointments. I was worried about Wendy's risk of falling, and she often did fall. Besides that, I'd noticed an unusual spot on my breast. My mother had endured breast cancer, and every time I got a mammogram, I feared a similar diagnosis. Amplifying my anxiety was the horrendous Houston traffic. I begged Jesus to give me the strength I so desperately needed.

We finally arrived, and I removed Wendy's walker from the back of my car. The valet took the keys from my trembling hands and gave me a ticket, which I promptly lost. My heart pounded, panic overtaking me. *Jesus, help!*

Wendy and I located the waiting room, and by the time my name was called, I felt faint. Where was the strength I'd prayed for? I was certain I was about to get bad news. *Jesus, be with me. My strength and courage come from You.*

As it turned out, the nurse practitioner who saw me prior to the mammogram told me the spot was not abnormal and my mammogram turned out to be okay. During the rush-hour drive home, I set my heart on Jesus, praising and thanking Him for providing me with *unexpected strength.* —PAT BUTLER DYSON

FAITH STEP: *In uncertain times, stand on your faith and beseech Jesus to give you courage.*

SATURDAY, JANUARY 22 ✓

God also has highly exalted Him and given Him the name which is above every name. Philippians 2:9 (NKJV)

You, my brothers and sisters, were called to be free. But do not use your freedom to indulge the flesh; rather, serve one another humbly in love. Galatians 5:13 (NIV)

EARLY IN MY SPIRITUAL JOURNEY, when something bad happened, I'd ask why God hadn't prevented it or why He had allowed it. I hear the same refrain from others when there are global catastrophes or smaller personal tragedies. But God isn't a cosmic puppeteer, moving people around in some galactic drama. The truth is we all have free will.

Free will means that, as I make good choices and bad choices, I'm subject to the natural consequences of those choices. The earth in which we live is no longer the paradise God designed. After the Fall, which was the direct result of Adam and Eve's free will, our world became a broken place where bad stuff could happen.

With Jesus's power within me, I can minimize the chance of harming anyone by choosing to serve others humbly with love, heeding Paul's command in this verse in Galatians. By His example, Jesus encourages me to use my freedom to help make the world a better place. —ISABELLA CAMPOLATTARO

FAITH STEP: *If you find yourself tempted to "indulge the flesh" today—choose instead to serve someone else with humility and with love.*

SUNDAY, JANUARY 23 ✓

You show that you are my intimate friends when you obey all that I command you. I have never called you "servants," because a master doesn't confide in his servants, and servants don't always understand what the master is doing. But I call you my most intimate friends, for I reveal to you everything that I've heard from my Father. John 15:14–15 (TPT)

SOMEHOW THE CONVERSATION WITH GRACE, our thirteen-year-old granddaughter, turned to friendships. "I only have seven friends," she said with a heavy sigh.

"Oh, honey, that's quite a few," I told her. As I counted on my fingers, I realized my close, trusted friends—the ones I share my hidden soul with—totaled five. One hand's worth.

"I have five," I told Grace. "And if you come to the end of your life and can say you have only one loyal friend, you are rich." I'd stolen that line from my stepdad, who said it to me when I was thirteen.

When Grace plopped into the passenger seat the next day after school, she chirped, "I made a mistake yesterday. I actually have eight close friends."

"Wow, that's marvelous," I said. "I thought of one more friend whom I forgot yesterday. And that's Jesus, my closest friend ever."

When I was Grace's age, I didn't think Jesus counted like other friends because I couldn't see Him. Five decades later, I realize Jesus is more real than my human friends. Because no matter what pain I experience or how much I hurt Him, He'll never stop loving me.

Grace tilted her head, pondered a minute, then said, "Jesus is my close friend too." —JEANETTE LEVELLIE

FAITH STEP: *Tell Jesus what an excellent friend He is. Then ask Him for an idea of a way to show Him your loyalty.*

MONDAY, JANUARY 24 ✓

The faithful love of the LORD *never ends! His mercies never cease.*
Great is his faithfulness; his mercies begin afresh each morning.
Lamentations 3:22–23 (NLT)

I LOOKED AT THE HUGE box outside my front door and knew I'd
made the same dumb mistake again. When shopping online, I often
forget to check the measurements of items. In this case, the piece of
wall art I'd ordered turned out to be forty-four inches wide—not a
good fit for the smaller space I had in mind.

Until I figure out its permanent home, it sits on top of the hutch
attached to my writing desk. The wood frame surrounds a single
Greek word: *tetelestai.* Underneath is a basic translation: "It is
finished." During New Testament times, people used the word in
everyday life. Merchant and tax receipts were marked with it to
indicate "paid in full." What makes *tetelestai* most significant is the
fact that Jesus spoke it from the cross just before He gave up His
spirit. Not only had His suffering been completed, but the debt for
our sin had also been paid in full.

Because of what Jesus finished on the cross, a new beginning is
waiting for me when I need it. Although the ultimate penalty for
my sin has been paid, I still frequently fall short in my daily life.
But Jesus promises forgiveness when I confess and repent. Each
day represents a chance to live with a clean slate, thanks to His
endless love and mercy. *Tetelestai*: a single word that represents
unlimited possibilities. Maybe that's why this wall art is oversized.
—DIANNE NEAL MATTHEWS

FAITH STEP: *Do you need a new beginning? Talk to Jesus about it, asking for*
His guidance. Write tetelestai *on a note card as a reminder of what He finished*
for you.

TUESDAY, JANUARY 25 ✓

When you pass through the waters, I will be with you; and through the rivers, they shall not overwhelm you. Isaiah 43:2 (ESV)

EVEN WITH ALL ITS FAULTS, social media sometimes serves up a devotional moment. Today I read a wise text image that said, "I asked Jesus why He was taking me through troubled waters. He answered, 'Because your enemies can't swim.'"

The children of Israel may have wondered why, after their nail-biting escape from the Egyptians, they ran smack-dab against a formidable sea. The enemy army was hot on their trail. Their only hope was through the waters, but they'd drown before they could say, "Let's rethink this."

The Red Sea story in the book of Exodus is popular. The waters parted. The Israelites crossed on dry land. Men, women, children, infants, and the elderly of Israel crossed safely to the other side. When the enemy followed, the waters closed over and drowned them. Not one Egyptian soldier could swim his way to safety—not with the ferocity of the walls of water swallowing them.

Jesus was well-versed with that story and the ancient promise, "When you pass through the waters…" Not *if*, but *when*. Jesus asked His disciples why they were afraid in the storm. He was there with them—wasn't that enough?

Is Jesus's presence enough for me when I'm faced with the impossible in front of me and an enemy fast approaching behind me? That's the very time for me to take courage. Miracles are about to take place. —CYNTHIA RUCHTI

FAITH STEP: *Think of a time when you stood facing impossible odds and the Lord "parted the waters" on your behalf. Share this story with a friend. Your testimony will serve as another thank-you note to Jesus.*

WEDNESDAY, JANUARY 26 ✓

How can I know all the sins lurking in my heart? Cleanse me from these hidden faults. Psalm 19:12 (NLT)

AT THE VACATION RENTAL HOME next door, guests scurried frantically back and forth to their car. I watched them hurriedly load up luggage and ski equipment—clearly past their checkout time—and couldn't help but laugh at the familiar scene. Many times, I, too, have scrambled to vacate a hotel room before checkout time.

Conversely, some "guests" sneak into premises, unseen, unwanted, without regard for the checkout time. It was a sad day when the trusty, old market in our little tourist town was discovered to have critters lurking in the attic. The store was shut down temporarily for a radical overhaul and deep cleaning to deal with the problem. During that time, people freely exchanged opinions around town. Some locals voiced empathy for the storeowner, some expressed disgust, and others wisely pointed out that no one is immune to such problems. "Troublesome secrets" scuttle about everywhere. The horror was that what had once been unknown was suddenly public knowledge.

Those pesky critters remind me of the "pests" that plague my mind: secret resentments, bad attitudes, negative thoughts. I certainly don't want my impurities and imperfections exposed for all the world to judge. Mercifully, Jesus doesn't humiliate me by posting Facebook videos revealing my secret sins, deficiencies, and shortcomings. Likewise, He doesn't kick me to the curb at checkout time. Thankfully, I can always come to Jesus for deep cleaning from my innermost hidden faults lurking in my heart. —CASSANDRA TIERSMA

FAITH STEP: *While bathing or showering today, ask Jesus to cleanse you from the inside out. While drying yourself off, thank Him for washing away any unknown secret sin. Praise Jesus that, with Him, there is no such thing as a checkout time!*

THURSDAY, JANUARY 27 ✓

Those who led the way rebuked him and told him to be quiet, but he shouted all the more, "Son of David, have mercy on me!" Luke 18:39 (NIV)

"STOP, STOP! PLEASE, HELP! STOP!" I heard her before I saw her.

An older woman who could barely stand was holding onto a lamppost and trying to hail a cab at a busy downtown intersection. Office workers on their lunch swirled around her and traffic was moving fast.

As soon as the traffic light halted the cars, I quickly crossed the street and asked the woman, who looked a bit shaken, if she needed a taxi. She said yes and I flagged one down. The woman held on to my arm as I helped her into the car and closed the door. She murmured her thanks and off she went.

For some reason, I thought about the blind beggar in Luke 18. You know, the one who kept yelling for Jesus to have mercy on him as the Lord approached the city of Jericho. Those around the man told him to be quiet, but he continued to shout to get Jesus's attention. And he did. Jesus asked him, "What do you want me to do for you?" He replied, "Lord, I want to see (verse 41, NIV)." And immediately Jesus restored his sight.

Persistence pays. The encounter with the woman was a great reminder that the Lord sees me and hears me. And He will show up at the right time. So, whether I need healing, courage, or even a cab, I want to keep calling on Jesus. In a whisper or a holler, I can tell Him what I want.

Lord, please help me to remember to say "thank you" when I receive what I asked for. —BARBRANDA LUMPKINS WALLS

FAITH STEP: *No matter what you're calling out to Jesus to do in your life right now, believe that He hears you.*

FRIDAY, JANUARY 28 ✓

If you believe, you will receive whatever you ask for in prayer.
Matthew 21:22 (NIV)

I WORK FROM HOME EVERY day, so I'm dependent on the internet to keep me connected to colleagues and to deliver my assignments to the people who expect them. Needless to say, frustration and anxiety take over my spirit whenever I'm close to a deadline and I see the message "Connection Failed" pop up on my computer screen.

This dreaded message showed up recently, right at the moment I was preparing to send a document to dozens of people that I'd spent a lot of time working on. Then, just like that, the connection to my work server failed. The clock was ticking. I frantically asked my husband to reboot our home router to see if that would help. It didn't. My mind began to churn in search of solutions.

Suddenly, my eyes spotted a silver medallion I keep on my desk. The words *Pray First* are embossed on it. Why hadn't I thought to do that right away? I immediately stopped and whispered a prayer: *Lord, You see what I'm trying to do here. Please fix this connection now.* Within minutes the internet was up and running again, and all was right with the world.

The hymn "What a Friend We Have in Jesus" says we can take everything to God in prayer. Nothing is too small. I've prayed for parking spots, no traffic delays, healing for my headaches, and much more. It's not just the big things that Jesus wants me to bring to Him. It's everything—even unreliable internet and Wi-Fi.
—BARBRANDA LUMPKINS WALLS

FAITH STEP: *What do you think is too small to take to Jesus? Remember you can take it all to Him.*

SATURDAY, JANUARY 29

For me it is good to be near God; I have made the Lord GOD my refuge, that I may tell of all your works. Psalm 73:28 (ESV)

I'VE BEEN A BELIEVER FOR more than four decades, but until recently I'd never read through the entire Bible. Though I had desired to do it. Some friends told me about their intention to read through the Bible in a year using an application called The Bible Recap. It included a daily, chronological reading plan with a short podcast recapping each day. They invited me to join them, and I said yes.

I'm grateful I committed! I learned so much. One recurring message was how God longs to be near us. Deuteronomy 4:7 says, "For what great nation is there that has a god so near to it as the LORD our God is to us, whenever we call upon him?" (ESV). Then came Jesus. He dwelled among us. People touched Him, saw Him with their own eyes, ate meals with Him, and talked with Him face to face. Mind blowing. No other god desires this closeness with humanity. James 4:8 also encourages me to draw near to God and promises that He will draw near to me.

Saying yes to reading the entire Bible in a year was the beginning of my commitment to draw nearer to Jesus with intention and consistency. I can emphatically say how good it was to spend those mornings with Jesus as He revealed Himself to me through His written Word and I discovered new and rich insights about Him. As I continue to daily hide myself in His Word and take refuge, I want to tell of His good works however I can. —JEANNIE BLACKMER

FAITH STEP: *To experience nearness to Jesus today, set aside thirty minutes to read and reflect on Psalm 73:23–28.*

SUNDAY, JANUARY 30

Set your minds on things above, not on earthly things. Colossians 3:2 *(NIV)*

I'VE LAMENTED OPENLY THE RISE and fall of my former business making products for kids who have special needs like my son Isaac, who has Down Syndrome. Despite my very best efforts, the business went down in flames, but it helped many people and eventually played a role in leading me to write for Guideposts.

Having had many mountaintop and valley experiences, I've learned to filter almost everything through the eyes of faith rather than using a worldly yardstick. I had a professional career that conveyed worldly status but left me feeling empty and lost. I've had awful low points.

When my business failed—as terrible an experience as that was—it proved to be a tremendous time of spiritual growth and intimacy with Jesus.

Any given day, things happen in my life that invite a response, an action, or some kind of judgment. I interact with people, information, and situations. Sometimes the matters are small. Other times, I have to contend with larger matters.

Whatever the case, I can either see everything from a worldly standpoint, influenced by news outlets, friends, family, and social media. Or I can filter everything through the wisdom of Scripture and an eternal view, focusing on Jesus first, last, and forever. My perspective of something changes dramatically by how I view it. And I choose to look up. —ISABELLA CAMPOLATTARO

FAITH STEP: *Draw a three-column chart. In the first column, list three things that are weighing on you today. In the second column, list a worldly view. In the third column, list a heavenly perspective. Reflect.*

MONDAY, JANUARY 31

Whether you turn to the right or to the left, you will hear a voice saying, "This is the road! Now follow it." Isaiah 30:21 (CEV)

CLUTCHING THE STEERING WHEEL, I negotiated a complex, multi-lane braid of on-ramps and off-ramps at breakneck speed. Trusting the GPS's navigational authority, I counted lanes, kept left or right, obeying its commands. Because I was swept up in the swift, unyielding current of seventy-mile-per-hour traffic, one abrupt, mistimed lane change in that rushing river of cars and trucks could have been fatal. I was driving to visit my daughter who lived out of state.

Suddenly three words on the GPS struck terror in me: "Lost Satellite Connection." I continued blindly, until the connection was restored. Periodically, it reconnected momentarily, only to be lost again. Finally, the connection was restored long enough to guide me through an intense series of critical lane changes.

When I was almost to my daughter's home, the dreaded "Lost Satellite Connection" message reappeared. By then, though, I was close enough to call my daughter, who guided me the rest of the way.

That harrowing experience revealed my utter dependence on technology, its unreliability, and my need for "connection." There's one connection that's paramount to all others and is always reliable: my spiritual connection with Jesus. Technology fails. GPS loses connection. But I'm always connected to Jesus, no matter what. I can depend on Him to navigate me through life, showing me the way He wants me to go. Ultimately, He's the One who'll guide me the rest of the way Home. No satellite connection required. —CASSANDRA TIERSMA

FAITH STEP: *Thank Jesus for being your spiritual GPS through life's twists, turns, and lane changes. Praise Jesus that, with Him, you're no longer lost. He'll guide you Home.*

TUESDAY, FEBRUARY 1

When this priest had offered for all time one sacrifice for sins, he sat down at the right hand of God. Hebrews 10:12 (NIV)

I LOVE CRAFTS AND RECENTLY stenciled a plaque for my office. This white board with black lettering speaks to my soul. The wording is simple and the message clear: "All Your Sins Are Forgiven—Even That One." The sign doesn't match my historic home's decor. Yet it's necessary. This reminder keeps me grounded in Jesus's limitless love. Just as important—maybe more—I need to trust that I am forgiven. For everything, even my sins that seem unforgivable.

When Jesus came into the world, He walked with tax collectors, prostitutes, the demon possessed, and lepers. He selected a man named Saul as His disciple, a Roman who'd spent his life persecuting believers. Jesus found the good in each of these people and taught them to see it in themselves.

In His supreme wisdom, as He hung on the cross, He forgave everyone. His purity covers us for eternity because He paid for every sin—past, present and future. Not just the tiny misdoings but even the worst, shameful, most vile thing we've ever done, been, or thought. Yes, even that.

I live in the joyful knowledge of Jesus's boundless devotion, but when I forget, I can look at the sign in my office and be reassured. Every person is forgiven, even me. Every sin is forgiven, even my worst one. Yours too. —HEIDI GAUL

FAITH STEP: *Make or purchase a sign that helps you accept the magnitude of His love and forgiveness. Hang it in a prominent spot to help you remember.*

WEDNESDAY, FEBRUARY 2

God is Spirit, and those who worship Him must worship in spirit and truth. John 4:24 (NKJV)

CANADIAN BRIAN DOERKSEN WROTE THE familiar worship song, "Come, Now Is the Time to Worship." In a lunchtime interview at his home, he told me that he composed it during a time of deep anguish in his soul. One day when he felt especially discouraged, he sensed the Holy Spirit nudging him to praise and worship the Lord despite the difficulties. He obeyed, and this song—which has blessed millions worldwide—was born.

Hearing about Brian's choice to worship in adversity forever altered my perspective. It's easy to worship Jesus for His goodness, presence, and power when life's going well. Not so much when life takes a sudden detour or someone hurts me. That's when I'm tempted to whine or doubt. But that's exactly when I most need to recall that song title and put it into action.

Now—in the middle of the muck—is the time to worship Jesus. He doesn't want me to wait until I've worked through my disappointment or healed from my pain to enter His courts with praise. Worshipping in spirit and in truth means coming to Him as I am, with all my warts, rather than putting on false airs or waiting until circumstances are ideal. It's acknowledging His beauty, faithfulness, goodness, and wisdom and inviting His Majesty to sit on the throne of my heart now, at this very moment.

Worship won't change my circumstances, but it changes the way I respond to them. I don't need to figure everything out before I engage in praise. I just need to worship, especially when life doesn't make sense. —GRACE FOX

FAITH STEP: *Praise Jesus for His promise to never leave you.*

THURSDAY, FEBRUARY 3

You make known to me the path of life; you will fill me with joy in your presence, with eternal pleasures at your right hand. Psalm 16:11 (NIV)

WHILE REVIEWING PHOTOGRAPHS FROM A recent hike, I was surprised how one snapshot drew my eye more than the others: the image of a canopy of trees sheltering a trail, its earthy surface dappled with mellowed sunlight. The path wound into a gentle curve and out of sight. When I saw that scene, with its carpet of autumn leaves piled along the walk's edge, pleasure swept over me.

Images of country lanes and dirt pathways that disappear past a bend—what makes me love them so? Why do they evoke such a sense of excitement and hope?

Paul likened his existence to a race. But for me, my faith walk— my life—more closely resembles a long hike through the wilderness. There is beauty to encounter and danger to face. Yet I move forward with anticipation, because I know this trail has been chosen just for me, and I trust the One who blazed it. Even though I don't know exactly what lies ahead in my future, I feel safe under the cover of His protection. I can round the bends in my world with confidence, enjoying every adventure that Jesus supplies along the way.

I look forward to the end of the trail, when I scale that final summit and see Jesus face to face. Until then, I remain happy with my journey. —HEIDI GAUL

FAITH STEP: *Next time you take a nature hike or walk through your town, reflect on the bends you've traversed on life's trail. How did Jesus guide you along the way? Thank Him for the blessings and the challenges.*

FRIDAY, FEBRUARY 4

He tends his flock like a shepherd: He gathers the lambs in his arms and carries them close to his heart; he gently leads those that have young.
Isaiah 40:11 (NIV)

I OFTEN SEE A NEIGHBOR taking his little terrier for a run. The man rolls down the road, balanced on a hoverboard. The dog races behind him. When the dog tires, his owner scoops him up and carries him. The animal nestles against the man's chest. He rests there, content and secure, able to ride for miles.

Watching these two reminds me of Jesus's promise to carry His children. Sometimes the path He leads us on feels long and tiresome. We grow weary, and our soul pants for water and rest.

I've experienced times like that. For years, I sweated over my ministry calendar. I wanted to be fully available to fulfill God's purposes for me, while being fully available for the needs and celebrations of my immediate and extended family. Stress and guilt from trying to do it all sapped my energy.

I finally learned what it means to let Jesus carry me. I asked Him to schedule my ministry trips in such a way that would leave me available for my family when they needed me most. He's answered in amazing ways three or four times every year since. No longer do I feel the need to do it all, and I don't entertain guilt if I'm overseas when my family needs help. I pray for them and encourage them from a distance, but I also leave the responsibility for their wellbeing with Jesus, whose promise to carry His children also applies to them. —GRACE FOX

FAITH STEP: *Recall a time when you carried a child who relaxed in your arms. Purpose to rest that way in Jesus's arms.*

SATURDAY, FEBRUARY 5

God saw everything that He had made, and indeed it was very good.
Genesis 1:31 (NKJV)

GROWING UP AS A BROWN GIRL in a mostly white neighborhood, I had daily opportunities to feel "not good." I knew I was smart, had hard-working parents, and even had some athletic abilities (thanks to my sporty Dad and our Sunday afternoon training sessions in the nearby concrete park). But as my preteen years approached, doubts encroached. I wanted so badly to get accepted into a particular private Jesuit prep school. One visit captured my heart—the gleaming hallways, high academic standards, and the clear diversity of the student body. I remember praying for the first time to a man named Jesus, who I was learning about in catechism class. I heard that He thought I was good! Back in my homeroom, the teacher said I was a B student and that the prep school only took A students. I was told to focus on other schools. Thankfully, I had learned about Jesus's sacrifice for me and that He died for me to succeed. I studied hard, thinking that if Jesus was for me, who could be against me?

The day the acceptance letters arrived, the tradition was for the teacher to read them aloud, for example: "Susie Parker. Accepted." Then she'd name the school. My turn came. I was beaming before she spoke: "Pamela Toussaint. Accepted?" (She said it as a question.) "Saint Francis Preparatory High School," she announced. I was accepted. But more importantly, Jesus had already accepted me! And that was very good. —PAMELA TOUSSAINT HOWARD

FAITH STEP: *Remind yourself of how good Jesus thinks you are, just for being you.*

SUNDAY, FEBRUARY 6

"Though the mountains be shaken and the hills be removed, yet my unfailing love for you will not be shaken nor my covenant of peace be removed," says the LORD, who has compassion on you. Isaiah 54:10 (NIV)

OUR YOUNGEST DAUGHTER, KIM, AND her husband, David, married in 2013. Since then, they've moved eight times for school and work. Gene and I have lent a hand each time. The four of us jokingly say we've mastered this moving thing. Maybe we should start our own business, right?

I think about how many dishes we've packed and unpacked. How many times we've assembled and disassembled their bed. How many kitchens and closets we've organized. I think about how many changes this couple has weathered and wonder how many more will come before David graduates and establishes his medical practice.

Change is not easy. Even a change for the better exacts a mental and emotional toll because it brings unknowns. It removes the familiar and comfortable and thrusts me into the new and uncertain. It calls me to adjust and realign my expectations with my new reality.

Change happens in a multitude of ways. No matter what it looks like, one thing remains consistent: Jesus's love for us. Our circumstances might be shaken and the familiar removed, but His love is steadfast, always and forever the same. Because He is who He is, we can face change with courage, knowing He will navigate the new with us, giving us everything we need to do it well. —GRACE FOX

FAITH STEP: *Identify a change you've either recently made or will make in the future. Tell Jesus your concerns about it and ask Him to help you adjust well.*

MONDAY, FEBRUARY 7

---

*The seed planted in the good earth represents those who hear the
Word, embrace it, and produce a harvest beyond their wildest dreams.*
Mark 4:20 (MSG)

AFTER I SPOKE AT A neighboring church when they were between
pastors, I got an email from their worship leader. He wrote, "We'd
like to have you preach for us on a regular basis until we find a
pastor. How often can you come back?"

Although I felt honored that they liked my message, I was also
a bit confused. The Lord had expanded my writing ministry to
include speaking—mostly for women's groups—but I'd never
aspired to preach. Yet the more I prayed about it, the stronger the
dream grew in my heart.

Yikes, I thought. *This is huge. Are You behind this, Lord, or is my
ego talking?* In my five decades as a Christian, I often believed Jesus
was speaking to me. Many times, it turned out that His voice was
the one I'd heard. Other times, when an idea backfired, I realized
my human desires had taken over.

I didn't want to start something that wasn't Jesus's plan for me.
I also didn't want to offend my husband, Kevin, a pastor for over
forty years. Would he resent me for suddenly preaching at different
churches, missing worship at our home church?

When I approached Kev, he gave me his blessing. Maybe he fig-
ured if I preached to others, I'd cut back on preaching to him!

Over the last year, Jesus has opened doors for me to preach at
several different churches. I like to think it delights Him to surprise
His followers with new dreams that are beyond our imaginings.
He's sweet like that. —JEANETTE LEVELLIE

FAITH STEP: *When you pray today, invite Jesus to surprise you with a new dream.*

TUESDAY, FEBRUARY 8

We are Christ's ambassadors. God is using us to speak to you: we beg you, as though Christ himself were here pleading with you, receive the love he offers you—be reconciled to God. 2 Corinthians 5:20 (TLB)

THEIR FACES FELL WHEN THEY saw the crowd. They'd hoped that Jesus could heal their paralyzed friend. But with so many people crammed in and around the house, they couldn't even see Jesus through the doorway—much less ask Him for help. In desperation, the four men made a hole in the roof and lowered their friend down. Jesus stopped teaching to tend to the man's needs. First, He told him his sins were forgiven, then He instructed him to get up and go home. The man walked out healed, physically and spiritually.

Whenever I read this story in Mark 2, I admire the determination that prompted these four men to use unconventional means to connect their friend with Jesus. As His ambassador today, I am also called to connect people with Jesus. In the biblical story, the crowd blocked the view of Jesus so that the men could not glimpse Him. It's my job to reflect Christ every day, to make Him visible to everyone around me.

Each day, I'm surrounded by people who are seeking Jesus, whether they know it or not. Serving as His ambassador means being sensitive to others' needs and responding appropriately. That might mean sharing the gospel, showing kindness, or initiating a friendship that will lead to deep discussions later. I don't ever want to be so busy with my own agenda that I fail to notice an outsider who needs to be introduced to Jesus. —DIANNE NEAL MATTHEWS

FAITH STEP: *Ask Jesus to show you someone who needs to be introduced to Him. Then keep your eyes open for that person.*

WEDNESDAY, FEBRUARY 9

Beloved, I pray that you may prosper in all things and be in health, just as your soul prospers. 3 John 1:2 (NKJV)

"YOUR KNEE'S FINE," THE DOCTOR said. "It's the muscles around it that need to get stronger."

Months after a major surgery, the pain I experienced seemed slow to recede. So I consulted the doctor to make sure nothing was wrong from a surgical standpoint. His reassurance was instructive on many levels.

When something is injured, the trauma to the surrounding area may be worse than the initial problem. A tornado sweeps through a town. Buildings can be repaired, but the emotional wounds of the people may be more difficult to assess and may take longer to heal. A young couple divorces, and it's heartbreaking. But even deeper pain may emerge as they attempt to coparent, or deeper pain may show up in the lives of the children. A woman is accosted on her way to her car. She survives, but fear takes hold and invites paranoia to join the party too.

The bruise we see may not be the worst of the damage. That may be why John, a Jesus follower, prayed that his friends would "prosper in all things." In other words, that God would heal and prosper both body and soul, keeping their faith strong and resilient to life's winds. Similarly, I must trust God to heal me and keep the muscles around my relational or emotional wounds strong, so I can prosper in all ways.

I love how Jesus uses everyday experiences, like a checkup with the surgeon, to communicate truths He needs me to understand.

—CYNTHIA RUCHTI

FAITH STEP: *Are you aware of a personal wound that is in the process of healing? Take steps to spiritually strengthen the muscles around that wound so you can fully heal.*

THURSDAY, FEBRUARY 10

The earth is the LORD's, and everything in it. The world and all its people belong to him. Psalm 24:1 (NLT)

WE HOSTED AN ISLAND-THEMED BACKYARD sleepover for my daughter's eleventh birthday. The girls played zany relay games and assembled island-themed kabobs to grill on the barbecue. Although the party was a success, I felt hurt that one of the mothers wouldn't allow her daughter to spend the night. I was deeply offended that she didn't trust me and my husband to protect her daughter in our backyard.

In time, I got over it. When my children grew up and I struggled with fears and worries about their safety in the world, Jesus reminded me of how hurt and upset I'd felt when that mom didn't trust my ability to keep her daughter safe in my backyard. He reminded me that the whole world is His backyard. And I realized how it offends Jesus when I don't trust Him to protect and care for my children.

Remembering my hurt that day of the sleepover, I asked Jesus to forgive me for not trusting Him with my children and releasing my children into His care, knowing He's always able to keep them safe in *His* limitless backyard. —CASSANDRA TIERSMA

FAITH STEP: *Spend some time with Jesus. Who or what have you had difficulty trusting Him to take care of? Entrust that individual or situation to His capable hands. Then tell Jesus you're sorry for forgetting the world is His backyard. He's fully able to protect us and provide what's needed.*

FRIDAY, FEBRUARY 11

But will God indeed dwell on earth? The heavens, even the highest heaven, cannot contain you. How much less this temple I have built! 1 Kings 8:27 (NIV)

DRASTIC TIMES CALL FOR DRASTIC measures. That became abundantly clear when life as I knew it came to a screeching halt during a worldwide health emergency. Out of necessity people became pretty creative to keep in contact with one another. I had videoconference calls to celebrate birthdays with friends and to meet with church leaders. I loved stories of neighbors who gathered to sing outdoors or applaud medical professionals and first responders for their important work and sacrifices.

I even noted how brick-and-mortar churches became virtual sanctuaries as worship services and Bible studies were held online. I was grateful to see my own pastor and other ministers deliver powerful sermons via the internet to encourage and uplift us. Despite the dire circumstances, God's work continued and Jesus was praised.

Although I know the Lord is everywhere, I became even more aware that He cannot be contained within the walls of any house of worship. And nothing can thwart His plans (Job 42:2). In 1 Kings 8, King Solomon had just completed construction of a magnificent temple in Jerusalem, and in his prayer dedicating the edifice, he, too, recognized that the Lord is much bigger than any dwelling. It stands to reason that our worship is not to be confined to a church building. While corporate worship is wonderful, there is still nothing like meeting with Jesus one-on-one in a quiet place. No live streaming. No apps. Just me and Jesus. There's no virtual God, but He is virtually everywhere. —BARBRANDA LUMPKINS WALLS

FAITH STEP: *Find a different spot to worship Jesus today—and experience His presence there.*

SATURDAY, FEBRUARY 12

The LORD bless you and keep you; the LORD make his face shine on you and be gracious to you; the LORD turn his face toward you and give you peace. Numbers 6:24–26 (NIV)

I HAVE A NEW SONG that I can't stop listening to. The habit of latching on to a song and listening to it over and over again harks back to my junior high days. I would find a song that I loved and tape it on my tape recorder. (Yep, I am that old.) Then I would play that song on repeat—for days. It drove my brother and sisters crazy.

Fast-forward a few decades, and I just replay my favorite songs online. Now I drive my husband, Scott, and my boys crazy. The thing is, when I listen to a single song on repeat, the truth of it starts to work its way into my soul.

The latest song I can't get enough of is a worship song. It has a refrain about Jesus's blessing being poured out on generation after generation. Its many truths are powerful: Jesus is for us. His blessing is covering us. Lifting us. Surrounding us. Hemming us in on all sides.

Jesus reminds me of these truths over and over again when I read His Word. It is almost as if I need to hear those words on repeat so that they can work their way into my soul. *Jesus loves me.* Repeat. *Jesus is with me.* Repeat. *Jesus is for me.* Repeat. It just doesn't get any better than that. —SUSANNA FOTH AUGHTMON

FAITH STEP: *Find your favorite worship song online. Put it on repeat. Ask Jesus to reveal the truth of His love and character to you as you worship and sing along.*

SUNDAY, FEBRUARY 13

We are hard pressed on every side, but not crushed; perplexed, but not in despair; persecuted, but not abandoned; struck down, but not destroyed.
2 Corinthians 4:8–9 (NIV)

I'VE BEEN BEEKEEPING FOR SEVERAL years, and each year I'm more astounded at the strength, ingenuity, unity—and especially the resilience of bees. During the warm months, bees face many threats to their survival: heavy rain, pesticides, wasps, bears, birds, and other critters that rob their hives of honey. Yet most survive. In Colorado, the winter months are especially difficult. Last winter, we experienced several weeks of temperatures below zero. To keep warm, bees huddle around the queen and shiver to generate enough heat to keep the cluster at 95 degrees. After each cold spell, once temperatures reached above 50 degrees, I would go look at my hives. If I saw bees flying around, then I knew they had survived.

Bees remind me of Jesus's promise to be with me when I'm hard pressed on every side. I was never promised that life would be a breeze. Jesus said, "In this world you will have trouble. But take heart! I have overcome the world" (John 16:33, NIV). When I face difficulties, I can cling to the promise that I will not be crushed. I might be perplexed and discouraged, but I'm never abandoned. Jesus is always with me. Like the bees, I can rely on the people in my life for help, and vice versa. Together we can survive our trials and bounce back from the events in life that try to strike us down.
—JEANNIE BLACKMER

FAITH STEP: *Who in your life is an example of resilience? Call that person today and ask her how she overcame her difficulties.*

VALENTINE'S DAY, MONDAY, FEBRUARY 14

Trust steadily in God, hope unswervingly, love extravagantly.
And the best of the three is love. 1 Corinthians 13:13 (MSG)

MY HUSBAND, KEVIN, AND I chose Valentine's Day for our wedding day forty-five years ago. (I was a child bride!) The idea of having our anniversary on that date sounded romantic. And it has been.

Recently, a worry threatened to curtail our usual anniversary fun. Our daughter, Marie, is not a fan of Valentine's Day because of her recent unwanted divorce. She was working in a superstore during and after the divorce, and scanning bouquets of roses and fancy cards before Valentine's Day added to her misery.

So, when she moved to our hometown last year, I wondered if Kev and I would need to tone down the excitement we usually exhibit around February 14. Should we refrain from telling her about the gifts we had bought for each other and what fancy restaurant we had chosen for dinner?

But Marie surprised me. Early in February, she asked what we'd like for our anniversary. When the day came, she excitedly handed each of us a lovely gift bag filled with thoughtful presents. She had set aside her own feelings of loss associated with the holiday so that she could show us love.

That reminded me of Jesus—how He set aside His glory and majesty to become a man and wash dirty feet, heal unclean lepers, and share meals with wicked people. He "endured the cross, scorning its shame" (Hebrews 12:2, NIV), for the joy of making me—and all of us—a part of His family.

Love is more than flowers or words on a fancy card. Love is a verb.
—JEANETTE LEVELLIE

FAITH STEP: *Ask Jesus to help you carry out deeds of love.*

TUESDAY, FEBRUARY 15

Stand your ground, putting on the belt of truth and the body armor of God's righteousness. For shoes, put on the peace that comes from the Good News so that you will be fully prepared. Ephesians 6:14–15 (NLT)

WE HAVE A RUG FOR shoes near our front door. Whenever my hubby and I leave the house, we grab the appropriate footwear. In the summer I have gardening clogs and sandals on that rug. In the winter, my warm boots wait for me.

Today as I slid my feet into slip-ons to take out the recycling, I thought about how important it can be to choose the right shoes. Each day, as I set out into the world, I have a choice to wear the ill-fitting clodhoppers of worry, anger, or selfishness. Or I can wear the spiritual armor that Jesus provides, with shoes that support an attitude of peace.

We can use our entrances and exits from our home as a place of remembering. Everywhere we go, we carry with us the good news. Jesus has come. His death and resurrection offer us forgiveness and salvation. And with each task we take on, we can follow in His footsteps. As we lace up tennis shoes or wriggle into church shoes, we can ask Jesus to help us walk the path of peace He has set before us, alert to anyone who needs to hear His good news. When we return home and take off our shoes, we can rejoice that our bare feet are always standing on holy ground—because we are always in His presence. —SHARON HINCK

FAITH STEP: *Be aware of your shoes today. Ask Jesus to help you walk in peace.*

WEDNESDAY, FEBRUARY 16

We know that in all things God works for the good of those who love him, who have been called according to his purpose. Romans 8:28 (NIV)

MY SENIOR CAT, JULIE, IS usually sweet natured. But her system occasionally succumbs to a recurring illness that requires antibiotics. My husband, David, holds her as I fill a syringe with medicine. Then the adventure begins. Seven pounds of aging feline transforms into a writhing, clawing mass of viciousness. We brace ourselves, keeping our eyes and hands protected. At last, we squirt the liquid into her mouth and she swallows. Sighing, we set her down. Our job is done, and the terror is over for another day.

As Julie's health improves daily, so does her attitude. When the cycle is over, she seems grateful.

Sometimes I need to swallow "bitter medicine" in my life to grow stronger faith. Bills, illness, or whatever unpleasant circumstances—I don't always accept them peacefully. I fight, kicking and screaming. Often, my fussing causes the trial to last longer or at least make it seem longer. When it's over, I've gained nothing from my rebellion.

I'm learning to accept life's tribulations with the quiet grace and obedience that Jesus wants me to display. I'm discovering a patience within as I acknowledge the reasons behind each situation and see their necessity for my soul's refinement. As I catch glimpses of the beauty of all things working together through Him and for Him, I'm filled with wonder. And I'm thankful. I am a witness to Jesus's movement in my life as He rescues me and reassures me. And I am healed.
—HEIDI GAUL

FAITH STEP: *Make a list of the "bitter medicines" you've encountered, and the wonderful ways Jesus strengthened your faith and your character as He walked you through them.*

THURSDAY, FEBRUARY 17

He performs wonders that cannot be fathomed, miracles that cannot be counted. Job 5:9 (NIV)

ON A RECENT VACATION, SEVERAL nurse sharks swam toward us on our first dive. One came directly at me! The closer she came, the more uncomfortable I was. When she rubbed against me like a kitten, I realized she was used to divers and was being playful. This dive was one of my best ever. I saw countless amazing creatures: colorful coral, turtles, a school of stingrays, and more. If I had been too uncomfortable to dive, then I would have missed the awe of seeing the miraculous underwater world.

I think Jesus wants me to step out of my comfort zone because then I'm forced to trust Him. When I do, I witness Him doing "wonders that cannot be fathomed, miracles that cannot be counted." The disciples definitely left their comfort zones when they chose to follow Jesus. They were terrified when Jesus walked on water and when He touched a leper. But when they trusted Him, they experienced awe when Jesus did what He does—miracles.

To experience Jesus's wonders, I want to keep getting uncomfortable. Not only while scuba diving, but also during other situations outside my comfort zone, such as taking food to the homeless, going on a mission trip, or volunteering for a prison ministry. I can willingly get uncomfortable and trust that Jesus will do His good work. —JEANNIE BLACKMER

FAITH STEP: *Write down an uncomfortable experience you think Jesus might be inviting you into today and pray about doing it.*

FRIDAY, FEBRUARY 18

When Jesus had called the Twelve together, he gave them power and authority to drive out all demons and to cure diseases, and he sent them out to proclaim the kingdom of God and to heal the sick. Luke 9:1–2 (NIV)

GENE AND I WATCHED AN animated movie with our grandkids while visiting them. The movie, *The Incredibles*, featured the Parr family—mother, father, and three children. This was no ordinary family. They were undercover superheroes, and each member possessed a unique superpower. They truly were incredible!

Dad possessed superhuman strength and durability. Mom stretched like elastic. The fourteen-year-old daughter could become invisible, the ten-year-old son was super speedy, and the baby could change his shape. When evil influences threatened civilization, this family combined forces and fought for the good of mankind.

Script writers and illustrators used their imaginations to create this family with superpowers. But know this: as members of God's family, we're filled with supernatural power that's real and enables us to experience victory as we fight spiritual battles.

Jesus gave His disciples special power to build God's kingdom, deliver people from demons, and heal diseases. Other Scriptures teach that the disciples received power from the Holy Spirit to also preach the gospel all over the world (Acts 1:8, Luke 24:48–49).

Jesus doesn't expect us to fight the battle against evil with our own strength. It's impossible to do so and win. Therefore, He's given us the Holy Spirit to empower us. He's Supernatural. Super strong. Super wise. Super everything. And when He fills and controls us, there's no limit to what He can do through us. —GRACE FOX

FAITH STEP: *Invite the Holy Spirit to fill you with His power to deal with the greatest challenge facing you today.*

SATURDAY, FEBRUARY 19

My dear brothers and sisters, take note of this: Everyone should be quick to listen, slow to speak and slow to become angry. James 1:19 (NIV)

I'VE JUST RETURNED FROM TEACHING at a writing retreat. As I reviewed my interactions, I was delighted by the way Jesus moved in the hearts of the attendees, bringing healing, encouragement, inspiration, and direction. But I also replayed many of the conversations and realized there were times I talked about myself too much. I had been quick to jump in and offer my opinions. I'd failed to listen as deeply and compassionately as I could have.

When Jesus walked this earth, He encountered many people. The Gospels record His unhurried and selfless responses. He wept with compassion. He celebrated at weddings. He asked searching questions. And He listened, listened, and *listened* to the hurts, needs, and doubts of those He met.

As I seek to follow His example, I will stumble. I'll get it wrong. Sometimes I'll feel defensive and instead of hearing the heart of the person across from me, I'll argue. I'm so grateful that when I miss the mark, I can turn to my Savior. He is quick to listen and to forgive. He offers to live within me to empower me to change and grow. Little by little, I can become more like Him, serving the needs of others by listening with love—and when appropriate, by holding my tongue. —SHARON HINCK

FAITH STEP: *In your next conversation, ponder this verse from James and listen purposefully. Before speaking, take a deep breath and pray that you'll respond with Jesus's love.*

SUNDAY, FEBRUARY 20

Blessed are the poor in spirit, for theirs is the kingdom of heaven.
Matthew 5:3 (NIV)

WHEN OUR CHILDREN WERE LITTLE and my husband and I were zipping up jackets and tying shoes on our way out of the house, our progress often stalled as one or more child shoved our hands away, saying, "I do it myself!" They didn't want to accept help. Their independence made me smile because I realized I wasn't that different.

Our culture idolizes rugged individualism. The athlete or entrepreneur who puts in solitary effort and achieves a great goal is lauded. A person with disabilities who fights through obstacles without relying on others is praised. I buy into this theme of "I do it myself!" Just this week, I received some bad news and felt bowed down by sadness. Yet I didn't want to tell my friends I was hurting; I wanted to put on a brave face and not come across as needy.

But Jesus challenges me in His Sermon on the Mount, which is why I wanted to write a series of devotions that will explore the blessings of the Beatitudes over the next week.

In Matthew 5:3, Jesus tells me that it is a blessing to recognize my neediness. When I'm poor in spirit, I should reach out with open hands, seek His help, and admit that I can't solve life's problems in my own power. That acknowledgment of my poverty of spirit clears the space for Jesus to step in and supply what I never could. The Word who created me, redeemed me, and continues to sanctify me invites me into His kingdom—the kingdom of heaven.
—SHARON HINCK

FAITH STEP: *Lift up open hands and admit your lack to Jesus. Invite Him to provide the blessings of the kingdom of heaven to meet your need.*

MONDAY, FEBRUARY 21

Blessed are those who mourn, for they will be comforted. Matthew 5:4 (NIV)

FIVE YEARS AFTER MY LAST novel came out, I published another one and copies arrived on my doorstep. That's usually a time of huge joy, gratitude, and celebration. But when I opened the box, I defaulted into stress and fear. Then I got mad at myself for those emotions, ashamed that I couldn't feel the excitement I wanted to feel.

As I prayed, Jesus reminded me that the past year had brought many forms of grief. The death of a family member, the Alzheimer's diagnosis of another, and my husband's cancer diagnosis. And empty nesting had hit harder than before when my hubby and I were alone at Christmas. How did I handle it? I had shut out my feelings and worked like crazy—writing, editing, and organizing book-launch events. No wonder I felt burnt out and my feelings were a confusing mess. Gently, I shared my grief with Jesus. Safe in His arms, I let tears fall and told Him how broken I felt and how much I was hurting.

When I allowed myself to mourn, He comforted me. The gratitude I longed to experience emerged naturally. Trusting that I would survive these painful times strengthened my spine. I even shared my sense of brokenness with a friend, and she thanked me because she was experiencing similar feelings. She was relieved to know she wasn't alone.

No one likes loss and grief, but when we are most vulnerable, Jesus pours out comfort. He weeps with us. He reassures us. And He points us to the joy to come. —SHARON HINCK

FAITH STEP: *Have you been trying to outrun grief? Stop and pour out your heart to Jesus today and let Him comfort you.*

Tuesday, February 22

Blessed are the meek, for they will inherit the earth. Matthew 5:5 (NIV)

Decades ago, I was serving at a mission base in Hong Kong. Each day, we would walk to a local streetcar to ride to the meeting place. As people surged toward the door of the tram, I found myself being elbowed aside. I often came close to missing the tram as others hurried aboard. A friend who had lived there a long time coached me to be more assertive. The city was fast-paced, and this was a time when meekness wasn't appropriate.

Most of the time, it is much easier to assert my own desires than appreciate the beauty of meekness. I may not elbow my way onto a tram, but I insert myself into conversations, focus on my own needs, and assert the priority of my struggles over the person next to me. I've wrestled with what Jesus means by meekness. Perhaps I fear that by making way for another, I'll never get *my* spot. Yet there is blessing in following His example: putting the needs of another before my own, listening more and talking less, being less of a drama queen about my own small struggles, and giving more compassion to the suffering of others.

Meekness is not cowardice or shrinking from gifts and callings. But it is a shift in priorities. I like how A. A. Milne's Winnie-the-Pooh said it: "Love is taking a few steps backward, maybe even more . . . to give way to the happiness of the person you love."

When I think of how Jesus left His throne in heaven to serve, comfort, and sacrifice, I'm challenged to find ways to let His type of meekness grow in my heart. —Sharon Hinck

Faith Step: *Think of one person you can make way for today. Find ways to elevate him and make him a higher priority.*

WEDNESDAY, FEBRUARY 23

Blessed are those who hunger and thirst for righteousness,
for they will be filled. Matthew 5:6 (NIV)

BECAUSE OF CERTAIN HEALTH CHALLENGES, my doctor recommended that I try intermittent fasting—a routine of eating during a short window of time each day, which gives the body a longer break from the work of digesting and processing meals. So my husband and I have been trying to have our meals early in the day and not eat in the evening. Of course, that means that right around bedtime I get cravings for all snacks ever invented. I usually manage to ignore that urge and am always grateful the next morning because I feel so much better.

Experiencing a tiny bit of hunger has been a good experience, reminding me of the sort of deep longing Jesus describes here in today's verse. My heart can get so saturated by the world that I lose the craving for righteousness. I fill up on junk—half-truths, material comforts, distractions for my mind and spirit. It is only when I come to the end of myself and my comfort that I will acknowledge my true emptiness and my need for my Savior.

So I ask Jesus to create a hunger in me for the right things. The longer I walk with Him, the more my desire grows to hear His voice, know His heart, and serve His people. He is the Bread of Life that fills my hunger for purpose and meaning. Whenever life leaves me feeling empty or hollow, I want to seek His righteousness.
—SHARON HINCK

FAITH STEP: *If possible, skip a meal today and let yourself feel hungry. Ask Jesus to make you even more hungry for His righteousness to fill your life.*

THURSDAY, FEBRUARY 24

Blessed are the merciful, for they will be shown mercy. Matthew 5:7 (NIV)

RECENTLY, A NEW FRIEND SHARED my personal and private information with a third party. When I found this out, all the warmth and sense of connection I had been building with her evaporated. I felt betrayed. I couldn't trust her. I tossed aside my plans to spend time with her.

Then Jesus prompted me to come to Him. As I prayed about the situation, I realized she hadn't meant any harm. She is an open, transparent woman, who is as chatty as I am. Then Jesus reminded me of the many times my words have been indiscreet or hurtful to others. If Jesus has forgiven me for those transgressions, shouldn't I show mercy and forgive my new friend for doing the same?

Thankfully, my friends have shown me mercy for my gaffes. A desire to show mercy to my new friend bloomed in my heart. Yes, for the time being, I may be a bit more cautious about what I share with her, but I don't want to slam shut the emotional door between us. Lack of forgiveness could easily become a habit, and I would begin to shut out more and more people as they disappoint me in some way.

I'm so grateful Jesus has poured out His mercy in my life. With His help, I hope to reflect that mercy to others. —SHARON HINCK

FAITH STEP: *Is there someone you have shut out of your life? Pray about whether Jesus is calling you to show mercy. If so, do it abundantly, remembering how He always shows mercy to you!*

FRIDAY, FEBRUARY 25

Blessed are the pure in heart, for they will see God. Matthew 5:8 (NIV)

I BLINKED, RUBBED MY EYES, and readjusted my glasses. "I'm having trouble seeing the page. I think I need a stronger prescription," I told my husband.

"Here, let me see." He took my glasses and held them up, then chuckled. After quickly spraying eyeglass cleaner and then wiping my glasses with a lint-free cloth, he handed them back. Sure enough, now my reading glasses worked just fine.

Because the Word tells me so, I know that Jesus is at work all around me. He reveals the true nature of God in profound mercy, gentleness, and power. But sometimes I don't see Him. As I muddle through my day, my vision is clouded by smudges of doubt, fingerprints of self-centeredness, and scratches of distraction. Or, in the same way that I often lose my reading glasses, I may forget to look at the world through the lens of faith.

When I spend time with Jesus, He cleanses my heart and makes it pure. He reveals attitudes I need to change. Then I'm able to view my circumstances and the people around me in a new way. I'm able to focus on the ways that Jesus is present. I look forward to seeing my Savior in a tangible way in eternity. But because of Jesus creating a pure heart in me, I can also see God right now in my ordinary days. —SHARON HINCK

FAITH STEP: *Ask Jesus to purify your heart and help you see Him today.*

SATURDAY, FEBRUARY 26

Blessed are the peacemakers, for they will be called children of God.
Matthew 5:9 (NIV)

WHEN I THINK OF PEACEMAKERS, I think of ambassadors and diplomats. I'm neither. In fact, on a recent trip to babysit our three grandchildren, I struggled to negotiate whose turn it was to pick a story or which child got to play with a special toy.

But Jesus spoke of peace in a different way: "Peace I leave with you; my peace I give you. I do not give to you as the world gives. Do not let your hearts be troubled and do not be afraid" (John 14:27, NIV).

He calls me to notice the troubled and fearful hearts around me and bring people the true source of peace: Himself. The world will continue to be full of conflict until His return, and if I focus on that, I can grow discouraged. Conflict and tension can arise between countries but also in my interpersonal relationships. As I learned while babysitting, making peace can be an exhausting effort. Yet I can still offer comfort and hope to people—at home or in the world—who are wounded. I can seek justice for those who are oppressed and remind others that Jesus offers peace the world cannot give.

In fact, sometimes I need to speak peace to my own troubled thoughts and remind myself to look to Jesus. Today I want to walk in His peace that surpasses understanding, ready to share it with others. —SHARON HINCK

FAITH STEP: *Do you have a friend who needs peace—from her own anxiety or a difficult relationship? Find a way to be a loving presence and reflect the peace of Christ today.*

SUNDAY, FEBRUARY 27

*Blessed are those who are persecuted because of righteousness,
for theirs is the kingdom of heaven. Matthew 5:10 (NIV)*

THIS ISN'T MY FAVORITE BEATITUDE, but it's an important one. As a Christian I like to focus on all that I gain by following Jesus: eternal life, a restored relationship with God, a life of meaning and purpose, a heart of worship, His friendship and guidance, peace that surpasses understanding.

But Jesus has always been honest that following Him on the path of right choices will sometimes cause suffering. Even small choices can require sacrifices. Giving the right of way to the car merging into your lane. Returning the money when a cashier gives too much change. Biting your tongue and changing the subject when someone starts to share juicy gossip. Dietrich Bonhoeffer wrote *The Cost of Discipleship*, in which he challenged Christians to let their faith make a difference in their choices—large and small. Bonhoeffer faced persecution, including imprisonment and death, for taking a stand against Hitler.

I may never face such heroic choices, but in whatever ways I endure persecution or sacrifice for Jesus's sake, He assures me that in the midst of it, I am still blessed. As I follow in His steps, He is on this road with me, and He is able to bring glory to God and further His kingdom even in the midst of persecution. —SHARON HINCK

FAITH STEP: *Today, go online and either read about the life of Dietrich Bonhoeffer or read something he wrote. Ask Jesus to give you the courage to make righteous choices.*

MONDAY, FEBRUARY 28

Blessed are you when people insult you, persecute you and falsely say all kinds of evil against you because of me. Rejoice and be glad, because great is your reward in heaven, for in the same way they persecuted the prophets who were before you. Matthew 5:11–12 (NIV)

A NOVELIST FRIEND SENT HER latest book to a review journal. The reviewer refused to look at it because the author identified as a Christian. Most of us rarely face such blatant rejection for being a follower of Christ. Yet we face subtler forms. Family members may be derisive of our faith. Coworkers may mock those of us who follow Jesus. The media often portrays Christians with unkind stereotypes.

It hurts when I'm insulted or misrepresented. Yet any opposition I face is a weak shadow of what Jesus faced for my sake. He endured injustice, scorn, betrayal, and physical suffering.

Hebrews 12:2 gives me a clue about how to endure: ". . . fixing our eyes on Jesus, the pioneer and perfecter of faith. For the joy set before him he endured the cross, scorning its shame, and sat down at the right hand of the throne of God" (NIV).

Jesus knew His persecution was a short-term trial as He carried out His long-term purpose of joy. When I feel battered by unkind comments about my faith, I can look to Him. I'd like everyone to be kind to me, but I know that's not realistic. It's far more important that I remain steadfast, fix my eyes on Jesus, and anticipate the reward of heaven. —SHARON HINCK

FAITH STEP: *Bring your wounded feelings to Jesus. Ask Him to remind you of the glories ahead and to give you the courage to endure any persecution you might face for His sake.*

TUESDAY, MARCH 1

If anyone has the world's goods and sees his brother in need, yet closes
his heart against him, how does God's love abide in him? 1 John 3:17 (ESV)

THE OMINOUS CLOUDS BURST, AND rain poured down as I left to run errands. Normally, I would have dreaded getting in and out of the car, but not today! I was the proud owner of a Better Brella, the nifty reverse-open umbrella that lets you open and close it without getting wet. I couldn't wait to try my new toy.

Driving down a busy street, heading for the mall, I stopped to allow a man pushing a shopping cart to cross the road. In the cart, a soaking wet dog crouched beside a bag that appeared to hold all the man's worldly possessions. The man dashed across the street and found shelter under the awning at Walgreens. I didn't need anything from the drugstore, but a nudge from Jesus sent me there. I sat in my car in the parking lot for a minute, resisting what I knew Jesus expected of me. Finally, I got out and handed the man my umbrella. I patted his dog, went inside, bought dog food, and got some cash. When I handed it all to the man, he thanked me and asked if I knew where he might find a job. As it turned out, our family hardware store was hiring.

The rest of the day, I dashed in and out of stores, getting thoroughly drenched, but it didn't matter. I wouldn't have been able to live with myself if I hadn't helped my fellow man. —PAT BUTLER DYSON

FAITH STEP: *Read Matthew 25:45. Remember that Jesus always expects you to reach out to "the least of these" (ESV).*

ASH WEDNESDAY, MARCH 2

He was beaten, he was tortured, but he didn't say a word. Like a lamb taken to be slaughtered and like a sheep being sheared, he took it all in silence. Isaiah 53:7 (MSG)

I LOVE THE SYMBOLISM OF Ash Wednesday: receiving a cross of ashes on the forehead, a token of Jesus's willingness to stoop in the ashes with me; acknowledging and asking forgiveness of my sins; fasting from a particular food or activity to show appreciation for all He's sacrificed. These reminders help me to not take Jesus's love for granted.

I'm not a champion faster. (Okay, I stink at it.) When I go without food, I get cranky. I recently thought, *Snapping at my husband and complaining aren't helping me grow closer to Jesus.* So I came up with the perfect solution: fast from speaking all negative words. I was pretty proud of this clever idea. Until I started.

Two hours into my no-complaining fast, I caught myself yelling at my uncooperative hair. Later that morning, I whined to a coworker about a picky customer. By lunch time, I longed to fast from potato chips instead of complaints. Controlling my words was harder than fasting from chocolate or coffee, and this made me appreciate Jesus for His sacrifice of silence.

In the accounts of Jesus's arrest, beating, mock trial, and crucifixion, we don't read once of Him speaking a single complaint. At His Last Supper, He sang a hymn of praise. In the garden where He prayed and sweated blood, He submitted His will to God's. Even on the cross, He spoke of forgiving His torturers.

Jesus was God's power personified. He proved it by what He said—and by what He didn't say. —JEANETTE LEVELLIE

FAITH STEP: *This Lenten season, consider fasting from a troublesome habit. As Jesus did, submit your will to God's.*

THURSDAY, MARCH 3

Blessed are the pure in heart, for they will see God. Matthew 5:8 (NIV)

MY BOAT'S GALLEY CUPBOARDS ARE stained a deep reddish-brown. The glossy doors look beautiful set against the surrounding off-white walls. Their interiors, however, are a different matter. Humidity levels run high from November through April because we live in a wet climate. As a result, condensation collects and mildew grows easily and often unnoticed in dark, damp places—like deep inside my galley cabinets. All looks good on the outside, but I must be aware of what lurks in the hidden places and then deal with it.

A couple times each year, I dig into the recesses of my cupboards and do a deep cleaning. I wash the walls and treat them with a solution that kills mildew and helps slow future growth. I never relish doing this job, but I always feel good when it's done. The sanitized space is now safe for storing dishes and food again.

In the Sermon on the Mount, Jesus spoke of the need for cleanliness in another hidden place—the heart. Looking good on the outside and behaving according to religious expectations doesn't impress Him. He's more concerned about those secret recesses that no one can see, and He wants to ensure I keep them clean from ugly things, such as lust, jealousy, greed, and unforgiveness. Just as my cabinets need a regular deep cleaning, so does my heart. It's not pleasurable to invite Jesus to inspect my heart and reveal the sin I've harbored there, but doing so brings blessing. —GRACE FOX

FAITH STEP: *If you're able, clean the interior of one cupboard or drawer today. As you do so, ask Jesus to cleanse your heart from anything that grieves Him and to open your eyes to see more of His glory.*

Friday, March 4

Jesus turned around, and when He saw her He said, "Be of good cheer, daughter; your faith has made you well." And the woman was made well from that hour. Matthew 9:22 (NKJV)

FOR DECADES I BATTLED INSOMNIA, lying awake at night gripped by a nameless anxiety. As life became simpler and my faith deepened, worries no longer filled my nighttime hours. Yet my body wouldn't shut off. I tossed and turned, grabbing a few moments here and a couple of hours there. I felt tired and scatterbrained. I resorted to using herbal and over-the-counter sleeping aids nightly. It seemed there was no choice.

Weeks ago, something unusual happened. I felt sleepy at bedtime. I decided to forego the medication. Within minutes of getting into bed, I slumbered. This rarely occurred. The next morning, I awoke refreshed and rested. The same thing occurred the following evenings. Now close to a month has passed, and this has continued to happen. I'm already reaping the benefits of quality sleep—energy, better concentration, emotional stability.

What happened here? I had prayed about the situation but not often; it seemed too minor a problem to focus on. But Jesus, the Great Physician, wanted me whole and strong. He saw fit to take away my condition and restore my health, without me pleading and crying. He healed something I'd resigned myself to and accepted as part of my life. In His love, He saw my need and filled it. He does the same for all of us, in His perfect timing. —HEIDI GAUL

FAITH STEP: *What problem have you dealt with for so long that you've stopped praying over it and have even accepted it as part of your life? Ask Jesus to remove it. Trust in His healing touch and His perfect timing.*

SATURDAY, MARCH 5

O Lᴏʀᴅ, you hear the desire of the afflicted; you will strengthen their heart; you will incline your ear to do justice to the fatherless and the oppressed, so that man who is of the earth may strike terror no more. Psalm 10:17–18 (ESV)

Oɴᴇ ᴏꜰ ᴍʏ ꜰʀɪᴇɴᴅꜱ ᴛᴏʟᴅ me today that she has cancer. She was already on my prayer list because her husband had been recently diagnosed with dementia. When I heard my friend's news, my heart sank and I prayed, *Lord, it's too much.*

I offered her what comfort I could: love and compassion and support of her adamant trust that Jesus was walking this road with her. But I longed to be able to do more than comfort.

As I floundered in my helplessness to solve my friend's problems, this psalm reminded me that Jesus is never helpless. These verses reflect the Savior who acts. He hears, He comforts, but He doesn't stop with a hug and a whispered word of reassurance. He does justice on behalf of those who are hurting. I treasure the fact that Jesus hears our cries and strengthens our hearts with His comfort.

Returning to my prayers, I thanked Jesus with new conviction that He is at work on my friend's behalf. For some of the trials that confront us, He conquers quickly. Others ultimately will be conquered in eternity. But we can face each day knowing He hears, consoles, and acts. —Sʜᴀʀᴏɴ Hɪɴᴄᴋ

Fᴀɪᴛʜ Sᴛᴇᴘ: *Think of a friend who is afflicted today, and cry out to Jesus on her behalf, knowing He is taking action for her.*

Sunday, March 6

In your strength I can crush an army; with my God I can scale any wall. God's way is perfect. All the LORD's promises prove true. He is a shield for all who look to him for protection. Psalm 18:29–30 (NLT)

I KNEW NOTHING ABOUT ROCK climbing until my daughter met her future husband. The guy is crazy about scaling rock walls, and his passion sparked enthusiasm in her. This became their favorite activity during their dating days.

One Sunday afternoon, they invited me and Gene to join them for a climb. They chose a climb that was like child's play for them but nigh impossible for me, a woman with neither previous experience nor the desire to claw my way up a wall while roped to a partner with whom I was entrusting my life.

This couple exudes confidence about climbing because they understand the ins and outs. They've invested in safety gear and, as partners, they trust each other's skill implicitly.

Sometimes life's journey leads me to walls of a different type. They tower above me and intimidate me. My palms sweat and my heart pounds. How can I muster the courage to climb and conquer?

The secret lies in knowing Jesus, equipping myself with the truth of His promises, and trusting Him with every detail of my life. Without this, I might be tempted to give up without trying. But when I walk in the truth of who He is and what He says, I am equipped and able to scale any wall no matter how difficult it may appear. —GRACE FOX

FAITH STEP: *Go online and google a picture of a rock climber scaling a wall. Thank Jesus that you can climb any wall, no matter how steep, with His help.*

MONDAY, MARCH 7

Humble yourselves before the Lord, and he will lift you up in honor.
James 4:10 (NLT)

WE CAN'T CALL THE KITTEN I adopted last summer "Wee Wally" anymore. At eleven months, Wally weighs almost twenty pounds. I often ask him how he got so big. But I know the answer. It's all my fault.

Whenever I let Wally venture outside, I entice him back in by rattling a bag of kitty treats. As soon as he hears that happy sound, he races to the door and zips in. I also give him treats for good behavior: letting me pet him without biting my hand, looking cute and innocent—you name it. Wally is fat because his mama spoils him.

I'm thankful Jesus doesn't act like me. He doesn't give me whatever I want when I want it, for no particular reason. I've often asked for things that I later realized weren't wise. If Jesus had said yes to my requests, I wouldn't be a healthy Christian—I'd be spiritually fat and spoiled.

Hearing "no" isn't fun. I often ask "Why not?" when the Lord refuses my desires. Months or years down the road, I look back and say, "Thank You, Jesus, for not giving me that." I realize my ultimate good was at the center of His heart. Jesus's love compelled Him to give me His best, even if He had to deny me the harmful treats I craved.

I need to improve my boundary-setting skills with Wally, so he'll go from fat to fit. Because Jesus loves perfectly, He's never afraid to say no. —JEANETTE LEVELLIE

FAITH STEP: *Tell Jesus you've let go of all your selfish desires. Then open your hands and ask Him to fill your heart with His perfect plans for you.*

TUESDAY, MARCH 8

Jesus said to him, "I am the way, the truth, and the life. No one comes to the Father except through Me." John 14:6 (NKJV)

IN ONE OF MY KITCHEN drawers, I keep an ingredient-substitute chart, and this list has proven to be a lifesaver at times. But I hear real-life horror stories of someone accidentally or unwittingly making a substitution that ruins a dish. Like measuring out salt instead of sugar. Or using whole cloves instead of ground cloves in a cake. Sometimes substitutions work out fine; other times, not so much.

When it comes to a recipe for a satisfying, meaningful life, I'm finding that it's best to ignore suggestions for substitutions. For example, we're surrounded by people who clamor for the opportunity to lead and guide us. But Jesus is the Good Shepherd who laid down His life for us. Only by following Him can I find protection, purpose, and rest for my soul. There are many things I can cling to, but Jesus is the true vine. I'll only experience healthy growth and abundant fruit when I abide in Him. There are many sources to go to for nourishment, but Jesus is the Bread of Life. Only He offers life-giving sustenance that will keep me from ever being spiritually hungry again.

If I feel as though something is missing from my life, I might want to examine my habits. Am I following the Good Shepherd and allowing Him to guide my decisions—or someone else? Am I clinging to the true vine in times of need? Am I nourishing my mind with the Bread of Life? It might be that I've tried to substitute something else for the One who has no substitute.
—DIANNE NEAL MATTHEWS

FAITH STEP: *Good Shepherd, Bread of Life, True Vine—which of these three titles for Jesus do you need to meditate on today?*

WEDNESDAY, MARCH 9

Jesus replied, "You are in error because you do not know the Scriptures or the power of God." Matthew 22:29 (NIV)

BEFORE THE COFFEE MAKER FINISHED its routine of pressing water through coffee grounds, the day had already started to fall apart. My plans disintegrated before they'd been fully formed. Appliances started a mutiny. Decisions demanded attention but nothing made enough sense to give even a breath of confidence. Casual conversations quickly turned to confrontations.

I knew only one thing for sure. I needed to run. Not the sweat and earbuds with cute workout gear kind of running. What I needed most was to run to my Bible, quiet my heart, and temporarily ignore the problems as I turned to the problem-solver—Jesus.

This pattern had served me well before. Trouble swells? Stop focusing on the trouble and lean on the truth of Scripture and the power of Jesus Christ. Is this inclination automatic? No, it has to be intentional. I have to choose to open the pages that will redirect my heart back to the real truth to keep me from living in error, worries, or powerless.

The Word never disappoints. Jesus never disappoints. He cannot fail. Within moments of opening the sacred pages, the sharp edges of the day's concerns dulled. The impossible-to-figure-out questions had the start of answers. Plans realigned themselves according to what Jesus had wanted all along. The dryer was still broken, but I could honestly respond, "Oh, well," and not take the burden back.

Jesus said it long ago in today's verse. I am weak, prone to error, and susceptible to bad decisions if I neglect the Scriptures. There's power in its pages. —CYNTHIA RUCHTI

FAITH STEP: *When you feel yourself drifting toward dark thoughts, despair, or even a bad mood, remember the antidote of Scripture.*

Thursday, March 10

You will feel as if you were out on the ocean, seasick, swinging high up in the rigging of a tossing ship. Proverbs 23:34 (GNT)

EVERYTHING TILTED LIKE A CAREENING sailboat and began whirling around. Feeling dizzy, I hugged the floor, crawling like a drunken sailor wary of being knocked overboard by the boom. Seasick, I couldn't eat or drink anything except a sip of ginger ale or a saltine cracker.

I'd like to say that was my first experience onboard a sailboat. But it wasn't. I was dealing with a bout of vertigo that incapacitated me for days. Similarly, other unexpected upsetting events have caught me off guard and thrown me off balance: the death of a loved one, a family tragedy, the loss of a valued relationship, a financial setback. Sudden bad news can knock us off balance.

My bout with vertigo caused me to reflect on challenging events that have brought sudden major change to my life. Each was akin to being afflicted with vertigo when my whole world tilted. Caught off guard, I lost my balance and got knocked down. Each time, it took a while to regain my equilibrium.

But when I'm experiencing emotional vertigo—feeling as if I'm crawling on my knees, struggling to regain my balance—I can call on Jesus. And I know He'll stay with me until the events in my life stop spinning and return to order. Jesus helps me stand on my feet again. He has brought me safely through all the emotional, financial, and spiritual vertigo episodes thus far. And, I know He always will. —CASSANDRA TIERSMA

FAITH STEP: *Has life knocked you off balance, causing you to lose your spiritual equilibrium? Thank Jesus for staying with you, for helping you get off the floor, and for restoring balance.*

FRIDAY, MARCH 11

He comforts us in all our troubles so that we can comfort others. When they are troubled, we will be able to give them the same comfort God has given us. 2 Corinthians 1:4 *(NLT)*

MY HUSBAND'S PHONE RANG WITH the news we dreaded. The biopsy had come back, and he had cancer. In our shock, we felt the grace of Jesus surround us in what I called a "grace bubble."

As we shared the news, our friends had different reactions. Some reassured us that they knew someone who had this same cancer who was successfully treated. Others reminded us of God's faithfulness and promised to pray for us. Many offered to help if there was anything we needed—although we were too dazed to know what we needed. Others offered to listen as we processed all that was happening. I was grateful for each friend who expressed love in any possible way. As the bubble began to wear off and harsh realities intruded, every kind word, every prayer, and each listening ear was a treasured gift.

One friend's visit helped me the most. Her husband had been battling the same cancer. She fully understood the mix of hope and fear and the practical concerns we were facing. Her experience on this same path made all the difference and offered unique comfort and courage.

Jesus has experienced our human condition. Like my friend, He understands. Whatever painful circumstance we are enduring, He sees, He knows, and He can offer comfort that soaks deep into our spirits. And He can then enable us to give unique support and help to others because of our experiences. —SHARON HINCK

FAITH STEP: *What life experiences uniquely qualify you to offer hope to someone facing the same trial? Reach out to someone today and point them to Jesus, who fully understands.*

SATURDAY, MARCH 12

*So this is what the Sovereign L*ORD *says: "See, I lay a stone in Zion, a tested stone, a precious cornerstone for a sure foundation; the one who relies on it will never be stricken with panic." Isaiah 28:16 (NIV)*

MY GRANDSON REED IS A Lego master. He absolutely loves those building blocks and takes them wherever he goes. Reed spends countless hours putting them together to create all types of things, from cars to spaceships and homes and hospitals. He can even make Transformer robots. I marvel at how those small pieces come together to make one solid object.

While Legos are the base of Reed's creations, the Bible tells me that Jesus is the cornerstone of my life's foundation. He came to give me hope and a future with Him in eternity. Jesus's words and teachings have come together to form the base on which I've built my faith and trust in Him. As a believer, I am part of the universal church; I'm one of millions who are the building blocks that form the kingdom of God. I bring the gifts and talents that the Lord has given me and add them alongside fellow followers of Christ.

Now when I see Reed's multitude of Legos scattered throughout the house, I can view the blocks in a different way. They're not just a child's toy but are also a reminder that each one of us is a piece of the puzzle that is built upon the Savior, the One who sustains and protects His great church. —BARBRANDA LUMPKINS WALLS

FAITH STEP: *Where do you fit in the building of the kingdom of God?*

SUNDAY, MARCH 13

Behold, I am with you always, to the end of the age. Matthew 28:20 (ESV)

ONE OF THE WOMEN IN my Bible study showed up to our small group with red-rimmed, watery eyes. She quietly told me that she'd been sobbing in her car because of her impending divorce. We scheduled a hike so we could talk more, and then she took a few minutes to pull herself together before joining the group.

A few days later, as we walked, she described how scary it was for her to think about a future alone. She'd recently moved into her own apartment. Initially she was excited about living alone for the first time in her life, but moving caused a tumultuous emotional reaction. I tried to offer her words of encouragement to assure her that Jesus is always with her and that she's never alone. But my words felt trite and hollow.

Then she told me an incredible story of how Jesus had intimately communicated with her through a country song on the radio as she was driving to buy furniture for her new apartment. The words of the song were about buying furniture to make a home. Through this song, she felt Jesus uniquely speak to her in a moment of sadness, assuring her He is with her and helping her make a new home. Jesus comforted her much better than I could have.

—JEANNIE BLACKMER

FAITH STEP: *Do you have a special song in which you sense Jesus speaking uniquely to you? Play it on repeat today, letting it encourage your soul as you remember He is with you.*

MONDAY, MARCH 14

Better is one day in your courts than a thousand elsewhere; I would rather be a doorkeeper in the house of my God than dwell in the tents of the wicked.
Psalm 84:10 (NIV)

OUR DOG, FLASH, HAS A new best friend. Our neighbors across the street have a half-Corgi, half-Chihuahua mix named Zito. Zito sits by his front window and waits for Flash to come outside. When I mention Zito's name, Flash cannot contain his excitement. He starts barking, his entire body wriggling with joy. He rushes to the front door, whining until I open it. I make sure that no cars are coming, because as soon as I open the door, he bounds across the lawn and meets Zito mid-street. His happiness is palpable. This is what he has been waiting for—time with his friend. His life is complete. Chasing each other and rolling in the grass together, you would think that they had been separated for months. This doggie meet-up happens every day, sometimes more than once. They never get tired of seeing each other. Whether animal or human, time in the presence of the ones we love is the best, isn't it?

Jesus invites me into His presence every single day. He flings open His arms and waits for me to come to Him, alive with anticipation. He loves me more than anyone ever will. He cares for my body, mind, and spirit. He longs to calm my anxious heart and fill me with peace. What could be more beautiful and life-giving than being in His presence every single day? —SUSANNA FOTH AUGHTMON

FAITH STEP: *Today, enter your time with Jesus with sweet anticipation. Ready your heart and mind with thankfulness as you come into His presence.*

TUESDAY, MARCH 15

According to the eternal purpose which he purposed in Christ Jesus our Lord: in whom we have boldness and access with confidence by the faith of him.
Ephesians 3:11–12 (KJV)

A FEW MONTHS AGO, SOME local people asked me to consider running for public office. I'm a teacher and a writer and have never had any political ambitions whatsoever. But after a lot of prayer, I said I'd give it a try.

One of the coolest things that has come out of the race so far is the people I've met. A few people (who are well-known in Arkansas) took an interest in my campaign, and that has led to a great network of helpers. Without such people supporting me, I would have never gotten the access I have now. And that access has led me to relationships and resources I could not have previously imagined.

This is not unlike our relationship with Jesus. Like Paul writes in Ephesians, our faith in Jesus gives us access to God and all the riches that relationship brings. Through Him we can go to the Father for help in times of trouble and He'll provide for all our needs, whether that be protection, guidance, strength, wisdom, joy—you name it. God's divine power has given us everything through Jesus. The door to the throne room is wide open. —GWEN FORD FAULKENBERRY

FAITH STEP: *Call a friend whom you know is struggling. Remind her that she has access to everything she needs in Jesus. Offer to pray for her right then on the phone.*

WEDNESDAY, MARCH 16

Peace I leave with you; my peace I give you. I do not give to you as the world gives. Do not let your hearts be troubled and do not be afraid.
John 14:27 (NIV)

IN ONE SECTION OF OUR yard, weeds had formed an overgrown tangle that begged our attention. We decided to replace the mess with pavers. I knelt and shoved my spade into the soil to loosen it, then yanked with all my strength. As I removed a mass of dirt and roots, a worm popped its head into the daylight. Inch after inch, more of the squirming creatures appeared. Worms terrify me. Acknowledging their benefits to the soil doesn't change that fact. I froze. No shrieks, just me, a woman kneeling statue-like in my garden. As soon as I could breathe, I stood and raced out of reach. My husband investigated and noted the offender was at least nine inches long.

The idea of something moving around underfoot while I'm blind to its presence… it's unacceptable. *Why can't they make noise?*

Life sometimes seems full of "worms"—things developing beneath the surface, then suddenly appearing, as if from nowhere. Health concerns are discovered during routine tests or a car's engine stops running. Unforeseen situations can and often do occur, reminding us that we need something—Someone—to settle our broken but beautiful world.

Jesus knows all things, so nothing shocks Him or shatters His peace. And because He is with us always (Matthew 28:20), we can rest in Him.

Soon a patio will complete this area in our yard, a place to sit and relax, in Jesus's perfect peace. —HEIDI GAUL

FAITH STEP: *When you face an unexpected situation, remember other challenges that Jesus has walked you through. Trust Him to guide you through this one as well.*

THURSDAY, MARCH 17

Devote yourselves to prayer, being watchful and thankful. Colossians 4:2 (NIV)

GIVING THANKS IS SOMETHING I incorporate into every prayer in two specific ways. First, I thank Jesus for what He's done for me in the past, and then I thank Him for what I trust He'll do in the future.

Recalling prayers that He's already answered bolsters my faith to believe He will do it again. This practice gave me courage to trust Jesus when my husband and I began the process of buying and moving aboard a sailboat. I thanked Jesus for providing suitable housing for our family every time He'd moved us to a new location in the past. I thanked Him that His timing for our moves had always proven perfect and that He'd gone before us to prepare a place for us in the hearts of our new neighbors. Focusing on His faithfulness and wisdom that oversaw our past relocations brought courage to trust Him for the next.

Then I expressed gratitude in advance for what I trusted Jesus would do. I thanked Him for providing finances necessary to buy the boat and a suitable place to moor it. I thanked Him for providing a vessel with every amenity necessary to serve His purposes. I thanked Him for helping my husband learn about the systems needed to keep the boat livable. Expressing gratitude for things yet to be seen or done grew my faith. It squelched uncertainties and birthed anticipation.

Prayer is more than making requests. It includes giving thanks. God's Word issues this command over and over again for my benefit. Making it a regular practice is helping me to have courage to trust Jesus in every situation. —GRACE FOX

FAITH STEP: *Thank Jesus for a specific prayer He's answered in the past. Now thank Him in advance for caring for the details of a concern yet to be resolved.*

FRIDAY, MARCH 18

You are my rock and my fortress; therefore, for Your name's sake,
lead me and guide me. Psalm 31:3 (NKJV)

WHILE HIKING A ROCKY TRAIL in one of Oregon's wilderness areas, my husband, David, and I marveled at the natural beauty surrounding us. Tall trees canopied a dense undergrowth of ferns and delicate wildflowers. The lightly used trail soon became difficult to discern, and we questioned whether we were even on the path. Divides in the lush foliage created decoy openings into the forest, and we retraced our steps. But then we spotted a cairn, a stack of rocks constructed by fellow hikers. These markers are left beside the trail to provide direction for others by helping them spot the route more easily. Like the encouraging voice of a friend, those stones guided us back in the direction we needed to follow. We continued our journey without problems.

Jesus sometimes sets special stones along the path of our lives. By offering us words of wisdom through a loved one, a Bible verse read at just the right time, or an answer felt during deep prayer, He leads us back from our spiritual wanderings. When the world overwhelms us, we can search for His "cairns" and trust we'll find the right direction. We are never lost or alone on our journey. —HEIDI GAUL

FAITH STEP: *Gather (or purchase) some smooth river rocks. Stack them where you can see them daily to remind you of Jesus, your guide. Give thanks for His steady direction in your life.*

SATURDAY, MARCH 19

Do not be afraid, you wild animals, for the pastures in the wilderness
are becoming green. The trees are bearing their fruit; the fig tree
and the vine yield their riches. Joel 2:22 (NIV)

YEARS AGO, MY HUSBAND AND I planted a small flowering tree in
the landscape bed along the back of our house. This spring, the
branches remained brown and empty of buds. Dead. Perhaps the
repeating patterns of winter's thaws and harsh freezes took a toll.
Perhaps a deer nibbled away too much bark. We planned to cut
down the thin, lifeless trunk, but we never got around to it.

Later in the summer, I noticed flowers poking out from the bushes
surrounding that barren trunk. Somehow, a branch sprouted side-
ways from the tree, unnoticed by me until its shoots reached toward
the sun and flowered.

Have you ever felt as if a part of you has withered away? I sometimes feel as if my service to Jesus's kingdom has shriveled like that
tree—work I've poured my heart into dries up or precious relationships grow as bare as dead twigs. Time passes while hopes and dreams
show no signs of life.

Yet as I trust my Savior, He constantly surprises me. His resurrection life overcomes the deadening discouragement. My life blooms
in new places, love reaches out with new vigor, and new dreams
stretch toward His sunlight—out of what seemed to be forgotten
roots. No matter how desolate my surroundings appear, Jesus can
bring beauty back into my life. He prunes me, He nourishes me,
and He never gives up on me. He rejoices over me when new life
blooms. —SHARON HINCK

FAITH STEP: *Take a walk and look for signs of new life growing from a plant that*
seems lifeless. Thank Jesus for constantly producing new blossoms in your life.

SUNDAY, MARCH 20

Heaven and earth will pass away, but my words will never pass away.
Matthew 24:35 (NIV)

YEARS AGO, I HAD A simple vision of homeownership. I pictured a pretty house with an office space where I could write wonderful, inspiring words. This was a big dream for a single woman living in a major city where house prices started at a half a million dollars. Still, Jesus showed me in Deuteronomy 6:11 that I would live in a house "filled with all kinds of good things [I] did not provide" (NIV). I hung onto it.

Later, when I finally purchased my fixer-upper townhome, I was excited. The Word He had spoken was coming to pass! I was glad and thankful, but something bothered me a bit. It was not exactly "filled with all kinds of good things" the way the Word had stated. The house was forty years old, and it seemed no amount of "zhuzhing up" could make it right. I filled it with most of the "good things"—a stove, a fridge, and other appliances—by myself. Instead of complaining, I saw it as a proving ground, and I focused on thanking Jesus and taking care of the home I was given.

But Jesus hadn't forgot His Word to me. When I met Andrew and got married, we were blessed to buy the newly renovated home we live in now. As I look around, I realize that I am in the house "filled with all kinds of good things" that I hadn't filled, just like Jesus had promised back then! Good things are everywhere I look. Whatever Jesus says in His Word, He will do. His Word stands the test of time. —PAMELA TOUSSAINT HOWARD

FAITH STEP: *As you read the Word, know that His promises to you are "yes and amen."*

MONDAY, MARCH 21

When Jesus spoke again to the people, he said, "I am the light of the world. Whoever follows me will never walk in darkness, but will have the light of life." John 8:12 (NIV)

FRED ROGERS, THE BELOVED CREATOR of *Mister Rogers' Neighborhood*, is one of my heroes. I love his soothing voice, his compassion for children, and his godly wisdom. So when the movie *A Beautiful Day in the Neighborhood* came out, my husband, Kevin, bought two tickets for the first showing on opening day.

My favorite scene takes place in a Chinese restaurant. The main character, Lloyd Vogel, tells Mr. Rogers—played by Tom Hanks—that he knows why Fred loves people like him: "Because we're so broken." In a voice rich with kindness, Mr. Rogers replies, "I don't think you're broken." I wanted to stand up and cheer. Right there in the second row.

As we left the theater, I started to make an inner commitment to emulate Mr. Roger's Christlike behavior. But the Lord interrupted my thoughts. "No," He said. "I want you to be the unique individual I created you to be, and I want you to follow Jesus. He is the only one worthy of worship."

I had to smile and agree. If I copy the attitudes and behaviors of any human, no matter how noble he or she is, I'm settling for second best. When I study how Jesus loved, forgave, and helped, I'm choosing to follow the best example of God's heart.

I can still be compassionate, kind, and empathetic. Like Fred. And most of all, like Jesus. —JEANETTE LEVELLIE

FAITH STEP: *On a 3x5 card, list all the character traits of Jesus that you admire. Now circle the one you'd most like to pattern your life after. Ask God to give you the grace to follow in Jesus's footsteps.*

TUESDAY, MARCH 22

As he walked along, he saw Levi son of Alphaeus sitting at the tax collector's booth. "Follow me," Jesus told him, and Levi got up and followed him.
Mark 2:14 (NIV)

I ENJOY READING MEMES ON social media, whether they're laugh-out-loud funny or a simple statement packed with truth that makes me think. Even more, I love finding the perfect one to send to a family member or friend, something that I know will either make that person laugh or say, "Exactly!" I recently came across a meme that seemed custom-made for me that said, "Give me a minute while I overthink this."

My tendency to analyze everything can be a good thing when I'm learning something new or thinking through complicated decisions. But it's a bad habit when it causes me to waver in my faith walk. Jesus simply spoke two words to Levi (who's also called Matthew), and the tax collector left his job and followed Him. Levi didn't wonder what the Romans would think about him leaving his post or about how his choice might affect his future. He instantly obeyed. And his life changed forever.

When I feel certain that Jesus is prompting me to act, I don't need to weigh all my options. I don't need to look ahead and reason out possible outcomes or examine the logic of the action. If I drag my feet too long, I may miss the opportunity or assignment He has for me. When Jesus calls me to follow Him, I can hold back and spend time overthinking, or I can step out boldly and follow Him into the unknown. I won't regret it, because instant obedience brings great rewards. —DIANNE NEAL MATTHEWS

FAITH STEP: *Do you sense Jesus prompting you to take a new step? Ask Him for the courage to obey without hesitation.*

WEDNESDAY, MARCH 23

. . . the kingdom of the Son of His love, in whom we have redemption through His blood, the forgiveness of sins. Colossians 1:13–14 *(NKJV)*

As A BOOK LOVER AND a person who is catching up on movies everyone else has already seen—including the video production of *Hamilton* (yes, I'm that far behind)—I'm always on the alert for places where Jesus and His truths show up. I watch for threads of forgiveness, sin's consequences, the power of a pardon, self-sacrifice, and redemptive moments. Those reflections of biblical truths thrill me, whether they're intended or not by the author, screenwriter, or playwright.

Several "Jesus messages" stood out clearly the first time I streamed *Hamilton* on TV. Based in part on both historical events and fictionalized imaginings, the story of Alexander Hamilton, the birth of our nation, the cost of freedom, and the price of foolishness, all revealed themselves on the stage.

I leaned toward the screen and pressed my hands over my heart during one moment in particular. It's a scene I'm sure Jesus wrote, although His Name isn't listed in the credits. Hamilton's infidelity eventually led to his young son Philip's unnecessary death in a duel to defend Hamilton's honor. Eliza—Hamilton's wife and Philip's mother—had been crushed by her husband's infidelity, which was then compounded by the loss of her cherished son. The character playing Eliza—agony ripping through her very soul—stretched out her hand toward her husband in a silent gesture of forgiveness as the cast sang, "Forgiveness. Can you imagine?"

Because of Jesus, my heart wanted to tell the cast, "Yes. Yes, I can."
—CYNTHIA RUCHTI

FAITH STEP: *Think about a scene from a movie, TV show, or play that is poignant because it reflects the love, power, and grace of Jesus Christ. Start a conversation about it.*

THURSDAY, MARCH 24

For there is hope of a tree, if it be cut down, that it will sprout again, and that the tender branch thereof will not cease. Job 14:7 (KJV)

LIVING IN THE WILD WILDERNESS of Arkansas provides endless opportunities for observing nature. It's amazing to me—and even terrifying sometimes in a way—to witness its power, its strength, its impulse toward life. Nowhere is this more obvious than in the immediate vicinity of my house, where my husband, Stone, battles trees, brush, and briars with a chainsaw. Just like Pa Ingalls carved out a homestead. Stone is determined we will have a semblance of order in our small section of the big woods. Nature has other ideas.

Last year he cut down a tree that threatened our roof. The roots were too deep to pull out without making a big mess of things with the tractor, so he just cut it off at ground level. It looked done for. However, in the spring, there was a brave little branch sprouting from the stump.

The life of Jesus in me is like that little branch—it's the overcoming nature of hope. Martin Luther said, "Our Lord has written the promise of resurrection, not in books alone, but in every leaf in springtime." But I think perhaps I see a greater picture of it in a branch that sprouts from a stump. Hope says there is nothing I can do that will stop me from believing—reaching, through darkness and difficulty, toward the Light. —GWEN FORD FAULKENBERRY

FAITH STEP: *Plant some bulbs in an area you see every day. In the spring, let the flowers remind you that Jesus lives in you, and that He is your hope.*

FRIDAY, MARCH 25

Set your minds on things above, not on earthly things. Colossians 3:2 *(NIV)*

MY CHURCH DOES A CORPORATE fast every year, when hundreds of members engage together in a dedicated time of prayer and fasting. My husband, Hal, and I decided to step out on faith and commit to a monthlong Daniel Fast, which involves consuming only fruits, vegetables, grains, and water. That's no small order for two self-proclaimed carnivores who love fried chicken, macaroni and cheese, and apple pie.

A week before we began the fast, I researched vegan recipes and stocked up on brown rice, bulgur, vegetables, and every type of bean imaginable. I got tips from my vegan friends on how to transition to meatless meals. I became fixated on food.

What I wasn't focused on was praying and reading God's Word. While I did spend time with the Lord, I concentrated more on the earthly (food) and not the spiritual. Near the end of the fast, I confessed to the Lord that I felt like I had failed. But after it was all over, I believed Jesus was pleased with my efforts, even if I hadn't done everything as I thought I should have.

The Bible tells us that we do not live by bread alone but on every word that comes from the mouth of the Lord (Deuteronomy 8:3; Matthew 4:4). I've learned that while fasting is a wonderful spiritual discipline, it does not replace spending time with Jesus. So, for my next fast, I'll ask Jesus to give me an urgent hunger for Him, one that will go beyond sacrificing earthly things.
—BARBRANDA LUMPKINS WALLS

FAITH STEP: *Take stock of what occupies your mind each day. Do meals, chores, social media, TV, and such consume you more than time spent with Jesus?*

SATURDAY, MARCH 26

Jesus said to his disciples, "Whoever wants to be my disciple must deny themselves and take up their cross and follow me. For whoever wants to save their life will lose it, but whoever loses their life for me will find it."
Matthew 16:24–25 (NIV)

I HAVE TAKEN GREAT JOY decorating our new home. I have been saying things like "pops of color" and "impact" and "a mix of modern and farmhouse." Scott bought me some bright yellow pillows that have the phrase *Hello, Sunshine* embroidered on them. I feel a zing of happiness every time I see them. The only problem with all the decorating is that I want to do more decorating. It has unleashed the beast within, the beast that says I should have everything I want—right now.

I've worked hard to tame this beast my whole life. It's my *selfish self*, the part of me that only thinks about me, lives for my own pleasures, and could care less about how my actions affect anyone else. I'm not going to lie; giving into the beast is ugly. There is no "pop of color" when my life is self-centered.

Jesus has something to say about my giving into the beast. He asks me to deny my *selfish self* and follow Him, the least selfish person in all history. The life of freedom and hope that I am longing for happens when I stop chasing after pleasing myself and start chasing Jesus. It unleashes the true impact of His love and grace lived out in me. —SUSANNA FOTH AUGHTMON

FAITH STEP: *Are you struggling with "the beast within" in any area of your life? Confess it to Jesus. Ask Him to re-center your heart and mind on Him.*

SUNDAY, MARCH 27

He predestined us for adoption to himself as sons through Jesus Christ, according to the purpose of his will, to the praise of his glorious grace, with which he has blessed us in the Beloved. Ephesians 1:5–6 (ESV)

AT THE AGE OF FIFTY-FIVE, I thought I was over feeling left out, but an old wound recently resurfaced that made we wonder if I really was. A group of women I knew in college scheduled a conference call, and it reminded me of a painful experience from years ago. I never truly felt like I was part of this circle of friends, but after college, I had become close friends with a few girls in this group. Back then, a weekend getaway was planned, and one of the girls invited me. I was excited! On the drive, we stopped to grab a bite to eat and I overheard arguing in the restroom. One of the girls complained that I wasn't a part of the group and shouldn't have been invited. I was crushed. The entire weekend was awkward and painful.

I'm still close to a few of the women. But when this recent group call occurred, I chickened out and didn't participate. I allowed a rejection, which had happened decades ago, to hinder me, and I missed out on what could have been a time of encouraging fellowship.

I long to belong, but first I need to believe I belong. Scripture says I am adopted into God's family through Jesus. I need to accept this as true. I am forever accepted in His group, so there's never a reason to feel insecure with others. Next time, I won't allow the enemy to whisper lies to my soul; instead I'll join the call.
—JEANNIE BLACKMER

FAITH STEP: *Write down five statements on what it means to you to always belong, based on Jesus's love for you, and read them when you feel insecure around others.*

MONDAY, MARCH 28

Be shepherds of God's flock that is under your care, watching over them—
not because you must, but because you are willing, as God wants you to be.
1 Peter 5:2–3 (NIV)

I LOVE WATCHING TV. MANY of my favorite shows had servants, especially those shows from back in the day. Among them was the ever-present Lurch from *The Addams Family*, sassy Florence from *The Jeffersons*, and the quick-witted Alice from *The Brady Bunch*.

All of these fictional servants had different personalities and ways to approach the situations that were presented to them by the hodge-podge group of people they served—some kooky, some sweet, some self-absorbed. I have similar types of folks—and more—among my family, friends, church members, and colleagues. They are my people, the ones whom the Lord has put within my reach to serve.

Peter says to be shepherds of God's flock, and not only willing shepherds but those who are eager to serve and be examples to the flock. That can sometimes be a pretty tall order for me. But with Jesus's help, I can willingly serve those who come with last-minute requests for help. I can eagerly assist people with personal challenges who on the surface may not be so lovable or easy to work with. And with Jesus's help, I can be an example of a true servant who walks humbly with Him.

This is part of the work that the Lord has given me to do. While I am watching over my flock, He is watching me as I represent Him. I like to think of myself as a servant in Jesus's everyday reality show.
—BARBRANDA LUMPKINS WALLS

FAITH STEP: *Reach out to serve a member of your flock in some way today.*

TUESDAY, MARCH 29

Call upon Me in the day of trouble; I will deliver you,
and you shall glorify Me. Psalm 50:15 (NKJV)

AHA, THERE IT WAS! THAT pesky sock I'd been searching for was right behind the dryer. I grabbed a broom and, using the handle, scooted the sock from behind the dryer to the tight space between the dryer and the wall. I couldn't quite get it, so I crammed my knee in that tiny space to get better contact. I was able to scoot the sock closer, but when I tried to move my knee, it was wedged tight. I tried to push the dryer away, but it wouldn't budge, positioned as it was next to the heavy washer. This could have been an episode of *I Love Lucy*, only Lucy wouldn't have been as dumb.

I didn't have my cell phone nearby and my husband, Jeff, wouldn't be home for hours. If I yanked my knee and was able to free it, I might break some bones. But if I stayed in this position, the knee would swell, making the space even tighter.

There was only one thing to do. *Jesus,* I cried. *Help!* In the Bible, people in trouble often cried out to Jesus, and He heard their pleas. Becoming more desperate by the moment, I prayed He would hear mine, despite my foolishness at being in this predicament. Fighting my panic, I took some deep breaths. With Jesus's help, I could do this.

With all my might, I pushed the dryer with both hands, and it moved a fraction of an inch. Just enough for me to free my knee. *Jesus, I praise You!* —PAT BUTLER DYSON

FAITH STEP: *In times of trouble, think of Jesus as your 911. He will rescue you!*

WEDNESDAY, MARCH 30

I wait for the LORD, my soul doth wait, and in his word do I hope.
Psalm 130:5 (KJV)

HAVE YOU EVER BEEN LIED to? I don't have to know your story to know the answer to that question—we've all been deceived at some point in our lives. Whether the lie is big or small, we learn something when someone is dishonest with us. We learn not to trust that person's word.

I recently had an experience with a person who promised to help me in a certain way. When receiving help took longer than expected, I tried to be patient, believing the person was just busy or that something else had come up and he would get to me eventually. He kept putting me off but never withdrew his offer to help. He just kept promising to help soon. Except he never did. Ever.

God's Word is different. I can put my hope in the Word and wait with confidence that I won't be disappointed. John 1:14 says that in Jesus "the Word was made flesh, and dwelt among us" (KJV). So when I wait, as the psalmist says, I can wait with hope because my hope is found in Jesus. What a world of difference it makes if I'm waiting on Him instead of waiting on people to fulfill my needs.
—GWEN FORD FAULKENBERRY

FAITH STEP: *Jesus is never late. He never provides the wrong thing or too little of it or too much. He's never confused about what you need. He's never too busy or too tired. He has the resources and the wisdom. His timing is perfect. Wait, with hope, for Him.*

THURSDAY, MARCH 31

Still other seed fell on good soil, where it produced a crop—a hundred,
sixty or thirty times what was sown. Whoever has ears, let them hear.
Matthew 13:8—9 (NIV)

OUR BACKYARD BACKS UPTO AN open field full of tumbleweeds. I didn't know a whole lot about tumbleweeds before moving to Idaho. Now, I know that whenever the wind kicks up, the dry brush breaks free from its stems and bounces over my fence. After one spring windstorm, there were twelve tumbleweeds stacked up in my yard. It was a tumbleweed party. What I didn't realize is that when the tumbleweeds were rolling through my yard, they were dropping their spores everywhere. And I mean everywhere. I can't keep track of the thousands of tiny sprouts growing up in the edges of the grass. They are prolific. I wish all my plants were like that.

Their growth reminds me of Jesus's parable about the sower and His seeds. Jesus said, "The seed falling on good soil refers to someone who hears the word and understands it. This is the one who produces a crop, yielding a hundred, sixty or thirty times what was sown" (Matthew 13:23, NIV). When I take the message of Jesus's kingdom to heart, allowing His grace, forgiveness, and love to take root in my heart, the spread of His goodness is prolific. His unstoppable love at work in my life not only changes me but also touches the lives of those around me. And that is great news!
—SUSANNA FOTH AUGHTMON

FAITH STEP: *What is the soil of your heart like? Rocky? Hard? Full of weeds? Ask Jesus to make your life ready for His good news to take root and then spread to everyone around you.*

FRIDAY, APRIL 1

Mary treasured up all these things and pondered them in her heart.
Luke 2:19 (NIV)

IT WAS APRIL, BUT A severe snowstorm was headed to Colorado. I'm a Colorado native, so such weather shouldn't be a surprise, but every spring when a snowstorm hits, I want to flee the harsh, disappointing cold. Harsh because the day before I was wearing flip-flops, and disappointing because the freezing temperatures threatened to destroy the precious spring flowers, including my daffodils. I couldn't escape the storm, but there was something I could do. I grabbed scissors and went outside. I cut a bounty of daffodils—beauty to combat the bleak days ahead.

Jesus knows that I'll experience challenges that threaten to devastate the splendor around me, yet He provides treasures in the midst of unhappy times. I love the story of the shepherds who hurried to Bethlehem after the angel of the Lord told them, "For unto you is born this day in the city of David a Savior, who is Christ the Lord" (Luke 2:11, ESV). When the shepherds found Jesus in the manger, they told Joseph and Mary that they believed their baby was the Messiah because of the angel's message. Then Scripture declares, "Mary treasured up all these things . . . in her heart" (Luke 2:19, NIV). I believe the Lord knew Mary would need a reservoir of treasures when, thirty-three years later, she witnessed Jesus's crucifixion.

My yellow daffodils cheered me greatly after the storm. Jesus knew I would need those golden treasures to sustain me through the snowy days. The flowers also reminded me to store up treasures of my own meaningful moments with Jesus to sustain me through life's storms. —JEANNIE BLACKMER

FAITH STEP: *Write down treasured memories with Jesus and place them in a special box so they're ready to read when needed.*

SATURDAY, APRIL 2

May the God who gives endurance and encouragement give you the same attitude of mind toward each other that Christ Jesus had, so that with one mind and one voice you may glorify the God and Father of our Lord Jesus Christ. Accept one another, then, just as Christ accepted you, in order to bring praise to God. Romans 15:5–7 (NIV)

I ENJOY PARTICIPATING IN MY town's historic home tours. Albany, Oregon, is known for its beautifully maintained historic structures, and twice a year, generous homeowners allow docents like me to share their homes with the public. It's a time of reflection, joy, and learning, as we witness the way past generations lived and recognize the craftsmanship of years gone by. During this season's tour, I was impressed with one couple. They had come together later in life, with one spouse divorced and the other widowed. As they welcomed us into their home, the wife shared how, by the time they'd wed, they each had their own collections of mementos. Neither wanted to part with the beloved items that had come to mean so much to them over their lifetimes. So, they compromised, starting a new tradition by mingling them together. The result was both charming and uplifting.

Like this couple, the church is as diverse as its members. Each individual's experience is as unique as the life each has lived, but varying perspectives don't need to divide us. Since Jesus walked among us, believers have set aside their differences to give Him glory. As I gather in worship, may my praises join with others to meld into a beautiful collection of acceptance and love. —HEIDI GAUL

FAITH STEP: *Think of fellow Christians who have a different outlook than you do. Find ways to accept your differences so you can better praise Jesus together.*

Sunday, April 3

When they came to the border of Mysia, they tried to enter Bithynia, but the Spirit of Jesus would not allow them to. Acts 16:7 (NIV)

How frustrating! Jesus called Paul to share the gospel, and he was raring to go—but then Jesus held him back. What's up with that?

I was invited recently to speak at a local writer's group. I was excited to support others in the body of Christ and felt called. But after I accepted, a group leader soon emailed me: "Sorry, I didn't realize someone else on the committee had already scheduled a different person." And with that, the door closed. I felt deflated. This is just a small example, but there have been other times when I was ready to charge ahead, but the Spirit of Jesus clearly didn't allow me to move forward. Disappointment made my heart ache, and my prayers held painful questions.

Perhaps you've experienced painful closed doors. You begin a ministry born from His prompting, but then He calls you to lay it down. You plan a move to a new job, but then the job dissolves. You invest in a relationship, but Jesus stops you from moving forward. When that happens, it's easy to feel confused. Yet I've learned that I can trust that when the Spirit of Jesus stops me from moving in my intended direction, He does this out of wisdom and love and for purposes I don't yet see.

Sometimes I struggle when Jesus says, "Go," but often I struggle even more when He says, "Stop." We can show our love and faith when we're willing to move forward, change directions, or even hold still—however Jesus leads. —Sharon Hinck

---

Faith Step: *Thank Jesus for the way He has guided and protected you through a time when He made you stop.*

MONDAY, APRIL 4

Delight yourself in the LORD, and he will give you the desires of your heart. Psalm 37:4 (ESV)

DURING THE LAST MONTH, EVERY time I looked out my window, I wanted to cry. Or at least yell at whoever had pruned our maple tree. Only stubs of a dozen huge branches and the trunk remained.

Because my husband, Kevin, is a pastor, we live in the parsonage, so I didn't have a say in the pruning of "my" tree. But how I loved that tree—and the two squirrels that lived inside.

Every morning while I prayed, pacing around my bedroom, I'd watch the squirrels skitter across the branches, chasing each other and washing their faces with their tiny paws. Even on days when my mood matched the murky sky, those critters made me smile. Now where would they live?

I knew the church leaders who decided to prune the tree were acting for our safety. If a bad storm hit, enormous branches that had grown over our bedroom might crack off and damage the roof and hurt us. I agreed with the logic of the decision. But I missed and worried about my little friends. *Jesus, please protect them. Help them find a new home.*

Jesus had created these delightful animals. He loved them more than I did. I found courage in the hope that when the branches grew back, the squirrels would return.

And then, yesterday morning when I opened the window shade, my heart leaped with joy to see my squirrels playing in the maple. They had returned! Jesus hadn't only given my furry friends a new home. He'd given me my heart's desire. What a Savior! —JEANETTE LEVELLIE

FAITH STEP: *Think of several little things that bring you enormous joy and thank Jesus for them.*

TUESDAY, APRIL 5

Therefore he is able to save completely those who come to God through him, because he always lives to intercede for them. Hebrews 7:25 (NIV)

I'VE ALWAYS BEEN A WORD lover, but there are some words I just don't care for, like *almost*. Kids get frustrated on long trips when they hear, "We're *almost* there." As adults, many of us have heard the word when we applied for an award or a job: "You *almost* got it." When my youngest granddaughter was born last year, I had *almost* finished knitting her lacy blanket. Maybe the real reason I hate the word is because while growing up, I felt "almost but not quite" in several areas: intelligence, looks, talents, social skills. Some days I still feel that way.

I'm thankful there is nothing almost or halfway about Jesus and His love for me. By dying on the cross, He fully paid my sin debt. Since I accepted Him as my Savior, I am wholly accepted and unconditionally loved. My past has been forgiven completely. My future destiny is secure and glorious. As I obey and trust His leading, my life is abundantly blessed. *Fully, unconditionally, abundantly*—now those are words I absolutely *love* to think about.

My walk of faith during this earthly life will never be perfect. I will make mistakes. I'll falter, stumble, or come up short. But what I'm learning day by day as I spend more time with Jesus is that in His eyes, I am never *almost*. Rather, I am completely His, and that makes me complete in every sense of that beautiful word.
—DIANNE NEAL MATTHEWS

FAITH STEP: *Write a list of ways you feel as if you don't quite measure up. Now beside each item, write a word or phrase that shows how Jesus feels about you. Cross out your original list.*

WEDNESDAY, APRIL 6

Always be prepared to give an answer to everyone who asks you to give the reason for the hope that you have. 1 Peter 3:15 (NIV)

IF ONLY I HAD A nickel for every time I've asked someone, young or old, this question: "What new thing has Jesus been impressing on your heart?" (Yet I *am* a rich woman because, as I've listened to the answers, the bank account of my faith has swelled.)

I've learned to pause and listen if the person I'm talking to doesn't have an immediate answer. Almost always, she eventually thinks of something. She reports that she's learning the real meaning of endurance. Or that Jesus is showing her new ways to cope with a hard-to-love coworker or an out-of-sorts friend. Or she'll share a Bible verse that won't leave her alone. Or she'll smile and say she's finally getting the hang of this contentment business.

If the answer is, "Nothing," then I let the person know I'll ask again next week. It's been a joy to watch that person seek me out the next time our paths cross, her eyes excited, to report what Jesus showed her or how she'd trusted Him with a sticky situation.

I also have to make sure that my "God stories" don't get dusty. I may have plenty to say about what Jesus did in my life over the last several decades—and for all those things I give thanks and praise—but I serve a living Savior. My relationship with Him is present tense. I want to be aware of what Jesus is doing this week, this day, this hour in my life, so I can always be prepared to give an answer for the hope I have. —CYNTHIA RUCHTI

FAITH STEP: *What new thing has Jesus been impressing on your heart? Who can you share that with before the day's over?*

THURSDAY, APRIL 7

On that day a person out on the deck of a roof must not go down into the house to pack. A person out in the field must not return home.
Luke 17:31 (NLT)

I LIVE IN A FIVE-SEASON climate: fall, winter, spring, summer, and fire. One fire season, when smoke from surrounding wildfires blanketed our little town, the sheriff issued an evacuation warning. In eerie stillness, parked vehicles waited—packed, ready to flee at a moment's notice.

Blessedly, it never came to that. Once the threat of danger subsided, we breathed sighs of relief, contemplating how we would prepare better or differently next time. "Grateful to have escaped total loss and devastation from wildfire, we returned to normal life." Gradually, we began to feel safe again. Eventually, emergency checklists were stored away. "Grab and Go" boxes were unpacked or shuffled off into basements, set aside until another fire season.

Preparing for an evacuation reveals our fears and priorities. During one fire season, I confess that, besides important papers and other essential items, I also packed a *huge* box of shoes, just in case.

Besides a quick getaway during a fire, what I *should* be preparing for is Jesus's return. What I want to have packed and ready to go is a heart devoted to Jesus. Not shoes. And not just during a fire season because Jesus said to always be ready (Mark 13:33).

Until then, I'll continue preparing for a possible evacuation—while praying through all five seasons, asking Jesus to prepare my heart for His return. —CASSANDRA TIERSMA

FAITH STEP: *Ask Jesus how to prepare for His return. Thank Him that the only checklist that matters, in the end, is the one in the Book of Life with your name written on it.*

FRIDAY, APRIL 8

Now all glory to God, who is able, through his mighty power at work within us, to accomplish infinitely more than we might ask or think. Ephesians 3:20 (NLT)

ABOUT SIX MONTHS AGO, MY husband and I got an idea to bless men in their first weeks after being released from prison. I read a study that said if something doesn't go right for returning citizens soon after their return to public life—the recidivism rate skyrockets.

So Andrew and I filled backpacks with toiletry items, socks, a New Testament, and a handwritten note of encouragement. Our plan was to invite men to our church and give out the backpacks, but that proved difficult to administrate because the returning citizens are released on staggered schedules. Prayer revealed that Jesus's plan was for us to keep a supply of backpacks in our car trunks for whenever and wherever He showed us a need. It's so like Him to want us to be ready "in season and out." (2 Timothy 4:2, NIV).

One day while running errands, Jesus told me, *Look around.* In no time, a man walked past me who looked as if he could use a backpack. I drove up to where he was standing, rolled down the window, and held up the pack. I asked him if he'd like one, and he nodded, skeptically. I handed him the backpack, smiled, and said, "Jesus loves you!" He smiled back and said, "Thank you. He loves you too!" In Jesus's name, I allowed the power at work within me to empower another person! —PAMELA TOUSSAINT HOWARD

FAITH STEP: *Walk boldly in the power Jesus has endowed you with today.*

SATURDAY, APRIL 9

Great is the LORD and most worthy of praise; his greatness no one can fathom. One generation commends your works to another; they tell of your mighty acts. They speak of the glorious splendor of your majesty—and I will meditate on your wonderful works. Psalm 145:3–5 (NIV)

I HAVE A SINGER-SONGWRITER FRIEND named Jenna. When we met, I was in junior high and she was in elementary school. I'd recently outgrown playing with dolls, but I wanted Jenna to have the same fun I'd had. I gave her my doll clothes, along with instructions to pass them on when she was done with them. It's fun to pass along good things. Jenna and I are still passing on good things to each other. Just today, she passed along encouragement, telling me how her friend loved one of my books. She passed along transparency, sharing about how Jesus is working in her. I passed along some hope, telling her about the miracles Jesus has done in our family this year, and some joy, telling her I couldn't wait to buy her latest album. We have a history of encouraging each other and sharing laughter and compassion. These precious things reveal how Jesus is working in our lives.

Jesus is in the business of passing along good things: outpourings of mercy, visions of hope, acts of great love. They are life-giving. As I follow Him, I get to do the same, sharing joy and words of encouragement and reminding others that Jesus is at work in my life. —SUSANNA FOTH AUGHTMON

FAITH STEP: *What good things are you passing along to the people around you? Make a point today to draw on the hope of Jesus and share His words of encouragement with those you see.*

PALM SUNDAY, APRIL 10

They led the donkey and colt out, laid some of their clothes on them, and Jesus mounted. Nearly all the people in the crowd threw their garments down on the road, giving him a royal welcome. Matthew 21:7–8 (MSG)

MY HUSBAND, KEVIN, IS A pastor and likes to illustrate his sermons in unique ways. One year on Palm Sunday, he arranged several styles of coats in the center aisle of the church building.

At the start of his message, Kev stepped into the aisle, held up a navy-blue suit coat, and said, "This first coat represents my career. It's one of my best, so I wear it when I preach. Next, I have a casual jacket that I might wear to a picnic with friends—my social life." He continued to pick up various coats, noting each one's purpose to use them as examples of all the aspects of our lives: work, family, finances, leisure time.

Kevin explained that the common person in Jesus's day owned only one coat, and it was used to keep warm, used as a covering at night, and used for protection from the weather. When the crowd laid their coats in the dirt for Jesus's donkey to walk on, they were declaring Jesus as Lord over their entire lives. If their coat was soiled and ruined, they couldn't go home to a closet full of replacements. They willingly sacrificed their most valuable garment to honor Jesus as their king.

Every year on Palm Sunday—what Kevin calls Coat Sunday—I need to ask myself, *Am I willing to give Jesus every area of my life? Am I willing to show Him—not just tell Him—how much I love Him?*
—JEANETTE LEVELLIE

FAITH STEP: *Online or in a hymnal, find the song "I Surrender All." Sing it to Jesus from your heart.*

MONDAY, APRIL 11

Going into the Temple he began to throw out everyone who had set up shop, selling everything and anything. He said, "It's written in Scripture, My house is a house of prayer; You have turned it into a religious bazaar."
Luke 19:45–46 (MSG)

WHEN MY BELOVED GRANDMA DIED, I helped Mom clean out my grandma's house. It took over a week to get rid of seventy-six years of junk (excuse me, *treasures*). That first day, Mom told me to set aside anything I wanted. I said, "All I care about are some of her paintings." Grandma was a self-taught artist. Her breathtaking oil paintings of mountain scenes and still-life flowers helped me feel close to her—as if she wasn't really gone.

But as the week progressed, my heart filled with greed. Every time I walked into a room, another item would catch my eye. By the time I left for my home, my car was filled with stuff. Most of which I later gave away.

On the Monday after Palm Sunday, Jesus demonstrated what God thinks of greed. Merchants who were selling animals for sacrifices and exchanging foreign currency in the temple were making a mockery of God's house. In a moment of justified anger, Jesus drove out the money changers and all their animals. He cleansed His Father's house, reminding them of the temple's original purpose: to meet with God.

Whenever I'm tempted to want more than I need, I remember that ugly feeling of greed I experienced while cleaning Grandma's house. I remind myself that God's house—my heart—is meant for fellowship with Him. —JEANETTE LEVELLIE

FAITH STEP: *Ask Jesus to show you if your heart needs cleansing of any type of greed. Imagine yourself, with Jesus beside you, driving out the greed and dedicating your heart—God's house—as a place of prayer.*

TUESDAY, APRIL 12

"I tell you the truth," Jesus said, "this poor widow has given more than all the rest of them." Luke 21:3 (NLT)

I HOPE NO ONE NOTICES, I thought, dropping a penny into the offering plate in church. Jesus's sweet voice in my heart had prompted me to give the penny, even though I could afford much more. As the pastor's wife, I worried that someone would think I was stingy. Nevertheless, I pinched my eyes shut and let go of the wee coin. In that instant, a delightful joy burst upon me. Despite my fear of others' opinions, I had obeyed. I felt Jesus's pleasure.

Two days after Jesus's triumphant ride into Jerusalem, He observed people in the temple as they put money in the treasury boxes. Some wealthy individuals gave huge amounts. Perhaps they saw Jesus sitting nearby and wanted to impress Him.

Instead of praising their large gifts, Jesus noticed the poor widow who gave all she had. He praised this destitute lady who emptied her purse of her last two coins (in our day, worth about two dollars). It wasn't the net worth of the money that impressed Jesus, but the attitude of this woman's heart: she trusted God enough to give Him her all.

Jesus was so pleased that He complimented the widow in front of all who were there with Him. I wonder if the rich people heard His mini-sermon on giving your all to God.

Several days later, Jesus practiced what He preached. He gave His all. —JEANETTE LEVELLIE

FAITH STEP: *Next time you give an offering at church or send a gift to a mission work, tell Jesus, I give not only my earnings but also my entire self to You, Lord.*

WEDNESDAY, APRIL 13

Just think how much more the blood of Christ will purify our consciences from sinful deeds so that we can worship the living God. For by the power of the eternal Spirit, Christ offered himself to God as a perfect sacrifice for our sins. Hebrews 9:14 (NLT)

DURING OUR SUNDAY AFTERNOON CALL with the grandkids, I complained to seven-year-old Jenessa how a strong wind had ruined my hairdo earlier that day. The twenty minutes I'd spent styling it before church was gone forever.

In her most serious tone, Jenessa said, "Don't worry, Grandma. People that always look and behave perfect are so annoying."

Although I laughed in agreement, I thought of one individual whose perfect behavior never annoyed me. In fact, I admired Him and even tried to live up to His standards.

Jesus never sinned. He never spoke a cruel word. He never acted out of spite or selfishness. Whatever He did was for the eternal good of others. He spoke nothing but the truth in love. He always trusted and followed His Father with a perfect heart. No one else in history could claim that He did and said only what His Father modeled (John 5:19).

As I meditate on Jesus's obedience during this week leading up to His death and resurrection, my heart overflows with wonder. That my Savior willingly took my sins and imperfections to the cross—*think of it!*—brings me to my knees in adoration.

The perfect Lamb of God, without blemish or fault, is the only one who could offer the perfect sacrifice: His very self.

Not annoying. Awe-inspiring. —JEANETTE LEVELLIE

FAITH STEP: *Watch the movie* The Passion of The Christ *or another film depicting Jesus's final days. Go ahead and weep or worship or do both—in gratitude to Him for His perfect act of love.*

MAUNDY THURSDAY, APRIL 14

When they had sung a hymn, they went out to the Mount of Olives.
Matthew 26:30 (NIV)

AS A VOCALIST, I HAVE many favorite hymns: "Be Thou My Vision," "Crown Him with Many Crowns," and "The Love of God." All hold deep meaning for me. They lift my spirits when I sing them. Recently I was surprised to learn the definition of the word *hymn*. It's not simply a song we sing *about* God or Jesus but is one we sing *to* Him. It means "to laud, to celebrate God in song."

Hymn is the Greek word *humneo*, used in Matthew 26:30 when Jesus and His followers ate the Passover meal together a few hours before Jesus's arrest. The final act of worship they participated in was to honor God in song. Imagine what was in Jesus's heart at this moment.

Jesus knew what was coming: betrayal by one of His closest friends, arrest under false pretenses, a whipping that had killed weaker men, and then crucifixion—the cruelest form of execution imaginable. Jesus knew that in less than twenty-four hours the Father would turn His face away from Jesus as He became sin for us (2 Corinthians 5:21). Yet He still sang adoration to God.

Our Savior dreaded the cross and the darkness of God's rejection. Yet in that anguish of His soul, Jesus worshipped the Father. And the Father listened.

I long to imitate Jesus. So that before, during, and after my darkest trials, I can raise my voice and extol God in song. It's the highest form of faith. —JEANETTE LEVELLIE

FAITH STEP: *Find a hymn you can sing or say to God, such as "How Great Thou Art," "Lord I Lift Your Name on High," or "I Bless Your Name."*

GOOD FRIDAY, APRIL 15

His life is the light that shines through the darkness—and the darkness can never extinguish it. John 1:5 (TLB)

EVERY FALL AND WINTER, I suffer from Seasonal Affective Disorder (SAD). It occurs when reduced exposure to sunlight produces a chemical imbalance in the brain. I'm thankful for the antidepressant that keeps my mood balanced and for the privilege of prayer. Talking to God and praising Jesus helps the most.

The Gospel of Luke tells us that during Jesus's final three hours, as He hung dying on the cross, darkness covered the entire earth "for the sun stopped shining" (23:45, NIV).

All of us who experience the darkness of depression—even for a short season—understand the hopelessness that Jesus must have felt in those hours. Not only did our Savior take on the sins of every person who ever lived during that time of darkness, I am convinced He also felt all our pain, shame, and despair, which accounts for His quick death (John 19:31–34). The Son of God experienced a staggering depression of the soul, like no other.

The Bible tells us that Jesus is not "unable to empathize with our weaknesses" (Hebrews 4:15, NIV). By entering into our darkness, Jesus understood and took on Himself all of our sin, weakness, and helplessness.

No wonder we call this day "Good Friday." —JEANETTE LEVELLIE

FAITH STEP: *Go into a secluded room or closet. Block out as much light as you can. Thank Jesus for His willingness to take on all the darkness of sinful humanity. Now open wide the door and windows. Turn all the lights on. As you do, sing a song of praise to Jesus, the Light of the world.*

SATURDAY, APRIL 16

Do not throw away your confidence; it will be richly rewarded.
Hebrews 10:35 (NIV)

WHEN MY DAUGHTER, ESTHER, CALLED last week to tell me some unfortunate news, my heart sank. The owner of Esther's dream house had decided not to rent it. Now Esther and her three teens would need to remain in their cramped mobile home.

I was disappointed. Jesus hadn't met my family's needs. After Esther's call, I plopped onto the couch and did everything but pray. Brain games. Facebook. Instagram. Finally, after abandoning my pout, I asked Jesus to show me a Scripture that would give me perspective. He reminded me of Hebrews 10:35, a sweet encouragement to not throw away my confidence in His good plan for my family. I recalled the many times He'd provided solutions far beyond our highest dreams.

I also recalled the account of that Saturday after Jesus's crucifixion and burial. His followers must have felt paralyzed with disappointment after watching Jesus die. They hid, fearing the authorities would crucify them, too, because they were Jesus's disciples.

God wasn't angry with these men's weakness. He knew the plan He'd had from before time. He could see ahead to the following day when Jesus would break out of the tomb, conquering death and fear forever. Soon the disciples would cast off their distress and see the fulfillment of Jesus's words: "I will rise again." The disciples' disappointment would turn to courage. Just as my disappointment will change to confidence as I trust Jesus's promise to meet all of my family's needs (Philippians 4:19). —JEANETTE LEVELLIE

FAITH STEP: *If you're disappointed that God didn't do what you thought He should have, find a Bible verse that will give you perspective and memorize it.*

EASTER SUNDAY, APRIL 17

Anyone who is joined to Christ is a new being; the old is gone, the new has come. 2 Corinthians 5:17 (GNT)

I LOVE THAT JESUS FIRST appeared to a woman after His resurrection—a woman with a past. According to Mark 16:9, Jesus had cast out seven demons from Mary Magdalene We aren't told how the evil spirits gained access to Mary. We can only imagine the torment she had experienced before Jesus set her free. After that miracle, she became a loyal follower of the Master.

Early on Sunday morning, when Mary visited Jesus's tomb, she was surprised to find it open and Jesus's body gone. She believed someone had stolen Jesus's body. While she wept about this, He showed up.

Mary had thought all was lost and that she'd never see her hero again. Now here He stood, speaking her name. And—wonder of wonders—He gave her a commission: "Go to my brothers and tell them..." (John 20:17, GNT).

For years I thought my ugly past would keep me from being used by Jesus in any significant way. I believed a lie—that my foolish choices had disqualified me from ministry—until I realized that when Jesus set me free from my past and I said yes to Him, He gave me His resurrection power and a fresh start.

Like Mary Magdalene on Easter Sunday, I'm no longer hopeless. I'm now filled with gratitude and eager to tell my story so others can discover Jesus's love and forgiveness.

I rejoice this Resurrection Day! Jesus has made me new and in writing this devotion I can "go and tell..." —JEANETTE LEVELLIE

FAITH STEP: *Imagine you are Mary Magdalene, kneeling at Jesus's feet after you realize He's alive. What do you say to Him? More importantly, what does He say to you?*

MONDAY, APRIL 18

Jesus spoke all these things to the crowd in parables; he did not say anything to them without using a parable. Matthew 13:34 (NIV)

I LOVE STORIES, so I was thrilled to attend The Moth Mainstage event in Breckenridge, Colorado. The Moth is a nonprofit organization dedicated to the craft of storytelling. The founder wanted to recreate the feeling of summer evenings in his native Georgia, when moths were attracted to the light on the porch where he and his friends would gather to tell spellbinding tales. The event features folks who tell their story to crowds across the country.

I was captivated as the speakers bravely told their stories. One young man had almost died while guiding tourists on a glacier trek in Alaska. One woman had survived the Chinese Communist Revolution. And another woman humorously talked about unexpectedly becoming a grandmother. You could hear a pin drop while they spoke.

Neuroscience has shown storytelling elicits joy and helps people pay attention and remember the points of the story. I love how Jesus already knew the power of storytelling. He told the best stories. His parables were full of powerful, life-changing lessons.

Who doesn't love a good story? What a creative God we have to provide such an amusing way to grow in our faith! Listening to The Moth speakers reminded me of Jesus's ability to tell fascinating tales that impart priceless wisdom. I was inspired to bravely share my own stories in hopes of encouraging others to experience a relationship with Jesus, who makes my life a story worth telling.
—JEANNIE BLACKMER

FAITH STEP: *Invite friends over for an opportunity to tell their "Jesus stories." Offer a topic such as child-like trust, overcoming fear, or facing the unknown. Encourage each person to share.*

TUESDAY, APRIL 19

Since we are surrounded by such a great cloud of witnesses, let us throw off everything that hinders and the sin that so easily entangles. Hebrews 12:1 (NIV)

A MUCH-LOVED MINISTER AT MY church recently made her transition from earth to her final reward in heaven. Reverend Gunn was one of the most faith-filled people I've ever known. She faced many difficult times in her life—sickness, pain, loss—but through it all, she always declared the goodness of God. With a dazzling smile and booming voice, she often offered encouraging, wise words to me and many others. Her life spoke volumes. She was a real cheerleader for Jesus.

Reverend Gunn is now one of my "cloud people," the folks whom the writer of Hebrews talked about, folks who have shown us what faith is all about. The writer points to how Noah, Abraham, Joseph, Moses, and Rahab, among others, exhibited faith during their lifetimes. "All these people were still living by faith when they died. They did not receive the things promised; they only saw them and welcomed them from a distance, admitting that they were foreigners and strangers on earth" (Hebrews 11:13, NIV).

I'm certain that Reverend Gunn is with Jesus in heaven and that she's meeting my other cloud people—my dad and grandparents and other dear friends and family who are no longer with me here on earth. Because of this great cloud of witnesses, I have wonderful examples of what it means to persevere through trials and know that, as a believer in Jesus, heaven waits for me too.
—BARBRANDA LUMPKINS WALLS

FAITH STEP: *Who's in your great cloud of witnesses, the ones whose lives tell you what faith means? How can you, too, be a witness of faith?*

WEDNESDAY, APRIL 20

So then, just as you received Christ Jesus as Lord, continue to live your lives in him, rooted and built up in him, strengthened in the faith as you were taught, and overflowing with thankfulness. Colossians 2:6—7 (NIV)

EVER SINCE THE SPRING SUNSHINE has hit our state, the lawn in the backyard has been thriving. Its verdant growth laid me out flat after the first spring mowing. It was so tall, I had to go over it twice. When I finished, I came inside and collapsed on the couch. My fourteen-year-old, Addison, told me, "Mom, your face is really red." And I said, "Too. Much. Grass." It was all I could manage to say.

But the front yard is a different story. There are patches of green woven with circles of dead grass. When we bought the house, the front yard had already been laid by the builders. The sod was put directly over dense clay. In the backyard, we topped the clay with three inches of nutrient rich topsoil before laying down the sod. The roots are digging into all that goodness. I think the front yard is jealous.

When Jesus came into my life, He laid down a nutrient-rich topsoil of love and grace. With my "roots" dug down into Him, I have access to all that richness. The richness of His mercy, truth, and wisdom strengthens and builds me up. In Him, I thrive. Anchoring myself in His amazing love leads to an overflow of thanksgiving. He is so good, isn't He? —SUSANNA FOTH AUGHTMON

FAITH STEP: *Jesus wants you rooted in His love. Plant a flower in a pot. Layer the soil with rich compost. Every time you see it, lift up a prayer of thanksgiving for His work in your life.*

THURSDAY, APRIL 21

This I recall to my mind, therefore have I hope. It is of the LORD's mercies that we are not consumed, because his compassions fail not. They are new every morning: great is thy faithfulness. Lamentations 3:21–23 (KJV)

MY FAMILY WENT THROUGH A situation this year in which someone we trusted completely let us down. It was one of those things you think can't possibly ever happen in a million years. And then it does. We were blindsided. We were all hurt, but those of us closest to the situation were devastated. When something like this happens, it's natural to think, *Well, if that happened, anything can happen. I guess I can't trust anyone.* It's probably not a healthy reaction, but it's human.

When I am shocked like this and the world seems upside down—like nothing I thought—I try to remind myself of the things I do know. It's kind of like grasping for something to hold onto in the dark. Calling those things to mind brings me hope, even if there aren't very many things I really know. But these verses in Lamentations speak to the few things that really matter: *His compassion never fails. He is always faithful.*

Always faithful. That's something no human can be, not even the best ones, not in every possible sense of the word. We fail each other, but Jesus never does. In Matthew 28:20, Jesus promises to be with us always. He doesn't say sometimes or most of the time or when He feels like it or when it is convenient. He is faithful. We have hope in Him because His word is always true, faithful, and trustworthy—we can depend on it. —GWEN FORD FAULKENBERRY

FAITH STEP: *Commit Lamentations 3:21–23 to memory so you can call it to mind when you need hope.*

FRIDAY, APRIL 22

Surely He has borne our griefs and carried our sorrows; yet we esteemed Him stricken, smitten by God, and afflicted. Isaiah 53:4 (NKJV)

AS JESUS SHARED HIS LAST Passover meal with His disciples, He told them distressing news: He would soon be going away. Someone in the group would betray Him. Stalwart Peter would disown Him three times that very night. All of them would fall away and leave Him alone. Then He urged them, "Do not let your hearts be troubled" (John 14:1, NIV).

Seems like a strange thing to say—or rather a strange time to say it. Their minds must have been reeling, trying to make sense of the awful things He had just predicted. After His triumphal entry into Jerusalem, Jesus had confided that His soul was deeply troubled (John 12:27). How could it be otherwise? Jesus knew full well the horrors He would soon face: the humiliation, the suffering, the agonizing death. And yet, He felt concern for His disciples' well-being and sought to comfort *them*.

When I'm reeling in shock from sudden trouble, the natural response would seem to be anxiety and fear. But Jesus still offers the same words of encouragement: "Don't let your heart be troubled." He paid a high price so I can know supernatural peace in all circumstances, despite how impossible that sounds from a human perspective. I honor Jesus when I refuse to let anything or anyone steal the peace He gained for me. His soul was troubled so mine doesn't have to be, regardless of what I face. —DIANNE NEAL MATTHEWS

FAITH STEP: *Is your heart feeling troubled? Read John 14 and list all the reasons Jesus gives for why you should not have a fearful, troubled spirit. Thank Him for His sacrifice.*

SATURDAY, APRIL 23

You will seek me and find me when you seek me with all your heart.
Jeremiah 29:13 (NIV)

IN THE KITCHEN, MY UTENSIL drawer was stuck shut *again*. I jiggled and yanked the handle, finally releasing whatever had blocked it. Staring at the jumbled contents, I sighed. All I needed was the ice cream scoop. Shuffling through various wooden spoons, silicone spatulas, and stainless-steel knives—each created for only one purpose—my fingertips found the familiar rubberized handle. Now to work it free from the tangled mass.

That drawer, with all its useful and helpful items, sometimes reminds me of the way life can get cluttered with busywork. Like the garlic press I recently purchased, I always find ways to cram one more volunteer opportunity or social engagement into my week. Sometimes I lose track of the point. Why am I doing it and who am I doing it for? With my focus split in a hundred directions, none of these things bring me—or others—closer to Jesus.

I've emptied the drawer, carefully selecting the utensils I'll keep and which to donate. Now I'll be able to find what I need with ease.

I'm doing the same with my free time. Things that distract me from Jesus or from serving Him better will be removed. Psalm 27:8 reminds me, "You have said, 'Seek my face.' My heart says to you, 'Your face, LORD, do I seek'" (ESV). I want to declutter my soul, to seek Him with all my heart and find Him, and to reach for Him and recognize His touch deep inside. —HEIDI GAUL

FAITH STEP: *Pick a cluttered drawer in your home and clear the unnecessary items from it. Now apply the same principle to your life. Remove the distractions and seek Jesus.*

SUNDAY, APRIL 24

Dear friends, do not believe every spirit, but test the spirits to see whether they are from God, because many false prophets have gone out into the world. 1 John 4:1 (NIV)

AT THE GROCERY STORE, I searched for a few healthy snack options. On a sale rack, I found crunchy peapod snacks. They sounded healthier than potato chips, with a similar crunch-salt value, so I grabbed them. After getting home I tasted them. Yuck. When I checked the ingredients, I saw they were super processed and packed with weird flavorings. Their resemblance to true peapods was only in the manufacturer's imagination. I shook my head. Why hadn't I just grabbed the real thing? Sweet, fresh peapods would have been a much more delicious snack.

As research for one of my novels, I've recently been studying cults. In cults, people substitute the real thing for a poor imitation. When a writer, speaker, or leader teaches about following Jesus, how can I know whether he or she is presenting the truth? Jesus provides ways to test for the truth. Through the gift of the Bible, I can make sure that any "new ideas" line up with the whole of Scripture. Through the gift of the body of Christ, I can receive wise counsel from others. As I daily walk with Jesus, He says I will learn to recognize His voice, as sheep recognize their true shepherd.

There's no need to ever accept a poor substitute when I have the true and only Savior. —SHARON HINCK

FAITH STEP: *Notice a thought from a book, magazine, podcast, or TV broadcast. Analyze it to see if it lines up with Scripture and ask Jesus to guide you in truth.*

MONDAY, APRIL 25

Make every effort to live in peace with everyone and to be holy;
without holiness no one will see the Lord. Hebrews 12:14 (NIV)

MY MOM, GLORIA, WAS A great woman who valued peace in her home and in her relationships. She was known for putting up her hand if a discussion got too heated and saying, "Peace!" Then she'd simply walk away, without holding a grudge. As a result of her commitment to keeping the peace, I grew up in a home where I can recall very few arguments. She didn't need to win every argument or prove she was right. As a result, there was an atmosphere of peace and holiness wherever she went. I have a similar desire for peace (though I admit I do like when I'm right).

In the verse above, the author of Hebrews states the importance of pursuing peace, and it's not just a suggestion. So my husband and I decided to adopt a technique we learned in a Christian marriage seminar. Every day we try to tell each other something we appreciate about the other. Sometimes we exchange comments back and forth until we're both grinning and twinkling and feeling appreciated. It actually becomes contagious as more and more qualities you enjoy in the other person come to mind. This is a surefire (and fun!) way to cultivate peace in any relationship. The result is that others will see Jesus in your peaceful and holy demeanor, and you will see it in them too. —PAMELA TOUSSAINT HOWARD

FAITH STEP: *Cultivate a peaceful atmosphere by regularly telling people you're in relationship with why you appreciate them.*

TUESDAY, APRIL 26

But those who wait on the LORD shall renew their strength; they shall mount up with wings like eagles, they shall run and not be weary, they shall walk and not faint. Isaiah 40:31 (NKJV)

LAUNDRY IS ONE HOUSEHOLD CHORE I enjoy. The gentle swishing of soapy water and clothes as they slosh together in the washer. The thumping of my four hedgehog dryer buddies as they bump against the walls of the dryer. The snappy cleanness of the clothes after I hang them up. It all makes me smile.

Last week a thought struck me: *Laundry won't be rushed.* I can set my washer for a small load, which does take less time, but it still needs to cycle through all the stages to clean our clothes. I can set my dryer temperature on "high" to speed up the drying, but then I'll need to give my shrunken jeans to our twelve-year-year-old granddaughter. If I try to cut corners, I won't be happy with the outcome—same as my relationship with Jesus. I get impatient to be grown up spiritually. I want that sparkly clean maturity right now. I don't like the endless agitation of painful relationships, fear of the unknown, and the darkness of grief.

Yet these are the situations that force me to rely on Jesus, to lean hard on His grace and compassion, and to trust Him with unanswered questions. All the things that help me grow up take time.

There's simply no rushing maturity in Jesus. —JEANETTE LEVELLIE

FAITH STEP: *Do some laundry today. As the clothes agitate, thank Jesus for helping you become more patient with the process of maturing in Him.*

WEDNESDAY, APRIL 27

Be imitators of God, as beloved children. And walk in love, as Christ loved us and gave himself up for us, a fragrant offering and sacrifice to God. Ephesians 5:1–2 (ESV)

WHEN OUR GRANDCHILDREN LIVED WITH me and my husband, we noticed they picked up habits and mannerisms from us. Our three-year-old grandson loved helping Grandpa vacuum and longed to copy anything he did.

My grandson also helped me clean up after dinner. Our garbage can is on a slide-out shelf in a low cabinet. One night he took a crumpled napkin and toddled over to the cabinet under the sink. After opening the door, he awkwardly hooked his foot over the slide-out shelf to pull the garbage can out and dispose of his napkin. I nudged my husband and giggled. "Why didn't he use his hand to pull out the shelf?"

My husband smiled. "Because that's how you do it. You always hook your toes over the shelf to pull out the garbage can, and he's been watching you."

Children are great at absorbing and copying others, but that incident reminded me that I am called to be an imitator as well. As I observe (through my study of Scripture) the way that Jesus responded to those around Him, I begin to pick up His habits and mannerisms. He forms a new spirit in me, one of love and sacrifice and forgiveness. —SHARON HINCK

FAITH STEP: *Choose one example of Jesus's actions in Scripture and imitate it today.*

THURSDAY, APRIL 28

The stone the builders rejected has become the cornerstone. Psalm 118:22 (NIV)

MY HUSBAND'S LATEST FISHING TRIP took him to a small lake with few private properties and great bass fishing. It also boasts a stunning log-and-stone house that captures his attention almost as much as the fish tugging on his line.

I've heard him talk about that lake home many times but hadn't seen any pictures until today. A massive structure, the home hugs the shoreline and boasts windows and decks that must afford the occupants indescribable views. "The stonework alone is magnificent, isn't it?" my husband said.

I took a closer look. Each stone fitted so perfectly, matched and artistic and...one stone at the far corner was unlike the others. Its color was slightly different, and it was larger in scale. Had it, perhaps, been rejected by the builders, but the owners insisted it serve as the cornerstone of their lavish home?

Jesus encouraged me even in my imagining. The Bible says that Jesus was rejected by people. This passage in the Psalms reminds us that the "rejected" stone—Christ—has become the cornerstone, the foundation of faith.

Writers like me face rejection every day. No matter how accomplished, my next project, next article, or next book is at risk of "unacceptance," as authors sometimes call it. But even in that, Jesus can identify with all that can rock my human heart. I can bravely face life's rejections because the One who loves me most walked that path before me and turned His rejection into an essential for my faith. —CYNTHIA RUCHTI

FAITH STEP: *In your garden or driveway or at the beach, find a rock that stands out from the others. Use it as a firm reminder that Christ alone is our cornerstone.*

FRIDAY, APRIL 29

*As a mother comforts her child, so will I comfort you; and you will be
comforted over Jerusalem. Isaiah 66:13 (NIV)*

I JUST FINISHED MAILING A stack of Mother's Day cards, as I do
each year at this time. I send greetings to my daughters and daugh-
ters-in-law and to a few friends. But the mothers I make sure never
to forget are those who, like me, are bereaved mothers—mothers
who have lost a child.

That first Mother's Day after Blake died, I didn't know how to
feel. Was I still a mother when my little boy was in heaven? I had
two other sons, so I was a mother to them, but I didn't feel worthy.
There was certainly nothing to celebrate and I didn't want gifts or
cards. Jesus felt very far away at that time—my choice, not His.

As time wore on, I was able to accept Jesus's comfort in my loss.
Much of my healing came from reaching out to other bereaved
mothers. We bereaved mothers are members of a club that no one
wants to join. We share unspeakable loss, but when we are together,
we don't really have to speak. We understand.

So every year as Mother's Day approaches and I send cards,
I make sure to remind my friends that they are definitely still Stephen's
mother, Brian's mother, Heather's mother, Terry's mother, Adalyn's
mother. I like to think our children are celebrating us on our special day, telling the angels in heaven that we were good mothers.
—PAT BUTLER DYSON

FAITH STEP: *Reach out to a bereaved mother. Even if you don't know what to
say, give her a hug. Listen. Say her child's name. It's the sweetest sound a mother
can hear.*

SATURDAY, APRIL 30

The thief does not come except to steal, and to kill, and to destroy.
I have come that they may have life, and that they may have it
more abundantly. John 10:10 (NKJV)

SOMETIMES I CAN STUMBLE ACROSS some real gems while surfing the internet. I came across one recently linked to the long-running animated show *The Simpsons*. In one episode, daughter Lisa asked her dad, Homer, if he knew that the Chinese used the same word for "crisis" as they do for "opportunity." Homer responded, "Yes, *crisitunity*."

Homer's mash-up caught my attention. Instead of *crisitunity*, I came up with my own word: *Christunity*—Christ + opportunity. Indeed, there is opportunity in Jesus.

Throughout the Bible, especially in the New Testament, I see people whose lives were changed because they chose to believe in the power of Jesus and availed themselves of an opportunity. There's the woman with the issue of blood (Luke 8:43–48) who was healed. On the cross beside Jesus, the thief was saved and forgiven in his final hours and wound up with the Lord in paradise (Luke 23:39–43). And Saul became Paul and was transformed from Christian persecutor to purveyor of the gospel, because of Jesus (Acts 9:1–19). Talk about opportunity!

In the Gospel of John, Jesus says He came so that we not only will have life but will have it more abundantly. For me, abundant life is peace, joy, and a constant awareness of Christ's presence and His power. I also have the assurance that after this earthly life is over, I'll land in heaven and live with Jesus forever—the greatest *Christunity* for all believers. —BARBRANDA LUMPKINS WALLS

FAITH STEP: *Write down the opportunities available through Jesus. Who can you share your list with as a testimony of Christ's love and presence?*

SUNDAY, MAY 1

The LORD is my shepherd, I lack nothing. He makes me lie down in green pastures, he leads me beside quiet waters, he refreshes my soul. He guides me along the right paths for his name's sake. **Psalm 23:1–3** *(NIV)*

I RECENTLY VISITED ONE OF Oregon's natural areas, a level path edged with mature oaks and ancient hawthorns. Native grasses spiked skyward as western meadowlarks and red-winged blackbirds sang from the treetops. Early wildflowers bloomed underfoot, testimony of the changing seasons. Hiking here brought me a sense of peace. My spirits rose along with the birds taking flight.

This park focuses on reestablishing a population of western pond turtles, native to the region. Seasonal watersheds form during the wet months, often drying up completely before the rains return. Until that happens, these creatures can be spotted basking on logs or boulders along a pond's bank. During the cooler months, the turtles hide in the undergrowth along the water's banks, preparing their nests, invisible to the average hiker. Spotting one is rare.

Jesus is continually at work in my life, unseen but not idle. Like the turtles He created, I can "nest" in comfort under His watchful eye, secure in the knowledge that He protects me from the predators of my world. He leads me in the direction I should go, guiding me to righteousness. As I walk through the wonders of His creation, He restores my soul. —HEIDI GAUL

FAITH STEP: *Visit a lake or pond near you. Walk the shoreline or follow a trail. Let Jesus restore your soul as you take in the quiet peace found in nature.*

MONDAY, MAY 2

I would hurry to my place of escape, far away from the wind and storm.
Psalm 55:8 (NCV)

This covering will protect the people from the heat of the sun and will provide
a safe place to hide from the storm and rain. Isaiah 4:6 (NCV)

EVERY SPRING, A FLOWERING PINK dogwood tree steals the show in my garden when blossoms cover its bare limbs. Next, leaf buds unfurl into fresh green foliage. As spring wind currents and rainstorms blow the flowers from the leafy boughs, fallen petals transform the lawn below into a carpet of pink confetti.

As I was enjoying my morning with Jesus today, something outside the window caught my eye: Although the dogwood flower show is over, a trio of blossoms remain securely attached to the trunk. While thousands of blossoms along the outstretched branches had been shaken, ruffled, blown about, and knocked down by the wind and rain, those three tenacious flowers prevailed, unaffected by outer circumstances.

I understood what Jesus was showing me. That was how I need to be clinging to Him amid the storms of life. Not fluttering out on a limb, being blown about by the changing winds of current events. Not hurrying to escape by complaining, consuming junk food, or pointlessly browsing the internet. Rather than being shaken, ruffled, and knocked down by circumstances outside my control, I need to snuggle up closer to the One called the Branch of Life, drawing close to Him through His Word. Jesus is my safe place when the winds of change and storms of life bluster around me.
—CASSANDRA TIERSMA

FAITH STEP: *Is something going on in the world that has you feeling shaken? Write it down. Then write, "Thank You Jesus for being my covering."*

TUESDAY, MAY 3

The fruit of the Spirit is love, joy, peace, patience, kindness, goodness, faithfulness, gentleness, self-control; against such things there is no law.
Galatians 5:22–23 (ESV)

YESTERDAY, MY ELDEST SON, WILL, and I drove to pick up some raised plant beds that I had ordered from a carpenter online. We took the back roads to get there—beautiful farmland surrounding our growing city. As we drove, we passed grazing cattle and goats. We saw cute farmhouses and irrigation canals. It was a patchwork quilt of newly budding fields and freshly tilled soil. Our Idaho town is the perfect region to start a garden. I'm attempting to grow my own vegetables this summer—I know it's a big leap, but I am excited to try. I want to plant peppers, green beans, and herbs, but mostly I am driven by my love for tomatoes. Beautiful red orbs of summer deliciousness. Who doesn't love a summer salad with olive oil, fresh basil, and sun-ripened tomatoes? The promise of this goodness is inspiring me to plant.

Like the garden I hope to have, my life is meant to yield the fruit of the Holy Spirit: love, joy, peace, patience, kindness, goodness, faithfulness, gentleness, and self-control. When it comes to planting, Jesus does the heavy lifting. His firm hand uproots all the anxious growth that chokes out His peace. His grace unleashes kindness toward others. His presence alone yields ever-present joy. When we invite Jesus into our hearts, the promise of His goodness is worked out in our daily lives. —SUSANNA FOTH AUGHTMON

FAITH STEP: *What kind of fruit is Jesus's presence yielding in your life right now? Ask Jesus to unleash the power of His Holy Spirit in your life, growing your life to look like His.*

WEDNESDAY, MAY 4

Whatever you ask in My name, that I will do, that the Father may be glorified in the Son. John 14:13 (NKJV)

MY SIXTEEN-YEAR OLD GRANDSON TY was scheduled to retake his driver's test. Last week he'd failed because he'd hit a curb while attempting to parallel park. The tester had sent him home to practice and then return the following week. Ty had been devastated. A chronic illness had kept him housebound for almost three years. He went to school online and rarely left his home. But this past summer, he'd found a bright spot when he took driver's training. He'd reunited with old friends he hadn't seen since middle school. He'd laughed, chatted, and had fun. When he'd passed the written test, he'd been able to drive with an adult in the front seat. Driving would give him freedom, and he'd proved to be an excellent driver. His folks had also surprised him with a truck. Getting his license meant the world to Ty.

On my knees, I prayed, *Jesus, is it wrong to pray for something so small—a boy to pass his driver's test? Ty so desperately needs a win. Please help him pass the test.* Over the years, many people had prayed for Ty to be cured, but it hadn't happened. Getting his license and being able to go out would bring joy to Ty and to his family, who yearned for him to be happy. I felt certain Jesus wanted Ty to be happy too. I remembered the verse, "Ask, and you will receive" (Matthew 7:7, CEV). So I stayed on my knees until I got the call. Ty had passed! —PAT BUTLER DYSON

FAITH STEP: *Ask Jesus to reassure you that it's okay to pray for anything in your heart.*

THURSDAY, MAY 5

This mystery . . . is Christ in you, the hope of glory. Colossians 1:27 *(KJV)*

JESUS IN ME—THIS IS A mystery indeed. When my daughter Grace was tiny and curious about faith, I tried to explain to her what it means to have a relationship with God through Jesus. I told her, "It's like Jesus is standing at the door of your heart and He's knocking. When you hear His voice, you open that door and ask Him into your heart, and He comes in and stays there forever."

I will never forget the look of deep concentration on her face, like she was putting together a puzzle. A few minutes later, she bowed her head and prayed out loud, asking Jesus in. As soon as she finished, her head popped up and her eyes searched mine. "Is He there?" She asked, pointing to her heart.

I've spent a lot of time since then working on a better explanation of what salvation means. One thing I'll never quite capture—and I think this is a good thing—is the mystery. As a Christian, sometimes I'm uncomfortable with mysteries and uncertainties, things I can't fully explain or even understand. By faith, I'm learning to accept what I don't understand. But faith is also a mystery! I have an intimate relationship with a God I cannot see.

While I sometimes fear the unknown, Jesus's perfect love for me casts out fear. And every time He casts out fear from my life, I'm left in a state of wonder, awe, and reverence. I can point to my heart and know He is there. Jesus in me. —Gwen Ford Faulkenberry

FAITH STEP: *Go outside tonight and look at the stars. Meditate on the mystery that the same God who set the stars in the sky lives in you.*

FRIDAY, MAY 6

Everyone who hears these words of mine and puts them into practice is like a wise man who built his house on the rock. Matthew 7:24 (NIV)

ONE OF MY PREVIOUS HOMES was a double-wide mobile. It sat on concrete blocks that were a bit of an eyesore, so we installed metal skirting around its base to hide them from view.

One afternoon, I felt our house sway. At first, I thought my imagination was messing with my mind, but then I saw the dining room fixture swing from side to side. That's when I suspected an earthquake. A radio report confirmed it.

Thankfully the tremor was mild and left our home standing. I have no doubt that a stronger quake could have toppled it. No matter how we tried to hide or disguise the concrete blocks, the truth remained—they could never provide the stability that a proper foundation offered.

Our culture encourages me to build my life on money and material possessions. I recently watched a TV ad in which a man said, "My [big] closet makes me so happy." His comment made me so sad. The size of a closet is a pretty shaky foundation on which to base one's happiness.

Culture also nudges me to build my life on my career. But what happens when an economic earthquake hits and devastates the working force? I might instead build my life on my family, but tragedy or bad decisions could leave me in a heap of emotional rubble.

There's only one foundation that stands firm forever—Jesus and His teachings. Building my life on Him keeps me secure when everything around me shakes and shifts. —GRACE FOX

FAITH STEP: *Read Matthew 7:24–27. Ask Jesus to show you if you've built a foundation on anything other than Him.*

SATURDAY, MAY 7

*Let us hold fast the confession of our hope without wavering,
for He who promised is faithful. Hebrews 10:23 (NKJV)*

TWO YEARS AGO, ON MOTHER's Day, my daughter Brooke gave me
a lovely orchid plant and my heart soared. Then my heart sank.
I have a brown thumb. I love plants so much that I kill them. I
overwater, overfeed, and offer too much sunshine or too much
shade. I didn't have much hope for this gorgeous purple orchid.
But I thanked Brooke and kept my fingers crossed. Two months
later when Brooke came to visit, my lovely orchid was on its last
leg. *"Mom!"* Brooke said, groaning. All I could do was apologize and
sink into my old familiar guilt that I sometimes feel about plants. I
couldn't bring myself to throw the orchid away, so I stuck it in the
bushes near my back porch.

A few days ago, I was in the backyard when a splash of purple
caught my eye. I peered into the bushes to find my long-dead orchid
plant blooming profusely, sporting ten buds that looked ready to
open. It had been two years! And my orchid was coming back. This
had to be a sign.

Jesus, those unanswered prayers—there's still time. I can't lose hope.
Hope is essential for me to keep going. But there's a partner that
goes with hope: trust. One of my favorite hymns, "'Tis So Sweet
to Trust in Jesus," comforts me. I love the chorus: "Jesus, Jesus,
precious Jesus! / Oh, for grace to trust Him more." I have to trust
that Jesus will answer my prayers. At the same time, I must understand that my desires will be fulfilled in His time and in His way.
—PAT BUTLER DYSON

FAITH STEP: *Make a list of prayers Jesus has answered. Praise Him for those
answers!*

MOTHER'S DAY, SUNDAY, MAY 8

Let them give thanks to the LORD for his unfailing love and his wonderful deeds for mankind, for he satisfies the thirsty and fills the hungry with good things. Psalm 107:8–9 (NIV)

BEING A MOM IS ONE of the most beautiful, challenging, difficult, exhilarating, anxiety-ridden, and hopeful jobs in the world. Moms walk around with their hearts split wide open with love for their kids. I know this because I'm a mom. My oldest son, Jack, left for college this year. I felt like a piece of my heart moved to Southern California. He was ready to spread his wings. And I couldn't stop wondering if he was getting enough snacks. But since he'd just turned nineteen, I'm pretty sure he was good on snacks.

Making sure that her people are alive and well is the blood that courses through a mom's veins. We are constantly enfolding the ones we love with care and protein bars. This never stops. I know this because I am way older than nineteen, and yesterday my mom called me to say that she wanted to help pay for my summer garden. She wants to make sure I have enough snacks.

Moms are a whole lot like Jesus. He thinks about us all the time. His heart is split wide open with love for us. From conception until the moment we'll see Him face to face, He cares about our minds, our spirits, our hearts, and of course, our daily snacks. He supplies our every need and fills up our hungry souls with His nourishing love. —SUSANNA FOTH AUGHTMON

FAITH STEP: *Thank Jesus for the moms (any woman who has been like a mom to you) who have influenced and touched your life. Take time to pray for them by name, asking Him to surround them with His rich love and peace.*

MONDAY, MAY 9

Whoever dwells in the shelter of the Most High will rest in the shadow of the Almighty. I will say of the LORD, "He is my refuge and my fortress, my God, in whom I trust." Psalm 91:1–2 (NIV)

THE LAST FEW YEARS HAVE been a season of transition for me, and over the next week, I'll be writing about it. For instance, my family of five has moved three times in the last three years. That's a whole lot of change. Our first move was across town. We downsized from our 1,400-square-foot home to a two-bedroom, one-bath 800-square-foot cottage. The cheap rent was great, but we kept bumping into each other. Our second move was a thirty-minute drive north, from our sunny hometown of Redwood City to foggy Daly City, getting us closer to my boys' school. We added a bathroom and bedroom with that move…*thank You, Jesus*. Our last move was the biggest. My husband's job took us from California to Idaho. We now have two and a half baths. Utter bliss. Mostly.

If happiness is linked to the ratio of bathrooms per person, I should be the happiest I've ever been. But this move has left me missing the closeness of family and friends. I have space, but I miss my people. Each move has had both advantages and drawbacks. But no matter what my address, Jesus calls me to the same space spiritually. Even in transition. He views "home" differently than I do. Square footage doesn't figure into the equation. He invites me to shelter in Him, finding comfort and hope in His presence. I can take refuge in His mercy. My address can change, but His immense love for me never does. —SUSANNA FOTH AUGHTMON

FAITH STEP: *Walk throughout each room in your home and ask Jesus to help you find your shelter in Him. Invite His peace and comfort to flood your heart.*

TUESDAY, MAY 10

One who has unreliable friends soon comes to ruin, but there is a friend who sticks closer than a brother. Proverbs 18:24 (NIV)

I HAVE THE BEST FRIENDS ever. (Of course, I'm completely biased!) The hardest thing about moving from California to Idaho was losing the face-to-face connection with them. My middle school colleagues—Crystal, Joanna, and Bethany—were my sisters-in-arms. They brainstormed and laughed with me daily, while we drank copious amounts of life-giving coffee. Their strength buoyed me. I met Jenn fourteen years ago at a park, by the beautiful working of the Holy Spirit. She is my long-lost sister. We both have three boys and knew all the dance moves from the early '90s. (Our children cringe when we bust them out now.) Despite distance and work, we connected with coffee dates, funny texts, and prayers shared over the phone. Marie France, my college prayer partner, and I, used to meet up on Saturdays to walk our Jack Russell-Chihuahua mix pups. She was my spiritual anchor. Not having these ladies close the past eight months has been difficult. I miss them like crazy.

Making new friends takes time. There is no such thing as an instant friendship. But the beautiful thing is that Jesus calls me His friend. When the people I love seem far away, He is near, no matter what. In times of upheaval and stress, He is there offering peace and comfort. His strength is a prayer away. He understands my heart and heals my mind. His presence surrounds me this morning. And that's the kind of friend we all need, isn't it? —SUSANNA FOTH AUGHTMON

FAITH STEP: *Reaffirm your friendship with Jesus. Thank Him for how He has been present in every beautiful moment and difficult struggle in your life.*

WEDNESDAY, MAY 11

I am the true vine, and my Father is the gardener. He cuts off every branch in me that bears no fruit, while every branch that does bear fruit he prunes so that it will be even more fruitful. John 15:1–2 (NIV)

THIS IS MY FIRST SPRING in Idaho. The flowers that my mom and dad helped me plant in my garden last summer weathered snow, hail, and ice. I was anxious to see if all the flowers survived. As the days have grown warmer, it has become clear that the lavender in the backyard did not make it. At all. One of the rose bushes is sprouting little green leaves. The other one has areas of green growth along a couple stems that are black and withered. My mom instructed me to trim back anything that was dead. This was so the new growth could take over. If I left the dead stems in place, it would stunt the overall growth of the rose bush. Good to know.

This is something that Jesus knows to be true in my life. He is the vine, the supply line of faith, hope, and life in the Father. If there is an area of my life that is keeping me stuck or dead in Him, it has to go. If there is a sin or habit keeping me stagnant or withered, it can hold back my growth. I am designed to flourish in Him. His love and hope are meant to blossom through me. I want to let it!
—SUSANNA FOTH AUGHTMON

FAITH STEP: *Are you being pruned? Jesus wants you to flourish in ways that you never have before. Meditate on this Scripture verse. Ask Jesus to remove anything that is keeping you from growing in Him.*

THURSDAY, MAY 12

I trust in your unfailing love; my heart rejoices in your salvation. I will sing the LORD's praise, for he has been good to me. Psalm 13:5–6 (NIV)

EXERCISE IS NOT MY FAVORITE thing. Some of my closest friends love to work out. I love to sit on the couch and read fiction. While this is wonderful for stretching my imagination, it does very little for my hamstrings. The other day, I had a few hours to sit and read. It was great until my shoulders started to seize up, my hips started to ache, and my neck got sore. I had to get up and stretch. I felt like the Tin Man from *The Wizard of Oz* needing a tune-up. My muscles need to be moved. It is what they are made for.

I don't just need to exercise my body; I need spiritual exercise too. When life is uncertain and I don't know what is coming next, I have to rely on my "trust" muscles. If I am a spiritual couch-sitter, paralyzed with worry and anxiety, those spiritual muscles get rusty. Jesus calls me to action. *Do I trust Him to supply all my needs? Or with loved ones who seem far from Him?* Trust is what I am made for. When I trust Him, He promises to come through for me…over and over again. He has in the past. He will in the future. And as I trust Jesus more each day, my ability to move in His will and His ways will increase and grow. —SUSANNA FOTH AUGHTMON

FAITH STEP: *Go for a prayer walk outside, inviting Jesus to take over your worries and cares. Ask Him to help you strengthen your "trust" muscles.*

FRIDAY, MAY 13

See, I am doing a new thing! Now it springs up; do you not perceive it? I am making a way in the wilderness and streams in the wasteland.
Isaiah 43:19 *(NIV)*

LEAVING OUR HOME, FAMILY, AND friends in California was hard for our sons. Jack, a college freshman who stayed in California, wasn't able to travel home on the weekends like his buddies. Sixteen-year-old Will and thirteen-year-old Addison had to adjust to new way of life in Idaho. Everything was different. Neither wanted to attend youth group at our new church—there were too many new faces. The first time we drove to school, Will said, "Mom, you brought us to the country." As a city boy, he wasn't thrilled. When we were invited to a hot air balloon event, Addison was dead set against going. I tried convincing him that it would be a fun new experience. Finally, with a catch in his voice, he said, "Mom, I just can't take another new thing." I felt his heart in those words. Tears welled up in my own eyes. Sometimes "new" can leave us undone.

I don't always love change. During times of transition, I've felt like Addie and Will, as if I couldn't take one more new thing. But Jesus invites me into new spaces. He knows the ultimate plan for my life and wants me to rely on Him in the unknown. He moves me closer to Himself in the process. He wants to use each new thing that He allows in my life for my benefit and His glory.
—SUSANNA FOTH AUGHTMON

FAITH STEP: *What new thing is Jesus doing in you? Ask Him for courage and strength to navigate the unknown and remember that He will be with you every step of the way.*

SATURDAY, MAY 14

---

*Come to me, all you who are weary and burdened, and I will give you rest.
Take my yoke upon you and learn from me, for I am gentle and humble
in heart, and you will find rest for your souls. For my yoke is easy and my
burden is light. Matthew 11:28–30 (NIV)*

THE LAST TWO YEARS OF transition have been tension-filled. With
my high-stress teaching job, I developed the habit of going home,
grabbing a bag of chips, and collapsing on the couch. My body
craved salty, fatty comfort food. My former healthy eating had been
replaced by a chips-and-salsa habit. Unfortunately, the habit didn't
disappear when I quit teaching. Almost a year later, I still want
my afternoon chip fix. The pantry has a magnetic pull. Transitions
affect me in different ways. Anxiety spins me out, looking for a
way to find peace and comfort, but comfort food is a temporary
fix. Hence, the need for more chips. Every single afternoon. So I've
decided to exchange the chips for soul food—real comfort, the kind
that doesn't disappear after thirty minutes.

The truth is that lasting comfort is found in Jesus. Everything else
is a poor substitute. When I draw near to Jesus and lean into His
care, the pull of destructive habits loses its grip. By inviting Him
into my moments of anxiety and craving, I allow Him to begin
healing me. If I come to Him, He promises to give me rest. And
that's way better than chips. —SUSANNA FOTH AUGHTMON

FAITH STEP: *Where do you seek comfort when you are stressed out and anxious? Find comfort in the presence of Jesus today. Ask Him to relieve your anxiety
and replace it with His peaceful rest.*

SUNDAY, MAY 15

You will call on me and come and pray to me, and I will listen to you.
Jeremiah 29:12 (NIV)

THIS PAST YEAR, I HAVE experienced the power of the video call. Linking up with others online has changed how I live. For work, I coach clients who are writing books. FaceTime helps me offer constructive feedback as they progress in the writing process. Every Sunday night, my sisters and I have what we call the Sister Briefing. We connect to share stories about the stresses and joys of life, and pretty much laugh our heads off. I love their faces. My Zoom calls with my parents lead to chats about writing and parenting questions and walks in my backyard as I ask for gardening advice. I can show them my areas of concern. *Is this rose dying? Is this a gopher hole or a vole hole?* Even at my age, their presence continues to guide me. These online connections are priceless.

My connection with Jesus is even more priceless. I might not be able to video chat with the Creator of the universe, but I have a direct line to His heart. The One who spoke worlds into existence wants to have a connection with me. He loves my face. When I call on His name, He actually listens. He loves me so much. He wants in on the daily routine of my life. He invites me into an intimate conversation with Him and acts on my behalf. That's the kind of connection I always need. —SUSANNA FOTH AUGHTMON

FAITH STEP: *Take time to connect with Jesus. Come to Him. Call on His name. Spend time in prayer today. Know that your words are being heard by the One who shaped the universe.*

MONDAY, MAY 16

The seed falling among the thorns refers to someone who hears the word, but the worries of this life and the deceitfulness of wealth choke the word, making it unfruitful. Matthew 13:22 (NIV)

YEARS AGO, MY HUSBAND AND I put in landscape beds in our backyard. We used a wood-chip mulch around the bushes and perennials, but in no time, the beds were overrun with creeping Charlie, stinging nettle, and other weeds. These threatened to choke all the plants we wanted to thrive.

Jesus offers clues to the source of thorns that choke my spiritual life. He plants the seed of His kingdom in my heart, but if I'm not mindful, then anxiety about the day-to-day cares of life and belief in the false promises of wealth can hinder healthy growth. The cares of the world might include seeking approval from others, fear about the future, turmoil in relationships—any place where I'm not trusting Jesus. The hunger for wealth can show up as lack of contentment or gratitude and as envy for what others have (their tangible possessions but also their career success or popularity).

My hubby and I have begun to put a fabric weed barrier in our garden beds. Water can get through, but it holds back weeds from sprouting. Just as Jesus gives me clues about the weeds that endanger me, He also gives me clues about how to lay down a landscape barrier. I can daily turn my cares over to Him. I can cover the fertile soil of my heart with gratitude. Faith, trust, joy, and love will smother the pesky seeds of thorns and allow me to produce fruit for Jesus. —SHARON HINCK

FAITH STEP: *Draw a picture of a weed and label it with whatever spiritual issue you struggle with. Ask Jesus to create a barrier of trust and gratitude that will smother spiritual thorns.*

TUESDAY, MAY 17

For I am confident of this very thing, that He who began a good work in you will perfect it until the day of Christ Jesus. Philippians 1:6 (NASB 1995)

WHEN I ATTENDED BIBLE COLLEGE in Colorado almost ten years ago, I befriended an older couple who acted as house parents for the students. The wife told me of her dream to open a branch of the school back in their hometown of Boston. She felt there was an urgency to do it, but her husband—not so much. However, they both attended upper-level classes that would qualify them to be school directors someday. She shared with me the pain of waiting for it all to come together and for her husband to get fully onboard. I shared with her the things on my heart that were also taking a while to come to pass (i.e., *Where's my husband, Jesus?*) We commiserated and encouraged each other, holding on to the promise in the Scripture verse above. There were many opportunities for us both to question what we believed and wonder if our dreams would ever be realized.

Both dreams took more than ten years to "perfect." I had the privilege of attending the announcement that her school was officially launching, and she enjoyed hearing the news of my wedding. In time, Jesus perfected the good plans He began in our hearts, but it took patience and perseverance—two qualities that were very necessary for the road ahead. —PAMELA TOUSSAINT HOWARD

FAITH STEP: *Don't let anything deter you from the plan God has for you.*

WEDNESDAY, MAY 18

We know that in all things God works for the good of those who love him, who have been called according to his purpose. Romans 8:28 (NIV)

"WHY DON'T YOU GIVE AWAY those books?" my husband, Kevin, asked me. "Everyone loves bloopers!"

Kev was referring to a recent incident. A friend asked to buy five copies of my first book. She wanted me to sign the books with the names of the ladies she planned to give them to. One of the names was Kealah. In the first book, I misspelled it. Setting that one aside, I grabbed another book. And then made the same silly mistake!

I practiced writing the name several times to ensure I wouldn't end up with three unsellable books. Although I speak in public frequently and always give away a book, I doubted I'd ever meet another Kealah. Kevin's blooper idea perfectly solved my dilemma. I could turn my embarrassment into a fun event.

Most of us love to watch and hear about other people's blunders. When I openly share with someone that I misspelled a name— twice—or spilled grape juice on my boss at lunch or lost my temper with my husband, that confession breaks down barriers between us. We feel safe with each other, knowing that we're equally prone to human slipups.

The good news? Jesus can take any blooper and bring good from it. I'm excited to see how He uses my two books with misspelled names. He might even surprise me by having two Kealahs in my next audience. —JEANETTE LEVELLIE

FAITH STEP: *Tell Jesus about a blunder that's bothering you. Release it into His hands to change it into something beneficial to others.*

THURSDAY, MAY 19

So if the Son sets you free, you are free through and through. John 8:36 (MSG)

I CAME OUT OF HAND surgery with my forearm laid against a plaster splint and wrapped up like a huge mummy arm. As the nurse helped me dress, she shared a warning that sounded strange. Whenever I had to move my numb arm, I should hold it down with the other arm; otherwise, it would involuntarily fly up and hit my face. A minute later, she helped me arrange a sling over my shoulder and sure enough, my arm flew up and whacked my nose. Still groggy from the anesthesia, I giggled. Thirty-six hours later, when the nerve block *finally* wore off, I had bumped my face a lot. After the first few times, it ceased being amusing.

Mark 5:1–20 records a serious case of self-inflicted harm. Jesus met a demon-possessed man who lived among the tombs; no one could control him, even by binding him with chains. He spent his days and nights shrieking and cutting himself with sharp stones. After Jesus healed him, the villagers were shocked to see the former madman calmly sitting with Jesus, fully clothed and in his right mind.

Most of us probably engage in some form of self-destructive behavior, whether consciously or unconsciously. Toxic relationships, harmful habits, addictions, or unhealthy thought patterns, such as my tendency to worry and imagine the worst. Change is hard, but Jesus wants to deliver me from whatever holds me back from growing into the person He created me to be. Jesus wants to show me even the most subtle ways I cause myself harm so He can set me free. —DIANNE NEAL MATTHEWS

FAITH STEP: *Ask Jesus to reveal to you any self-destructive habits or thought patterns that you engage in. Trust His healing touch to help you make positive changes.*

FRIDAY, MAY 20

Jesus said to his disciples: "Therefore I tell you, do not worry about your life."
Luke 12:22 (NIV)

"IF I HADN'T BEEN IN such a worry..."

I mean, *hurry.* "If I hadn't been in such a *hurry*..." That's how the saying goes. I use it to explain away forgetting my phone at home. I chide myself with the phrase when I stumble or when I realize the food cooler for our camping trip is still in the garage sixty miles away. I pull out the phrase "If I hadn't been in such a hurry..." to defend myself when I fail to notice a new stop sign or a friend across the street.

But how many of life's "oopses" and agonies would fit "If I hadn't been in such a *worry*..."? If I hadn't been so worried about being on time for my appointment, I wouldn't have been in a hurry and would have noticed the stop sign. If I hadn't been so worried about the cost of a new washing machine and its effect on our household budget, I wouldn't have snapped at my husband. If I hadn't been so worried I could have heard the voice of Jesus reminding me that He's *well* aware of my needs.

Worry leads to poor choices, loss of sleep, stomach and blood pressure issues, ornery attitudes, and relationship fractures. But Jesus specifically, for good reason, tells me, "Do not worry about your life." It's both a word of comfort and redirection when life gives me plenty to worry about. "Just don't," He said (paraphrasing). Good counsel. —CYNTHIA RUCHTI

FAITH STEP: *In what area are you most vulnerable to worry? Children, finances, health? Picture relinquishing those concerns to Jesus. He knows what to do with worry.*

SATURDAY, MAY 21

For we are God's masterpiece. He has created us anew in Christ Jesus, so we can do the good things he planned for us long ago. Ephesians 2:10 *(NLT)*

THIS AFTERNOON I CHOSE TO take advantage of the beautiful spring weather. I grabbed a glass of iced tea and claimed a favorite spot in the backyard to relax. Sprawled across a chaise lounge, the air soft and sweet, I closed my eyes. I lay there for several minutes, surrounded by spring's fresh scents, with sunshine caressing my face. The everyday sounds of my neighborhood—children playing, dogs announcing the postal carrier's arrival, a bee buzzing past en route to a flower—hummed in the background. When I opened my eyes, feathery clouds cast lines across the sky. I sighed, refreshed and eager to take on the rest of the afternoon.

Every day is a gift, and I had been blessed to witness this simple perfection in the making. A masterpiece available to any who might notice. And I had.

But there was more to take in. Like all believers, I'm a part of this holy masterpiece, made new in Jesus. As I looked at the hours ahead, I scrutinized them with an artist's eye. How could I make my time worthy of the day and honor Jesus? Where could I add my own brushstrokes to further define this piece of art—our world? I reentered my home with my eyes, ears, and heart open to the beautiful possibilities. Like the bee, I'm ready for the good He has planned for me. —HEIDI GAUL

FAITH STEP: *Take a few minutes today to slow down and notice the subtle beauty going on all around you. Thank Jesus for this beautiful gift.*

SUNDAY, MAY 22

Imitate me, just as I also imitate Christ. 1 Corinthians 11:1 *(NKJV)*

WHILE TALKING VIA FACETIME WITH my younger sister, Nan, I felt as if I was looking at myself. I never thought we looked much alike while growing up—she was the spitting image of our mother. But now, the older we get, the more we both not only resemble Mom but also sound exactly like her. People tell us that all the time.

It's funny how that transformation took place. I never really paid attention to how my appearance was changing, but then—*bam!*—I could see the difference. The shift was subtle over time, but it was change nonetheless.

Like the apostle Paul, I want to imitate Jesus too. But that's going to take intentional change on my part. Every day I pray that I will become more like Christ and be a walking billboard for Him. I want to be more loving, patient, compassionate, kind, and obedient. I want those Christlike characteristics to replace my inclination to be critical, judgmental, selfish, and self-sufficient.

While I'm nowhere near being the perfect Christian, I know Jesus knows my desire to be and do better. He is changing my heart so that I can be all that He wants me to be. I can see, even feel, that I'm not so quick to fire back unkind words when someone says something hurtful to me. And I am more apt to extend grace than criticism. My quest to imitate Jesus is ongoing, but at least I know I'm making progress—a slow but steady transformation—and resembling Him more and more each day. —BARBRANDA LUMPKINS WALLS

FAITH STEP: *What changes do you need to make to be more like Jesus? Spend some time today asking Him to help you make the transformation.*

MONDAY, MAY 23

I am my beloved's and my beloved is mine; he browses among the lilies.
Song of Songs 6:3 (NIV)

SCOTT AND I HAVE BEEN married for almost twenty-four years. It is crazy how quickly time has passed…and how much gray I have in my hair. (Some of the gray is genetic. The rest comes from life with three teenage boys.) I love that Scott still calls me his girl. Despite the way my knees crack when I stand up too fast, I still feel like a girl. And I really like being his. Scott was my first boyfriend. That sense of possessiveness that we feel about each other is not a weird or jealous thing—it is a grounding, hopeful thing. We like belonging to each other. Even after all these years. I want to be his until the day that I die.

Jesus understands being possessive in a good way. He grounds me in eternal hope when He claims me as His own. I am His friend. His disciple. His adopted sister. And I get to claim Him right back. He is my Lord and Savior. My redeemer. My counselor. My comforter. My bright morning star. My teacher. My refuge. My deliverer. (Is it me or does it seem like I get the better deal here?) Jesus is the lover of my soul, who gave every single thing—even His life—so that I could be His. I don't know about you, but I want to be His until the day I die. —SUSANNA FOTH AUGHTMON

FAITH STEP: *How does it feel to know that Jesus, in all of His glory and goodness, chooses you as His own? Meditate on this thought today: you are His and He is yours.*

TUESDAY, MAY 24

Not only so, but we also glory in our sufferings, because we know that suffering produces perseverance; perseverance, character; and character, hope. Romans 5:3–4 (NIV)

WE HAVE A LARGE THREE-CAR garage with glass doors on the north and south sides. One morning, I found a bird flying inside the garage. The bird, desperate to get out, kept slamming into the glass. *Feisty little guy,* I thought. *He's not giving up.* This struck me because that morning I had felt like giving up. I felt burdened with worries about my aging parents, a friend in hospice, and our financial struggles. And I had a nagging stiff neck. I backed my car out and left one of the garage doors open, hoping the bird would find its way to freedom. When I returned home, before driving in, I checked for the bird. And there it sat, on the floor of the garage, dazed but still alive. As I opened all of the garage doors, the noise startled the bird. It flew up and easily found its way out. It just needed some help.

This tenacious bird reminded me to not give up, a reminder I really needed in that moment. That little bird was an example that if I persevere through hard times—even if I fly into obstacles—I'll build character, and then hope will come. And my ultimate hope comes from Jesus, my help. Jesus promises to restore me and make me strong (1 Peter 5:10). Sometimes I might feel dazed, but if I can endure difficulties and keep my eyes on Jesus, with His help, I will make it. —JEANNIE BLACKMER

FAITH STEP: *Write the word* hope *at the top of a piece of paper. Then list specific issues you need hope for and ask Jesus to help with each one.*

WEDNESDAY, MAY 25

For we are God's handiwork, created in Christ Jesus to do good works,
which God prepared in advance for us to do. Ephesians 2:10 (NIV)

I OFTEN SEE LETTERS AFTER a person's name in an email or document that indicate the individual is educated and certified in a subject matter or profession. Some of the letters are familiar, such as PhD, MD, JD and CPA. Others aren't as well-known. In fact, out of curiosity I recently asked a colleague what LPD stood for. Turns out it stands for "doctor of law and policy." Who knew?

I can't claim any academic letters after my name. But that doesn't matter. Before I was born, God prepared special works for me to do in my lifetime. He has equipped me with the ability to serve and encourage people, lead ministries and small groups, pray for others, and share my testimonies of His goodness and grace.

Perhaps Jesus has more good works for me to do. And I trust that He will reveal them to me in due time. One thing I do know: I won't necessarily need man-made credentials to do them. At the right time, He'll give me whatever I need to accomplish His purpose.

Now that I think about it, maybe I can add a few letters after my name: COG (Child of God), SBG (Saved by Grace), and FOC (Follower of Christ). Those are all the credentials that I need.
—BARBRANDA LUMPKINS WALLS

FAITH STEP: *Think about the skills and talents you have. How can you use them to do the good works that Jesus has for you? What godly initials would you place after your name?*

THURSDAY, MAY 26

Many are the plans in a person's heart, but it is the LORD's purpose that prevails. Proverbs 19:21 (NIV)

JESUS'S DISCIPLES WERE IRRITATED WHEN children flocked around Him, but Jesus was not. Interruptions were a frequent occurrence in Jesus's life. His mother called on Him to turn water into wine at Cana. The woman who was hemorrhaging accosted Him on His way to healing Jairus's daughter. He was interrupted when He was praying, when He was sleeping, and when He was speaking to a crowd. But the interruptions didn't seem to bother Jesus, no matter how inconvenient they were. He used them for good purposes.

My children have a way of interrupting me at inconvenient times when they need help editing papers, essays, or speeches. As a former English teacher, I usually enjoy fixing words, but sometimes I'm knee-deep in my own plans. I remember when my youngest daughter texted me late one afternoon: "Mom, can you please edit this paper? It's only ten pages. Oh, and could you help me write a conclusion? It's due at midnight tonight. Love you!"

I'm a perfectionist, so I'm going to make sure that my work, whatever it is, is as near flawless as possible. My kids know this. They also know I'd do anything for them. So when I get a request for help with a paper, I drop what I'm doing and get busy with the assignment, although not always cheerfully. I think I need to follow Jesus's model of service. He didn't get cranky. Interruptions didn't derail Him, no matter how inconvenient. He used them for good. All expressions of love can be inconvenient. But that doesn't mean I stop loving. —PAT BUTLER DYSON

FAITH STEP: *Ask Jesus to help you recognize that interruptions sometimes present blessed opportunities.*

Friday, May 27

But I would not have you ignorant, brethren, concerning them which are asleep, that ye sorrow not, even as others which have no hope.
1 Thessalonians 4:13 (KJV)

MY AUNT HAD A LONG battle with cancer. She suffered greatly and it was excruciating to watch. When she died there was peace at last— for the soul set free from her ravaged body, and for those of us who loved her. There was sadness, of course. But in the dark place of grief there was also a light to move toward. A place to warm my heart. A place for hope, because I know she is with Jesus. And because He is also with me, I believe I will see her again. My kids sang "Because He Lives" at her graveside service, and the words "as death gives way to victory, / I'll see the lights of glory" expressed my aunt's hope and also mine. When to live is Christ, dying is gain (Philippians 1:21).

It is hard for me to imagine the sorrow of losing a loved one without having the hope of heaven. However, it's really just the culminating event of a life lived without Jesus. I will face many difficulties—sorrows—before the final blow of death. What gets me through such situations is knowing that Jesus is with me. I may face a thousand tiny deaths as I walk through my days. But I have hope because I know He has a plan for my life. In all things, He works for my good. —GWEN FORD FAULKENBERRY

FAITH STEP: *Visit the grave of a loved one. To express the hope Jesus brings to your heart, take some seeds or new fresh flowers and plant them.*

SATURDAY, MAY 28

The LORD directs our steps, so why try to understand everything along the way? Proverbs 20:24 (NLT)

SEVERAL YEARS AGO, I ATTENDED a writers conference with a book proposal in hand. I showed it to three editors. One invited me to email it to her. I did but never received a response. Two shared it with their publishing committees, who said, "No, thank you."

I felt disappointed. The book's concept had lived in my head for months. Had I not developed it in obedience to the Holy Spirit's prompting? Or had I just concocted it myself? Perhaps my book-writing days were over. I filed the proposal and went on with my life. Every so often the title came to mind, and I sensed the need to change it. I toyed with various ideas, but nothing grabbed me.

Nearly two years later, a friend told me about caring for a woman battling the last stages of cancer. As she spoke, a title randomly popped into my mind: *Finding Hope in Crisis.* This one gripped me. I went home, updated the proposal with renewed enthusiasm, and added the new title. COVID-19 struck immediately afterward.

My literary agent submitted the proposal to several publishers. Several weeks later, an editor expressed interest. She'd acquired a similar project several months prior, but it had fallen through. Now she needed a substitute. She said she wanted to fast-track it and asked how quickly I could submit the complete manuscript. The committee approved the proposal the next day, and I signed a contract a week later.

Now I understood why Jesus allowed the earlier disappointment. He knew when people would be most desperate for hope, and He directed my steps accordingly. —GRACE FOX

FAITH STEP: *Draw a question mark. Write today's verse below it.*

SUNDAY, MAY 29

But the Lord is faithful, and he will strengthen you and protect you from the evil one. 2 Thessalonians 3:3 (NIV)

OUR BARN CAT, IVY, RECENTLY recovered from an illness requiring medication. We set up a feeding station and cozy bed for her in the basement. That's when I learned that the only thing she dislikes more than our other pets is being cooped up. Whenever I headed down those stairs, there she'd be, complaining loudly.

This week, Jesus chose to do the same for me. I'd strained my back, making bed rest necessary. Lying in bed, barely able to move, I wished I could get up and get out. But there was another problem, one of equal importance, that the Great Physician needed to tend to.

Sometimes illnesses affect our physical bodies and other times our emotional health. And sometimes both. I needed more than bed rest to heal. I needed Jesus. Those days I spent solo, tucked between the sheets, I sought both doctoring and solace. As long-held hurts came to light, there were no distractions I could use to escape.

But during those long hours, I sensed Jesus's presence and His love and divine healing. I've now come away refreshed and restored—body and soul—knowing I was under the care of One who loved me deeply.

Ivy is feisty again. It's time to set her free. Like her, I'm ready to rejoin my daily life. My period of being alone has strengthened me. But then, I never was alone, was I? —HEIDI GAUL

FAITH STEP: *Next time you're ill, give thanks for Jesus's constant presence. Pray for Him to heal you—body and soul—of illnesses known and unknown.*

MEMORIAL DAY, MONDAY, MAY 30

When Peter saw this, he said to them: "Fellow Israelites, why does this surprise you? Why do you stare at us as if by our own power or godliness we had made this man walk?" Acts 3:12 (NIV)

THIS PAST WEEK, I HAD the privilege of reading comments from an online book club discussing one of my novels. Several people shared ways Jesus had used the story to bring them encouragement as they applied its themes to their own lives. I was touched and grateful.

But soon after, my stomach began to knot. Free-floating anxiety swirled in my thoughts. I have a new novel releasing soon, and I suddenly felt pressure to measure up. What if the new story didn't touch hearts in the same way? What if people were disappointed? What if I wasn't skilled enough?

When Peter and John brought healing to a lame man outside the temple, they made it clear that it wasn't their own power of godliness at work. They acknowledged immediately that the only thing they had to offer of value was Jesus and that it was Jesus who brought the blessing of healing. Reading about their example lifted the pressure from my shoulders. If Jesus has used my efforts to bring a measure of healing to a weary heart, it isn't because of my wisdom, skill, or power. That means I don't need to live in fear of not being enough.

My role, as Peter and John demonstrated, is to simply bring Jesus to others and rejoice that God is glorified. —SHARON HINCK

FAITH STEP: *Do you have a need or task that causes anxiety? Or do you worry that you aren't enough? Ask Jesus to help you trust Him and to remind you that He is always enough.*

TUESDAY, MAY 31

Let all that I am praise the LORD; may I never forget the good things he does for me. Psalm 103:2 (NLT)

WE HAVE AN AMAZON ECHO in our kitchen that displays photos in a continuous slideshow. Every day I get to see a variety of images that remind me of good times and good people—a summer evening at a baseball game with my husband, visits with my spunky mother, birthday celebrations with girlfriends, my grandson as a toddler, and much-loved family and friends who are now with Jesus.

I can't help but smile as I view the photos throughout the day. I'm grateful for this slideshow of memories because it helps me remember the multitude of blessings that Jesus has poured into my life. He has provided me with a lot of laughter, love, and fellowship with others, along with provisions that I often take for granted.

Just like businesses that close to take inventory of their wares, this Amazon Echo helps me pause to take stock of my blessings. I've also gotten into the habit of jotting down blessings and answers to prayers whenever they occur. I fold the slips of paper, put them in a large glass jar and watch them multiply. It's a perfect visual of God's goodness and how blessings pile up daily.

The saying goes, "When the praises go up, the blessings come down." I always want to remember all the Lord's blessings toward me and give Him praise. Jesus has been too good for me to forget.

—BARBRANDA LUMPKINS WALLS

FAITH STEP: *Write down five blessings or answers to prayer that Jesus has bestowed upon you this week. How can you be more intentional about remembering His goodness and grace toward you?*

WEDNESDAY, JUNE 1

Then Jesus said to her, "Your sins are forgiven." Luke 7:48 (NIV)

CERTAIN HYMNS AND WORSHIP SONGS bring me to tears. With my husband on a fishing trip this week, I've used the alone time to crank up the volume on songs that touch something deep in my soul—music that reminds me of what a privilege it is to love and be loved by Jesus.

Lyrics and melodies marry and give birth to expressions of praise beyond what the tongue alone can tell. So this week, the house has been filled with worship and occasional teary outbursts of gratitude.

I'm overwhelmed that Jesus would choose to love me and die for me and will one day welcome me into an endless eternity with Him.

How interesting that this week—my "drench the house with worship songs" week—would be when I landed on Luke 7:36–50 in my Bible reading. It's the story of the woman with a reputation of having a sinful life who crashed the party at Simon's house, washed Jesus's feet with her tears, and poured an alabaster jar of perfume on them. She was overcome with love for her Savior and showed it in a tender and public way.

Jesus read Simon's mind. The Pharisee still thought of her as "that sinful woman" and couldn't understand why Jesus allowed her to weep all over Him. Jesus acknowledged that her sins had been many but that all of them had been forgiven (verses 47–48).

Her tears were part of her worship. Jesus's parting words to her that night were, "Go in peace" (verse 50, NIV). When I pour out my tears of gratitude, that's what I'm left with too—peace.
—CYNTHIA RUCHTI

FAITH STEP: *Which hymns or praise songs can bring you to tears? Let the gratitude flow.*

Thursday, June 2

Peter answered Him and said, "Lord, if it is You, command me to come to You on the water." Matthew 14:28 (NKJV)

WHENEVER I READ THE STORY of Jesus walking on water to reach the disciples' boat, I always pause when I get to Peter's request. It boggles my mind that such a thought even entered his head. It probably amazed the other disciples too. None of them seemed eager to join Peter. No one piped up and said, "Me too, Lord! Me too!" Only Peter asked Jesus to command him to walk on top of the water. On a dark night. In a storm. Jesus said, "Come" (Matthew 14:29, NKJV). And Peter didn't hesitate.

Everything went swimmingly until Peter got close to Jesus. He faltered when his eyes turned toward the wind-lashed waves. Fear replaced Peter's exhilaration, and he began sinking down into the water. But he cried out to Jesus, who simply reached out a hand and raised him up. The two of them together walked on the water the rest of the way to the boat.

I've never desired to walk on water, but this passage reminds me of how often I've limited myself in my Christian walk. Haven't I held back from serving Jesus in a certain area because I didn't think I was good enough? Haven't I ignored a long-cherished dream because it seemed impossible? Jesus is waiting for me to get out of my comfortable boat and join Him in doing something amazing. I want to always remember that when my courage falters, He'll be right there to reach out His loving hand. —DIANNE NEAL MATTHEWS

FAITH STEP: *Are you wondering if Jesus is calling you to do something that seems scary? Ask Him to give you clear commands to follow.*

FRIDAY, JUNE 3

Give me back the joy of your salvation. Keep me strong by
giving me a willing spirit. Psalm 51:12 (NCV)

ON ANOTHER OCCASION, PETER'S FAITH faltered in a more serious manner. During the night Jesus was arrested, Peter had vowed to lay down his life for Jesus. But before the rooster crowed three times, Peter denied even knowing Jesus, just as Jesus had predicted. When he later met the resurrected Jesus, Peter needed courage, but a different kind than the boldness that prompted him to walk on the water.

Peter needed the courage to be honest about his failure while accepting the forgiveness and restoration that Jesus extended. It took trust in Someone stronger than himself for Peter to publicly confirm his love and commitment to Jesus after failing Him so terribly. Yet soon Peter would preach about Jesus and see three thousand souls added to the kingdom. He would go on to become a leader of the early church.

It takes courage to get back up after a fall. Anyone can choose the easy way out—to give up and wallow in bitterness or self-pity. Jesus offers to raise me up after a fall; He longs to restore me to full fellowship with Him and renew my joy. If I'm willing to trust Him, He can use any mistake or failure to mold me into a better version of who I was before—strengthened in my faith and my resolve to obey Him, more teachable and usable for His kingdom work. My fresh start begins the moment I reach up and take His outstretched hand. —DIANNE NEAL MATTHEWS

FAITH STEP: *Is there an area in your life where you need a fresh start? Ask Jesus to give you the courage to take the first step. Then follow Him into forgiveness and restoration.*

SATURDAY, JUNE 4

Encourage one another and build each other up, just as in fact you are doing. 1 Thessalonians 5:11 (NIV)

THERE IS A DOWNWARD SLOPE in our backyard that invited all the runoff water from our next-door neighbors' yard to collect at the side of our fence. It looked like a baby pool, but one that was full of mud. When we had the sod laid in our backyard, the landscape designer noticed the flooding issue. He built up a small ramp of topsoil against the side of our fence with the runoff. He used this built-up slope to redirect the flow of the water. Since then, we have had zero flooding in the lawn. We love that landscape designer. He knew what he was doing!

Encouragement is a whole lot like a built-up ramp of topsoil for my spirit. The enemy of my souls would like to flood my life with anxiety and despair. Life circumstances and struggles can leave me feeling overwhelmed.

But Jesus refuses to let the enemy win. He builds up hope in my heart and mind. He wants to use me as His voice of encouragement to help shore up the souls of those around me. He knows what He is doing. Encouragement can be a healing balm to a bruised heart. When my actions are loving, it can infuse those around me with strength and peace. Jesus showed me how to encourage others with the way He lived out His life, speaking words of truth, hope, and healing. —SUSANNA FOTH AUGHTMON

FAITH STEP: *Write a letter of encouragement to someone who is in desperate need of it today. Include a Scripture verse to lift their spirit. Like Jesus, use your words to shore up people with hope.*

SUNDAY, JUNE 5

But God did listen! He paid attention to my prayer. Psalm 66:19 (NLT)

THE EMAIL'S SUBJECT LINE WAS "It's time, y'all." The message was an invitation from a friend to join several other sister-friends on a video call. We hadn't seen one another in quite a while, so there was great anticipation until the appointed time when we would gather together virtually.

When the call finally started, we excitedly greeted one another. Then several of us started talking at the same time—asking and answering questions, our words tumbling over each other's. From time to time I had difficulty following who was saying what among the constant chatter.

That's how I picture it must be for Jesus hearing us speak to Him 24-7. Along with my desperate cries, joyful praises, probing questions, pleas for peace, and fervent intercessions, I know He must hear the same and more from others. But unlike me, Jesus can keep it all straight with no problem—He knows His sheep (John 10:14). Jesus knows my voice from others, even when we're all bending His ear at the same time. For Him, there's no jumble of voices, chaotic conversations, or confusion. He hears each of us clearly.

The best part is, not only does Jesus hear us collectively and individually, but He also pays attention and answers our prayers. His response to my prayer is just for me, and He speaks specifically to my needs. The Lord listens patiently and my time with Him is limitless. I can drop in anytime. No appointment necessary.
—BARBRANDA LUMPKINS WALLS

FAITH STEP: *Gather several friends for a prayer call. Take a minute for everyone to pray aloud at the same time and imagine how it sounds to Jesus. Do you believe He knows your voice?*

MONDAY, JUNE 6

A new command I give you: Love one another. As I have loved you, so you must love one another. By this everyone will know that you are my disciples, if you love one another. John 13:34–35 (NIV)

MY OLDEST SON, JACK, IS home from college right now. My two younger boys, Will and Addison, are still in school, but are more than ready for summer. The other night after everyone had gone to bed, I tossed and turned until midnight. When I couldn't sleep, I finally got up to go check on the boys. Mom habits die hard. I checked Will's room, and he wasn't there. Neither was Addison. I opened the door to Jack's room to find all three of them watching a show on Jack's computer. They knew they were busted. They mumbled, "Sorry, Mom," and Will and Addison hurried to their rooms. I couldn't stay mad for long. I love that my boys like hanging out—even in the middle of the night. It hasn't always been that way. In fact, punching with a side of yelling used to be the way they communicated their love to one another. Now, nothing brings my heart more joy than seeing them love one another.

Nothing brings Jesus more joy than seeing us love one another. Too often I get caught up in disagreements or become irritated with those around me. But when I go out of my way to show kindness or forgiveness to people, I fill Jesus with joy. When I love others like Jesus loves me, I start to look like Him. —SUSANNA FOTH AUGHTMON

FAITH STEP: *What is a way that you can reach out in love? Ask Jesus to put a person on your heart who needs His love and pray for her throughout the day.*

TUESDAY, JUNE 7

Thy word is a lamp unto my feet, and a light unto my path.
Psalm 119:105 (KJV)

A FEW YEARS AGO, MY husband and I toured Israel with two other couples. One of my favorite moments was walking through Hezekiah's tunnel. Built during the reign of King Hezekiah, it brought water from one side of the city to the other. It is also the water shaft David led his army through to conquer the Jebusites and seize the city of David (2 Samuel 5:8). As we traveled through the dark, earthy-smelling tunnel in knee-deep rushing water, we imagined an army silently heading to fight for what is now Jerusalem. At one point, we turned off our headlamps. In the pitch-dark, we started to sing, "Thy word is a lamp unto my feet, and a light unto my path." It sounds hokey, but it was an amazing moment as I literally experienced some of the sights, sounds, and smells of this ancient story.

Later during our tour, I stood on the shores of the Sea of Galilee, possibly in a spot where Jesus stood. Maybe I stood where Jesus fed the five thousand or healed a man with leprosy? Struck by an intense feeling of Jesus's presence, I wondered, *Why does His presence feel more real here than anywhere else?* I had a deep desire to be just as keenly aware of Jesus back in my hometown of Boulder, Colorado.

But I learned from my trip to Israel that Jesus is the Word, a lamp for my feet, and a light for my path *wherever* I am. I've held onto this truth since then. Whether in the Holy Land or my homeland, Jesus's presence is real everywhere. —JEANNIE BLACKMER

FAITH STEP: *Where do you most sense Jesus's presence? Take time today to sit in that place.*

WEDNESDAY, JUNE 8

*Teach these new disciples to obey all the commands I have given you.
And be sure of this: I am with you always, even to the end of the age.*
Matthew 28:20 *(NLT)*

I'M NOT SURE HOW HE got there, but Jesus is in my car. Well, not Jesus Himself, but a card with His picture on it. My husband, Jeff, surmises a worker may have put it there during my car inspection. I don't care how He got there; having Jesus riding on my console has changed my life!

The picture features a close-up of Jesus's face, His hair long and shining, His eyes looking toward heaven. Some days, I think He's looking right at me! Each day, I get in my car, put on my seat belt, start the engine, and glance to my right at Jesus.

Having Jesus beside me while I'm driving makes me think twice before I shake my fist at the guy who cut me off or mutter unkind words about the woman who wouldn't let me merge. If I'm late and start to exceed the speed limit, I glance to my right, see Jesus looking at me, and slow down.

Other times, when I'm troubled or depressed, I look to Jesus and am reassured that I'm not alone and that things will be all right. In my heart, I know Jesus is with me every minute of every day, no matter where I go. But having a visual reminder of His constant presence gives me peace and comfort.

I'm grateful to the person who put Jesus's picture in my car. Having Jesus as my passenger makes every day better. —PAT BUTLER DYSON

FAITH STEP: *Find a picture of Jesus that comforts you. Put it somewhere you'll see it every day.*

THURSDAY, JUNE 9

*According to my earnest expectation and my hope, that in nothing
I shall be ashamed, but that with all boldness, as always, so now also
Christ shall be magnified in my body. Philippians 1:20 (KJV)*

IN MY LIFE I HAVE learned that there is a direct correlation between shame and fear. They go in a cycle: shame leads to fear, which in turn leads to more shame. Nowhere is this more obvious to me than in my own body.

For years, I was caught in a cycle of food addiction. I would feel afraid or stressed or lonely or bored or some other uncomfortable emotion, and I would try to medicate my feeling with food. Then I would feel ashamed, which added to my discomfort. So I'd medicate myself with more food. And then I'd feel even more ashamed. . . You get the picture. I finally got help with those issues and as long as I work on it every day and don't let down my guard, I pretty much stay healthy.

I love that the Bible offers a helpful anti-addiction cycle. In today's verse, we see that first comes hope, which then leads to no shame, which then leads to courage. And the result? Jesus is magnified in my body. The key here is that the cycle begins and ends with Jesus. He is the reason I have hope, which is more than mere wishful thinking. Hope is a thing of substance, an anchor for the soul. It means that because He overcame; so can I. —GWEN FORD FAULKENBERRY

FAITH STEP: *"O magnify the LORD with me, and let us exalt his name together" (Psalm 34:3, KJV). Make a list of five ways you can use your body to magnify Jesus, then incorporate them into your week.*

FRIDAY, JUNE 10

Like newborn babies, crave pure spiritual milk, so that by it you may grow up in your salvation, now that you have tasted that the Lord is good. 1 Peter 2:2–3 (NIV)

MY SON ADDISON IS GRADUATING from eighth grade. My baby is going to be in high school. The years have flown by. His school asked us to send in a baby picture and his school picture for the eighth-grade celebration. They wanted to show the amazing growth that has taken place in the years between. As I sorted through photos, it was fun to look back on all of Addison's milestones: his first birthday, his first day of preschool (we both cried), his first day of kindergarten (only I cried), starting at a new school in fourth grade, performing in his class musical, overcoming years of shyness, making the leap to middle school and making new friends. Each picture showed a new level of growth. Now my six-foot-tall son is completing one more rite of passage. I am one proud mom. I want him to mature, to become the young man that Jesus created him to be.

Even though I am long past middle school, Jesus wants me to mature too. My spiritual growth is a lifelong process of knowing and loving Him. Maturity requires perseverance. The milestones in my spiritual journey have drawn me into a place of dependence on Him. They are not always easy to achieve. They don't always feel good. But Jesus is good. With His mercy and grace, He promises to complete the good work He began in me. —SUSANNA FOTH AUGHTMON

FAITH STEP: *In what area of your life do you need to mature? Ask Jesus to continue His good work in you, helping you become the person He created you to be.*

SATURDAY, JUNE 11

Though you have not seen him, you love him; and even though you do not see him now, you believe in him and are filled with an inexpressible and glorious joy. 1 Peter 1:8 (NIV)

THE SUN WARMS MY BODY as I lounge on my favorite chaise. A gentle breeze stirs the air. Neighborhood sounds meld into calming white noise, and I smell a barbecue nearby. I reach for my glass and sip some iced tea.

Sprawled across my lap, my tuxedo cat, Milo, stretches his paws to knead the air. His adoring gaze never leaves my face. A loud purr rumbles against my ribs.

I haven't petted him or scratched his chin. I've done nothing aside from giving him a quiet place to rest. He's elated just to be here with me, sharing a few minutes together. Knowing this makes me smile.

I understand the simple joy Milo feels in my presence. Like him, I have a safe place to land when I need a break from the world's bustle. During the quiet time I spend alone with Jesus, the serenity I experience restores me. He need not *do* anything—the privilege of His presence is enough. I sense His love for me and am filled with deep, abiding joy.

My simple need for His company—along with my complete trust in Him—delight Jesus. As I smile at Milo, I suspect Jesus is smiling too.

He is peace. He is joy. He alone is enough. —HEIDI GAUL

FAITH STEP: *Take a few minutes today to close your eyes and meditate on Jesus. Let the Spirit lead you in silent prayer and thanksgiving. Share the joy you experience in Jesus's presence with Him and know He feels pleasure by your devotion.*

SUNDAY, JUNE 12

He said to them, "Follow me, and I will make you fishers of men."
Immediately they left their nets and followed him. Matthew 4:19–20 (ESV)

ON A WEEKEND GETAWAY, MY husband, Ted, and I took a boat tour of sandstone caves on the south shore of Lake Superior. The boat captain told us about fishing charters he led. When he spotted a boat of fishermen, he headed toward them. "How's it going?" he called. The men shrugged and admitted they hadn't caught anything in several hours.

Our captain held up a lure and asked if they'd tried it. He also suggested a better spot at a different depth. They thanked him, and after we motored away, we looked back and saw them moving to the new location.

Jesus taught his disciples—some of whom were already fishermen—how to draw in a much more valuable catch: human souls. But in a world where many have been wounded by those who carry His name and others simply resist the good news of the gospel out of rebellion, intellectualism, or lies from our culture, I find it hard to muster the courage to be a fisher of men.

My only hope is to do exactly what Jesus told His new disciples: "Follow Me." I can watch for where Jesus is at work in my community and follow Him there. I can listen for His guidance about which person to talk to, in which setting, and in His timing. I can cast my nets wide, trusting Him to gather more people into His kingdom, where one day we can all celebrate together. —SHARON HINCK

FAITH STEP: *Ask Jesus to show you one person to reach out to. Take a small step to build a relationship or share your faith with that person.*

MONDAY, JUNE 13

When the Advocate comes, whom I will send to you from the Father—the
Spirit of truth who goes out from the Father—he will testify about me.
John 15:26 (NIV)

MY HUSBAND, TED, SETTLED BESIDE me so we could watch a talent
show on television. I noticed the bowl in his hands. "Cherries?
Where did you get cherries?" I asked, my mouth watering.

He shot me a puzzled look and slid the bowl within my reach.
"We've had them in the fridge since I got groceries a few days ago.
I wasn't hiding them." I had missed several days of enjoying juicy
cherries because I hadn't looked on the bottom shelf.

Jesus has placed blessings of His Spirit in my life, but because
I'm not looking in the right places, I often miss them. The Holy
Spirit—the Advocate that Jesus gives me—offers fruit more deli-
cious than ripe cherries: love, joy, peace, and more.

Just this week I struggled to be happy for a friend's success, and
I was dismayed by my selfishness. At first I tried to muster up the
fruit of love with my own strength. Then I remembered to look in
the right place, remembering that when I open my hands and heart
to receive Jesus's gift, His Spirit forms the fruit I need in my life
each time I need it. Instead of striving in my own strength, I want
to welcome His gift. —SHARON HINCK

FAITH STEP: Eat some fruit today and ponder the fruit of the Spirit that Jesus
pours into our lives.

TUESDAY, JUNE 14

Now all glory to God, who is able, through his mighty power at work within us, to accomplish infinitely more than we might ask or think.
Ephesians 3:20 (NLT)

WHEN OUR DAUGHTER, MARIE, AND her three kids moved from 350 miles to 6 miles away, I was elated. Our teenage grandkids? Not so much. Especially Daniel, who had to leave his beloved orchestra, where he'd played bass viol for his first two years of middle school.

Our local schools have only bands. I told Daniel we'd seen a bass player in the high-school band last year at graduation. "Perhaps you can play next year, when you're a freshman." But Daniel refuted my every word of encouragement. He said that the school might not own the bass, and if not, his family couldn't afford to buy him one or even rent one.

So I got out my big guns: "Let's pray that Jesus will give you this desire, honey." I reminded Daniel of Ephesians 3:20—God's promise to go far beyond our best imaginings.

On the night of high-school orientation, the vice principal invited everyone to visit the gym, where leaders of extracurricular clubs waited to meet the incoming freshmen. Daniel beelined toward the music tables. When we spotted the band director, Daniel asked him about the bass.

"Sure," he said. "The school owns a bass, and the girl who plays it graduates this year." Daniel was happier than a chocolate lover on vacation in Switzerland.

On the way home, I reminded Daniel how we'd asked for this exact blessing and noted that it was Jesus who orchestrated every detail. Because Jesus was a boy once Himself, He understood. —JEANETTE LEVELLIE

FAITH STEP: *Ask Jesus to do something so big that when it happens, you'll know it came from Him.*

WEDNESDAY, JUNE 15

No wonder we are happy in the Lord! For we are trusting him.
We trust his holy name. Psalm 33:21 (TLB)

WHENEVER I GET TO VISIT my daughter's family, I always enjoy the dinner conversations. One evening, four-year-old Lilah gazed across the table at her big brother, age nine, and asked, "Roman, what's it like to be so handsome?" She sighed. We all chuckled and watched Roman shake his head as he kept on eating. Then, without looking up from his plate, he responded, "Okay, you want to know the worst thing about being handsome? Your legs get tired from running away from all those girls."

We got a good laugh out of Roman's observation, but later I decided it perfectly illustrates the old adage: "Be careful what you wish for." Wise words, because often what I long for may come with unexpected drawbacks. Our culture works overtime to make us dissatisfied with who we are and what we have. It's easy to fall into the trap of thinking how much happier we would be if we were only better looking, richer, thinner, more talented, more successful, or—whatever. Sometimes I forget that all these things can vanish in a moment's time or gradually fade with the passing years.

Although I may not always realize it, I am created with a need to know my Creator. The only path to true, lasting joy and fulfillment is to know Jesus personally. To live every day conscious of His presence and His everlasting love for me. I don't have to just wish for those blessings; He offers them freely. —DIANNE NEAL MATTHEWS

FAITH STEP: *Have you been wishing for something that you think would increase your happiness? Ask Jesus to take away that desire if it's not His will for you. Tell Him why He is your main source of joy and fulfillment.*

Thursday, June 16

As soon as Judas had taken the bread, he went out. And it was night.
John 13:30 (NIV)

OF ALL THE HEALTH PROFESSIONALS, phlebotomists are not patients' favorite people. I used to be a phlebotomist. We come with needles and tourniquets and extract what looks like too much blood.

During my years as a phlebotomist, I dealt with calm patients, nervous patients, and screaming patients (who were not necessarily children). Most took the approach of "Let's get this over with."

Why am I thinking about that today? Because I recently read an important but complex passage of Scripture from John 13. Jesus said something that sounds like "Just rip off the Band-Aid and get this over with." At the Last Supper, Jesus told Judas, "What you are about to do, do quickly" (John 13:27, NIV). The disciples were confused and didn't understand Jesus's words. Even though I have the advantage of the Bible and know exactly what Judas was about to do, I used to wonder why Jesus told Judas to "speed it up, buddy" (paraphrasing).

Some speculate Jesus was simply saying, "Let's get this over with," knowing that ahead of Him lay the cross. Others surmise Jesus was trying to minimize the guilt Judas would feel for selling Him out. Still others say Judas couldn't afford to dillydally since Jesus was the *Passover* Lamb, and Passover's clock was ticking.

Whatever the reason, Jesus did not lack courage. After His heart-to-heart "not my will, but yours" speech in the garden of Gethsemane (Luke 22:42, NIV), Jesus unflinchingly faced what I certainly wouldn't be able to stomach—paying the price for the sins of the world. I think Jesus told Judas to hurry because lives were at stake. Yours and mine. —CYNTHIA RUCHTI

FAITH STEP: *Express your gratitude to Jesus for the courage it took to give up His life for you.*

FRIDAY, JUNE 17

Do not swerve to the right or to the left; turn your foot away from evil. Proverbs 4:27 (ESV)

RIDING CLOCKWISE IN A BRITISH roundabout, I screamed when a car to my right sped straight at us. The rental car my husband and I were in was hit broadside! Our English holiday began with a bang! Literally.

Blessedly, the right front wheel received the impact—not the passenger side where I sat. Our vehicle was disabled, and our adventure continued with a ride in a British police car. The constable humored me, turning on the revolving lights while I took pictures of my husband in a police car on the first day of our holiday in England.

At our bed and breakfast, we tried to order a tow truck. That's when we realized we didn't know the location of the roundabout where we'd left the car! Our first day in a foreign country, and we'd lost the rental car! We set out on foot to find the abandoned car so that we could relay its location to the towing company. Eventually, we found it, scheduled a tow, rented another car, toured the Cotswold countryside, and recovered from the stressful day that began with a bang.

Motoring in a country with different driving rules is stressful. But not half as stressful as navigating through life without our universal driver's manual, the Holy Bible. When I first began enjoying mornings with Jesus and His Word, I was overjoyed to discover the book of Proverbs. Its rules for "the road leading to life" (Proverbs 6:23, NET) are applicable everywhere—regardless of the side of the road I drive on! —CASSANDRA TIERSMA

FAITH STEP: *Proverbs 4:27 says, "Don't turn off the road of goodness..." (NCV). Ask Jesus to keep you on the good road.*

SATURDAY, JUNE 18

*We say with confidence, "The Lord is my helper; I will not be afraid.
What can mere mortals do to me?" Hebrews 13:6 (NIV)*

MY DAD IS A DOER. Sitting around and doing nothing is not his gig.
When my parents visited our new home in Idaho for the first time,
Dad went out and bought us the essentials for our beautiful new
lawn: a lawn mower and an edge trimmer. Next, he set about teaching
me how to use them both. This took a minute, but my dad was
kind. He didn't make fun of me when I almost pulled my arm out
of the socket trying to start the lawn mower the first time. He was
also patient when I flooded the engine, causing us to wait another
fifteen minutes before we could mow the lawn. Next, he set up a
shelving unit in our garage to store my books. He followed this up
with detailing our car. He always helps us. He can't do enough for
us. I think it is because he loves us so much.

I get the same feeling about Jesus. He is a doer. He is not sitting
around waiting for things to happen. He makes them happen.
He sets me free from sin, heals my hurting heart, and fills me up
with love. Moreover, He opened the way for me to have a relationship
with His Father. My heavenly Dad. Day in and day out, Jesus
does good things on my behalf. All because He loves me so much.
—SUSANNA FOTH AUGHTMON

FAITH STEP: *Write down all the ways that Jesus has helped you this year. Put this
list up on your fridge to remind you that Jesus is in the business of overwhelming
you with His love.*

SUNDAY, JUNE 19, JUNETEENTH AND FATHER'S DAY

Now the Lord is the Spirit, and where the Spirit of the Lord is, there is freedom. 2 Corinthians 3:17 (NIV)

I WAS IN COLLEGE WHEN the ground-breaking TV mini-series *Roots* premiered in 1977. My friends and I gathered around the television on eight consecutive nights, riveted by the story based on author Alex Haley's family history that detailed the enslavement of Haley's African ancestor Kunta Kinte to his descendants' liberation.

While *Roots* was unsettling to me and my African-American friends, it gave us a real appreciation of our ancestors and all they overcame to survive. The characters in Haley's story talked about the Lord and called on Him for help and protection throughout their trials. Although they were in bondage, they dreamed of freedom. But when I stop to think about it, many of these people were already experiencing freedom in their minds and hearts because they knew Jesus.

I believe my own enslaved ancestors' faith in God and the presence of the Holy Spirit is what sustained them during dark times. They, too, believed they would be free someday. I'm not shackled in physical chains as my ancestors were, but from time to time I still battle things that try to hold me captive: fear of failure, guilt for sins past and present, and more. But as one who knows Jesus and the power of His spirit, I am free.

Unlike many of the enslaved people who had to wait to get word of their freedom long after their official emancipation, I have been free ever since the day I gave my life to Jesus. He gives on-the-spot liberation to all believers, and that's the main reason to celebrate today. —BARBRANDA LUMPKINS WALLS

FAITH STEP: *What is holding you captive? Your job? Financial worries? A past sin? Know that there is freedom in Jesus.*

MONDAY, JUNE 20

Jesus said to him, "'If you can'! All things are possible for one who believes."
Immediately the father of the child cried out and said, "I believe; help my
unbelief!" Mark 9:23–24 (ESV)

RECENTLY IN MY BIBLE STUDY, I shared my struggle with waffling between fear and faith during uncertain times. Sometimes I'm confident of God's control and have faith He is up to something incredible. Other times, I feel fearful. Sometimes I doubt God has meaningful work for me during this stage of life, or I'm afraid of aging and the aches and pains that come with it. I shared how I couldn't hold faith and fear at the same time; it was either one or the other that dominated my thoughts and actions.

Then one of the girls who recently graduated from college and was anxious about the job market spoke up. She'd just listened to a podcast on the topic of uncertainty, and she shared a quote from it: "Fear and faith need the same thing to grow: the soil of uncertainty." This perspective, that uncertain times are opportunities to grow in faith or fear, struck a chord with me. I thought about the man who came to Jesus to heal his son. He seemed uncertain when he approached Jesus with his request. The man said, "If you can do anything..." and Jesus's response assured him that the impossible is possible with Him. The man cried out, "I believe; help my unbelief!" These words have become my daily prayer. I'm learning that uncertainty does provide the perfect soil to grow faith or fear. But I'm committed to always choosing faith. —JEANNIE BLACKMER

FAITH STEP: *On one side of a notecard write* Believe *and on the other side write out Mark 9:23–24. Put this somewhere you'll see often.*

TUESDAY, JUNE 21

Whether you turn to the right or to the left, your ears will hear a voice behind you, saying, "This is the way; walk in it." Isaiah 30:21 (NIV)

I SLOWLY PUSHED THE SHOPPING cart along the aisle, my eyes scanning the shelves for liquid soap. I was in a new grocery store that had just opened in my neighborhood, so I wasn't familiar with its layout and where everything was located.

In my quest to find the soap, I heard a voice: "There are arrows on the floor. You're going the wrong way." I looked away from the shelves, and a woman near me was pointing downward as she passed by. Indeed, there were arrows pointing shoppers in the direction they should move throughout the store. I apologized and turned my cart around.

I was so focused on what I wanted that I hadn't noticed the signs. But the voice had grabbed my attention. I later remembered the brief encounter, and I thought about the times I had clearly heard Jesus tell me what to do. When I followed His direction, it was the right way to go. Many times I've sought His guidance and longed to hear His voice, but the silence was deafening. *Jesus, should I go left or should I go right? Should I even move at all?* Sometimes, I had to wait patiently for the answer.

Those fork-in-the-road moments can be challenging. But I've learned that's when I really need to be still and listen for Jesus's voice to guide me in the right direction. When I do, I never wind up going the wrong way. —BARBRANDA LUMPKINS WALLS

FAITH STEP: *What decisions do you need to make today? Jesus is there to direct you. Just ask.*

WEDNESDAY, JUNE 22

This I say for your own profit, not that I may put a leash on you, but for what is proper, and that you may serve the Lord without distraction.
1 Corinthians 7:35 (NKJV)

MY CAT KRIS LIKES TO drink water from the bathroom sink, preferring the water be running, so he can lick it as it flows. I indulge him because he's the boss. One recent day, I ran the water for Kris before jumping in the shower. I washed my hair and sang a song or two, and when I stepped out, the water was two inches deep on the floor, a stream still flowing merrily from the sink. Had the cat inadvertently pushed down the stopper? Kris sat in the closet, momentarily safe from the encroaching flow. It took every towel I owned to mop the floor as well as sop up every drawer and shelf in the bathroom. I was disgusted with myself, but I had to admit, this mishap was a symptom of a bigger problem.

For days, I'd felt a vague sense of unease. My life didn't seem to be running as smoothly as it might. I'd been so busy caught up in the cares of the world that I'd neglected my time with the Lord. *Oh, Jesus, when I take my eyes off You, things just don't go right.*

Distractions, the bane of my existence. But I knew what I had to do to get my life in order. Each morning, before the world intruded, I needed to get back to spending time with Jesus. I needed to read the Bible, pray for those on my list, and talk to Him about my cares. I could do it! —PAT BUTLER DYSON

FAITH STEP: *Set aside a time each day for Jesus. Don't skip! Nothing on your to-do list is as important.*

THURSDAY, JUNE 23

Give to the LORD the glory due His name; bring an offering, and come before Him. Oh, worship the LORD in the beauty of holiness! 1 Chronicles 16:29 (NKJV)

MY FRIEND DIANA NEVER SEEMS to age. On Facebook recently, her daughter Aimee posted a photo of Diana at an outdoor farmer's market. I've also viewed photos of Diana during a messy home repair or while cleaning out roof gutters. Somehow, she manages to look like a model even in those settings.

Whenever I compliment Diana on her youthful looks, she says, "I inherited good genes." But I know her loveliness runs deeper than genes. Diana takes excellent care of her health. And she has a close relationship with Jesus, resulting in what the Bible calls "the beauty of holiness."

Do I feel envious of Diana's looks? No. Other than Jesus and my husband, Kevin, Diana has helped me grow in the Lord more than anyone else. She has lovingly and willingly spent untold hours mentoring and advising me and praying for me and my family. Her beauty is a reflection of Jesus's love and compassion. I could never be jealous of her. Quite the opposite. I'm proud to call her my friend.

Jesus is my Lord and Savior. He's also my dearest friend. If someone asked me, "Aren't you envious of Jesus? He gets so much attention and praise," I'd be outraged. I'm not jealous of Jesus, and I'm also deeply grateful to Him. He laid down His life so I could join His family. He gave me His Spirit to strengthen and comfort me. He mentors and advises me and prays for me. Now that's beautiful.
—JEANETTE LEVELLIE

FAITH STEP: *Think of a friend who exemplifies Jesus's loveliness. Text her or send a handwritten note to say "thank you."*

FRIDAY, JUNE 24

For the Spirit God gave us does not make us timid, but gives us power, love and self-discipline. 2 Timothy 1:7 (NIV)

JUST OFF OREGON'S COAST, MASSIVE rock monoliths jut skyward, hundreds of feet above the sea. Every year atop those pillars of stone, mother murres lay their eggs. As the babies grow, both parents tend to their needs. But soon the time comes for them to seek food on their own.

Floating on the water's surface below, the fathers call up to their offspring. The hatchlings' answering cries fill the air as they realize what they must do. They'll need to leave their colony, the only home they've ever known, and not return. But they've never flown, never touched down on the ocean.

These babies recognize their fathers' voices, coaxing and encouraging. One step at a time they move closer to the edge, an action that spells new life but also risks of the unknown. They cluster and stall. At last, a single bird jumps, then another and another, each one trusting it will be safe and will not be alone.

Watching this gut-wrenching scene leaves me speechless. I remember times Jesus has called, nudging me from my comfort zone into leaps of faith much like the baby murres' leap.

Though I am tempted to dawdle on the edge, my faith is strengthened with every trusting step I take. And as I step off into the unknown—into His will—my spirit soars. I'm confident Jesus will be there to catch me and teach me how to ride life's waves. I'm not alone. —HEIDI GAUL

FAITH STEP: *Place a picture of an empty nest where you can see it daily. Add the words of Matthew 6:26. Be ready to answer—and take a leap of faith—when Jesus calls.*

SATURDAY, JUNE 25

We are hard pressed on every side, but not crushed; perplexed, but not in despair; persecuted, but not abandoned; struck down, but not destroyed. We always carry around in our body the death of Jesus, so that the life of Jesus may also be revealed in our body. 2 Corinthians 4:8–10 (NIV)

MY FRIEND JOYCE CAME OVER on a lovely summer day to take a walk with me to a local creek. At the park across the street, a city employee drove a huge riding mower back and forth across the field. The sound roared, so we walked quickly to the corner, eager to get past it. But in the parking lot between us and the creek, a man was using a leaf blower. Once again, the sound escalated so much that we couldn't carry on a conversation.

After getting around him, we spotted a bench by the creek, but a different man was circling it on yet another riding mower. We turned back, but now someone with a weed wacker blocked our path, just as a helicopter thundered overhead, almost skimming the treetops. Any way we turned, we were assaulted by noise.

Life can feel that way sometimes. A problem confronts me, and I try to find a way around it, only to run into yet another obstacle. Following Jesus doesn't guarantee peace and quiet in my life. As I serve Him, I might still feel hard pressed, perplexed, or even perse-cuted. But because of His life in me, I'm not crushed. Because He never abandons me, I don't need to despair. As I follow the loving Shepherd, He will lead me to still waters. —SHARON HINCK

FAITH STEP: *Find a quiet place. Write down any problems that surround you. Thank Jesus for being bigger than those problems.*

SUNDAY, JUNE 26

You are my friends if you do what I command. John 15:14 (NIV)

MY FATHER WAS HANDY, BUT also thrifty. The techniques he chose for household repairs could lean toward the unconventional. Paper clips and bubble gum sometimes found their way into his "fixes."

Not so with my husband, Dave, whose grandfather constructed houses using conventional building materials. When one of the windows in our historic home required work, I scrutinized every step Dave took to restore it. Like an interrogator, I questioned the supplies he'd selected. When I continued demanding to know the point behind each process, he grew tired of my endless queries. I heard the frustration in his voice. He knows repair work. I don't.

Like Dave with household maintenance, Jesus knows which areas of my faith need attention and how best to restore them. My body is His temple and He was a carpenter, after all. He understands which aspects of my spirit require removal and a full rebuild, and which can be set right with a paper clip and some gum.

He doesn't need my questions, my doubts, or my advice. He only desires my acceptance of His will for my life. When I live in obedience instead of a constant struggle to do things my way, He can "fix" me more efficiently, and the results are beautiful. I can hand Him a hammer or steady the ladder, but He's the one capable of restoring and redeeming my broken parts. I am His creation, His project. And He's still working on me. —HEIDI GAUL

FAITH STEP: *Consider yourself a DIY project. Which part of you is Jesus working on? Pray for wisdom and a willing spirit as He restores you.*

MONDAY, JUNE 27

"Lord," Ananias answered, "I have heard many reports about this man and all the harm he has done to your holy people in Jerusalem. And he has come here with authority from the chief priests to arrest all who call on your name." But the Lord said to Ananias, "Go! This man is my chosen instrument to proclaim my name to the Gentiles and their kings and to the people of Israel." Acts 9:13–15 (NIV)

HAS JESUS EVER ASKED YOU do something you're sure is a bad idea? Ananias had good reason not to seek out Saul. He explained the problem to his Savior, but when Jesus affirmed His call, Ananias obeyed.

Recently, Jesus challenged me with an opportunity to teach college classes in an online format. My conversation was similar to Ananias's. "Do I really have anything of value to offer the students? I haven't spent my life in academia. And what about my health challenges? Not to mention my writing deadlines?"

Yet Christ's quiet voice was insistent. I continued to be fearful, as I'm sure Ananias was as he approached the house on Straight Street where Saul was staying. But over and over, Jesus reassured me of His presence and fulfilled His purposes. Joy is found on His improbable path.

The next time I sense Jesus sending me in a new direction—instead of reminding Him of the potential hazards—I'll remember that He invites me to share my concerns with Him. He understands that I can't always see the big picture. But if He affirms and still says, "Go," then I can step forward with confidence. I'm learning that Jesus always equips me for the tasks He asks of me. —SHARON HINCK

FAITH STEP: *Have you felt a nudge toward an improbable task? Take your concerns to Jesus and ask Him for courage to obey.*

TUESDAY, JUNE 28

For out of the abundance of the heart the mouth speaks. The good person brings good things out of a good treasure, and the evil person brings evil things out of an evil treasure. Matthew 12:34–35 (NRSV)

I HAPPENED TO BE VISITING my daughter Holly's family, when two of my grandkids, Lilah and Roman, had dental checkups. After their exams, the office assistant dragged out a big cardboard box shaped like a pirate's chest. Roman and Lilah leaned over and rummaged through the pile of rings, bracelets, whistles, and tiny animals—all made from thin plastic. What looked like treasure to my grandkids looked like a pile of junk to me. I knew something they didn't: whatever they took home would likely be cracked or broken by the next day.

While growing up, I had learned that what others call "treasure" isn't necessarily something valuable—it may be worthless. Jesus taught that treasures can even be evil. He explained that speech reveals the true spiritual condition. My words will be worthwhile when I've stored up good treasures in my heart: prayer, Scripture passages, memories of God's goodness, time spent with godly people, noble thoughts as described in Philippians 4:8. Or my words will tend toward evil if I've accumulated evil treasures: anger, resentment, unresolved issues from my past, dwelling on my disappointments, exposure to ungodly reading material and images.

What comes out of my mouth reflects whatever I've stored up in my heart and mind. Jesus wants me to store up only good treasures so that my speech and conversations honor Him and bless those who hear me. With His help, the words that come out of my mouth can be treasure worth keeping. —DIANNE NEAL MATTHEWS

FAITH STEP: *Think about recent conversations you've had. What kind of treasure did your words reflect?*

WEDNESDAY, JUNE 29

You are my hiding place; you will protect me from trouble and surround me with songs of deliverance. Psalm 32:7 (NIV)

I DON'T LOVE MESSY. I like tidy. When I drive past a well-manicured lawn, I get a sudden craving for a full-time groundskeeper, someone who will take our property's Northwoods-casual to a pristine yard with crisply defined edges, trees in neat rows, and every weed banished. I'm not looking for yard accolades. In our neck of the woods, I don't even have a homeowners' association with a manual full of guidelines. But I do appreciate a well-tended, symmetrical, neat yard.

Though I'm rethinking that stance today. Through my office window, I can see what I would otherwise consider an unsightly, overgrown corner of a pasture. It's messy. Hundreds of varieties of grass and weeds crowd that corner. A doe and two fawns bravely emerged from the grass where they'd escaped from the midday heat. They danced as if a voice had called, "Recess!" Their tawny bodies cavorted, then they retreated back into the tall weeds.

That untidy pasture provides protection, a safe place, and shade for all kinds of animals. I don't want to take that away, because all of those things are much more important than grooming the grounds for a *Better Home & Gardens* magazine photoshoot.

The lesson from Jesus? The messiness of my life just might serve as a safe place for someone else or offer them the kind of courage I've found through Jesus. My willingness to show I'm not perfect or to be vulnerable with my untidy edges may mean another person can find a hiding place in Jesus too. —CYNTHIA RUCHTI

FAITH STEP: *Recall a time when your messy edges brought someone closer to Jesus or offered them shade. Thank Him for redeeming and using even that.*

THURSDAY, JUNE 30

We ourselves heard this voice that came from heaven when we were with him on the sacred mountain. 2 Peter 1:18 (NIV)

I LIVE NEAR A WORLD-FAMOUS mountain considered by many to be sacred. People from around the globe worship Mount Shasta, claiming, "The mountain called me." Myths and legends associated with this majestic, snow-covered volcano include everything from extraterrestrial activity to beings from ancient civilizations dwelling underneath this mountain.

Enhancing its mystique are the extremely rare and fantastical cloud formations, called lenticular clouds, which often encircle this mountain like a halo or float above it. Consequently, this local geographic celebrity—with its spectacular, ever-changing beauty and ephemeral cloud formations—is photographed daily by tourists and locals alike, and is often featured on the front page of local newspapers.

Granted, this mountain in all its glory is breathtakingly beautiful. However, it's never the object of my worship, but rather evidence to me of our creator God's magnificence. The mountain's towering 14,000-plus-foot elevation serves to remind me how much more vastly immense is the One who created it. This area's beloved mountain is but one part of God's wonderful creation—as is the fresh air, blue sky, evergreen forest, and abundant waters around it.

Whenever I see Mount Shasta, I thank Jesus for His divine artistry in nature. I take comfort that, no matter how overwhelming my present problems may appear, they are tiny in comparison to the work of His hands. —CASSANDRA TIERSMA

FAITH STEP: *Are you facing a challenge that feels like more of a mountain than a molehill? Talk to Jesus about it. Ask Him to give you an elevated perspective, to show you the situation as He sees it. Thank Him for being with you on the mountains and in the valleys of life.*

FRIDAY, JULY 1

Study to show thyself approved unto God, a workman that needeth not to be ashamed, rightly dividing the word of truth. 2 Timothy 2:15 (KJV)

LAST SUMMER, I VOLUNTEERED AT my church's Vacation Bible School and worked with a group of rambunctious fifth graders. Some regularly attended children's worship services; others were newbies to the Bible. One day, the VBS lesson required the children to match Scripture passages with their locations in the Bible—book, chapter, and verse.

We didn't have much time to complete the activity, so I helped a few kids find the specific Scriptures. One boy named William used the Bible's index to find the book of the listed Scripture passage, and from there he found the chapter and verse. To help him navigate more quickly through the index, I told William whether the book was in the Old Testament or New Testament. After about three hints from me, he looked at me in amazement. "You must have studied the Bible a lot," he said. "You know where to go!"

While I had never really stopped to think about it, all those Sunday School lessons and Bible drills I experienced as a child must have taken root. A little at a time, I learned about the Bible, and more importantly, Jesus and salvation. I'm still learning as I spend time reading Scripture and pause to hear what the Lord is saying to me.

My time spent in the Word and with Jesus has been time well spent. A little bit at a time adds up to a lot. As my pastor says, "Read your Bible. It'll make you a better Christian." That's the truth—in more ways than one. —BARBRANDA LUMPKINS WALLS

FAITH STEP: *What will you do today to build your knowledge and relationship with Jesus?*

SATURDAY, JULY 2

A time is coming and in fact has come when you will be scattered, each to your own home. You will leave me all alone. Yet I am not alone, for my Father is with me. John 16:32 (NIV)

MY HUSBAND, GENE, AND I spend two weeks in Poland every July for ministry. One year, I received an invitation to speak at a retreat two weeks before our scheduled camp. Gene and I agreed that I should say yes. I would fly to Poland alone, and he would join me closer to the camp date.

I felt okay about flying on my own because I'd traveled that route before. However, after the retreat, I would have to take a seven-hour train ride from Warsaw to a small city where I'd stay with friends until Gene arrived. That part made me nervous.

Personal experience had taught me that Eastern European train rides often become adventures. Sometimes they arrive or leave from a different platform than expected. A loudspeaker usually announces schedule changes, but they happen at the last minute and are hard to decipher, especially for anyone who doesn't speak the language. What if I missed a connection?

A dear friend tried to dissuade me from going alone. My emotions agreed. But in my heart, I knew better. I knew enough to be cautious with my bags, safeguard my passport, and avoid sketchy situations. More important, I knew Jesus would be my constant companion.

Several weeks later, I made the train journey. I was by myself, but not truly alone. Jesus, the best travel companion ever, was with me.
—GRACE FOX

FAITH STEP: *Find two small identical objects, such as beads or stones. Place them by your sink or on your nightstand. Use them as a visual reminder that you are never alone. Jesus is with you.*

SUNDAY, JULY 3

---

*The Spirit of God has made me, and the breath of the
Almighty gives me life. Job 33:4 (ESV)*

ON A VACATION WITH MY family in Belize, I almost ran out of air
while scuba diving. About ten minutes into a dive, I checked my air
supply—it was in the red zone. My heart rate escalated. I signaled
to my husband that I was low on air. His eyes widened, and he
motioned for me to swim to our guide. I showed the guide my air-
supply gauge. He locked eyes with me, pointed to his extra regulator and calmly handed it to me. I replaced mine with his extra, took
a deep breath, and relaxed. Then he looped my arm into his, and we
swam side by side, buddy breathing, for the remainder of the dive.

The fear of running out of air was terrifying. Then having the
guide calmly share his air and swim side by side reminded me of
what Jesus does for me when I'm afraid. Just like when a drop in
real-estate value presented the real chance that we could lose some
of our needed income. Or when my husband was going in for a
life-threatening surgery. When I feel fear, then I need to remember
to "buddy breathe" with Jesus. I must depend on Him for all things
just as I depend on air to live. It doesn't mean tough circumstances
will disappear, but He will link arms with me, offer His breath of
life, and get me through. —JEANNIE BLACKMER

FAITH STEP: *Are you experiencing fear? Try a "breath prayer." Inhale deeply
and pray, "Jesus is with me." Then slowly breathe out and pray, "He gives me life."
Do this several times until you feel more peaceful. (You can also come up with
your own phrases.)*

INDEPENDENCE DAY, MONDAY, JULY 4

*Those who are wise will shine like the brightness of the heavens,
and those who lead many to righteousness, like the stars for ever
and ever. Daniel 12:3 (NIV)*

SOME DEAR FRIENDS OF MINE have a home that sits high on a hill overlooking the nation's capital and surrounding areas. For the Fourth of July, they often invite family and friends to come over and gather on their deck at dusk to enjoy the festive fireworks shows. Because we have such a spectacular view, we can see jaw-dropping fireworks in the District, Maryland, and Virginia. Everywhere we look we *ooh* and *ahh* as the flashes of colors and designs appear and disappear. Even the neighbors below us on the street get into the act, setting off Roman candles, rockets, and poppers.

Whenever I view these awesome displays, I think of them as representative of the lives of individuals. Some of the fireworks are quite memorable because of their fantastic colors that light up the nighttime skies. Some are very pretty but not as explosive, while still others start out with a bang and quickly die out. I pray that I am one that steadily glows bright and, like today's Scripture verse says, will lead others to righteousness and shine like the stars forever.

Jesus tells me to let my "light shine before others" (Matthew 5:16, NIV). As long as I'm shining for Him, I can dispel the darkness around me and glorify Him. I'm striving to be a real firecracker—one with a long fuse and lots of light. —BARBRANDA LUMPKINS WALLS

FAITH WALK: *How can you let your light shine brightly for Jesus today? Will you explode on the scene with goodness and light? Or will your flame die out quickly?*

TUESDAY, JULY 5

Suppose one of you wants to build a tower. Won't you first sit down and estimate the cost to see if you have enough money to complete it? Luke 14:28 (NIV)

I REMEMBER HEARING THAT "HAVING kids is infinitely more demanding than you can anticipate but infinitely more rewarding too." Boy, this advice is so true and completely incomprehensible before having children. Having now had two kids, one with Down syndrome, I can testify that it's a costly undertaking in every way. Being a good parent means exuding more heart, sacrifices, emotional energy, and money than I could imagine, but reaping way more joy, satisfaction, and love than I could anticipate too.

There have been times in my twenty years of being a Christian when being a believer seemed very costly. I reluctantly confess that I've bristled or grieved at the rejections, difficult choices, or personal sacrifices my life as a Christian has required. Sometimes these challenges were hard even if I definitely felt motivated and empowered to meet them. On the other hand, I've had extraordinary experiences and rewards that I cannot quantify—and that's not even counting the promise of heaven!

Today's Scripture verse is one morsel of a speech in which Jesus shares a few parables to describe the cost of discipleship. Later, He says we must be willing to give up everything to follow Him. He urges us to count the cost of following Him. The price is worth every penny. —ISABELLA CAMPOLATTARO

FAITH STEP: *Make a list of what being a disciple of Jesus has cost you. For each item, list at least one of the extraordinary rewards you receive in exchange.*

WEDNESDAY, JULY 6

*Be completely humble and gentle; be patient, bearing with
one another in love. Ephesians 4:2 (NIV)*

OH, NO, THERE HE WAS again—that guy on the bike who didn't follow the rules of the road. Here he was, zooming toward me on *my* side of the road when he should be riding with the flow of traffic. Well, I wasn't moving. Ha! He swerved at the last minute, giving me a dirty look. I gave him one back. If there's such a thing as bike rage, this was it. When I told my husband, Jeff, about my encounter, he said, "Really, Pat? Is it so important for you to be right? You could've had a serious accident!"

Deep inside, I knew Jesus wasn't pleased with the way I'd acted. Jesus had been right plenty of times when others weren't, but He'd practiced restraint. He is the epitome of patience! As a child in Sunday school, I memorized Galatians 5:22–23: "The fruit of the Spirit is love, joy, peace, patience, kindness, goodness, faithfulness, gentleness, self-control" (ESV). Hmm. It might be a good idea to repeat those verses to myself.

I knew I needed to find a way not to be so angry with the guy on the bike. To live and let live, or in my case, "ride and let ride!" I asked Jesus to show me how I should handle this pesky biker, and He gave me an easy solution. Now when I see the biker coming, I move peacefully and lovingly to the other side of the road.
—PAT BUTLER DYSON

FAITH STEP: *Find examples of Jesus practicing peace. Then follow suit!*

THURSDAY, JULY 7

Delight yourself also in the LORD, and He shall give you the desires of your heart. Psalm 37:4 (NKJV)

MY HUSBAND AND I JUST bought our first home together. With our son in high school, this will give him more opportunities in a better district. I am still awed by the space and the newness of everything. After living in fixer-uppers for years, I had to push myself to say, "Yes!" when we viewed the fully renovated home. Buying furniture in a real gallery was another mind-shift—a big change from the hand-me-down dinette set and the box-store bargain couch that sagged in the middle. The latter always felt like the prudent way to live—the godly way. But Jesus showed me that it's okay to ask big when our heart's desires line up with His Word and our minds are on Him.

Jesus often did more than people asked for or even seemed to need. In doing this, He reveals His character, His generous spirit, and His ways. Jesus's very first miracle in John 2 is an example of His wonderful habit of giving us more than we need. In John 2:7, Jesus asked the servants to "Fill the jars with water," before He turned it into wine. Those jars held 20–30 gallons of water! He provided above and beyond. If more sandwiches than a lunch crowd could eat and more fish than folks could fry in a month is our Father's way of showing us love, then let's honor Him and receive! —PAMELA TOUSSAINT HOWARD

FAITH STEP: *Strengthen your friendship with Jesus by sharing your heart's desires with Him today.*

Friday, July 8

For am I now seeking the approval of man, or of God? Or am I trying to please man? If I were still trying to please man, I would not be a servant of Christ. Galatians 1:10 (ESV)

I USED TO BE A compulsive poll taker. I'd ask eleven people their opinion on some decision, large or small. This wasn't seeking wise counsel, as the Bible repeatedly suggests, particularly in the Old Testament. This was getting someone—anyone—to rubber-stamp my decisions. I see now that this was both because of my own insecurity and because I wasn't really relying on my heavenly Counselor when making decisions. I wanted human approval rather than trusting Jesus alone.

The impulse is still there, but now I have the awareness to redirect myself. When I sense I'm wanting the quick fix of a worldly seal of approval, I take the time to talk to Jesus about it. Sometimes, it's as simple as asking, "What's Your will?" Then waiting for the answer.

The Bible is clear about its instructions for living. But through Jesus, the Counselor, my relationship with Him has become infinitely more intimate and personal. This is an amazing and practical privilege. Still, like any relationship, it requires time and effort to cultivate deep, trusting connection. But that closeness helps me to hear from Jesus and trust His direction with greater confidence. The very good news is that I already have His eternal approval, thanks to the cross. —ISABELLA CAMPOLATTARO

FAITH STEP: *Next time you face a decision about which you're inclined to poll others, take the time and effort to connect with Jesus on a deeper level by praying, listening, journaling, and waiting for His direction.*

SATURDAY, JULY 9

Accept one another, then, just as Christ accepted you,
in order to bring praise to God. Romans 15:7 (NIV)

I LIVE AT THE EDGE of town, so a variety of wildlife often overlaps into my neighborhood. Flocks of wild turkeys—one tom and several hens—often stroll the lane. They strut and gobble to my delight.

But this year I noticed a new group making the rounds. I sensed there was something different about them long before they came into the view. The sounds I heard caught my attention. Gobbling, yes, but also—*Was that a cockle-doodle-doo?*

They rounded the corner. A tom, a hen—and a proud rooster. My jaw dropped.

Yet, aside from the obvious differences, they were like any other flock. They munched at the seed that smaller birds had scattered below our feeder. They searched for pebbles along the road's edge. And they talked and talked, perfectly happy in one another's company, despite the fact that they didn't speak the same language.

Unlike those birds, I sometimes catch myself focusing, not on the similarities I share with others but the disparities. I fail to see that the very beauty of our relationship lies within our contrasts.

When Jesus invited me into His family, He didn't judge the way I dress. He never asked me whom I voted for or how much money I make. My skin color and gender were of no interest to Him. He cared only about what was in my heart, welcoming me with arms spread wide.

I choose to do the same, to crow to your gobble and to join in the holy, discordant chorus of life. To accept you just as you are.
—HEIDI GAUL

FAITH STEP: *Thank Jesus for accepting you. Offer that same acceptance to those you meet.*

SUNDAY, JULY 10

Be careful not to practice your righteousness in front of others to be seen by them. If you do, you will have no reward from your Father in heaven.
Matthew 6:1 (NIV)

MY DESIRE TO APPEAR LIKE a good girl was deeply rooted in my childhood. I'm not sure if it was my traditional Italian upbringing or my desperate desire for approval, but it was ingrained. As a child, I'd help my teachers at every turn, eager for the accolades. I had almost fastidious manners and soaked up compliments from my parents' friends. Even after becoming a Christian, the habit persisted for a long time.

I wanted people at church to know how much I volunteered. Many times, I'd say yes to requests for help solely for that reason, never thinking to ask Jesus if it's what He wanted me to do. Eventually I burned out on serving in ways Jesus hadn't called me or equipped me to do. Ironically, I became anything but people pleasing as I grew resentful or dropped commitments after overdoing it.

Today's verse tells me that if I do good deeds solely for human praise, I won't get any credit with God. Sounds harsh, but the point is that if I'm not doing it out of loving gratitude to God and by His strength, then it's really all about me. I've learned to ask Jesus what He wants me to do and wait for an answer. I can then serve Him and enjoy the enduring rewards of helping others with no strings attached. —ISABELLA CAMPOLATTARO

FAITH STEP: *Next time you have an opportunity to do a good deed, consult Jesus first and then try doing it without telling anyone at all.*

MONDAY, JULY 11

For this world in its present form is passing away. 1 Corinthians 7:31 *(NIV)*

UPDATING AND FLIPPING HOUSES HAS become a hobby of mine and my husband in the past few years. It really can become another full-time job if you let it. From searching the internet for deals to setting up showings and doing calculations and researching the areas and estimating renovations, we've discovered that this can easily become an obsession. Not to mention my budding interest in interior decorating. Just entering a home store and seeing the amount of choices there are for hand-soap dispensers is astounding—it took me all afternoon to simply outfit a bathroom!

But in the midst of this, Jesus gently reminds me every so often that all of it will pass away someday soon. When He does this, I pull back for a minute and refocus on what is eternal. The Bible says that, as believers, we are called to bear fruit that lasts (John 15:16). This means I need to frequently check whether or not I'm moving forward with the ministry callings Jesus has given me. We were taught in Bible school that we will not fulfill these callings by accident but that it would take deliberate effort to eschew the things of this world to pursue it. This doesn't mean that I can't enjoy my home and other niceties (like the patio I'm planning on retiling), but my main focus should be on Jesus and on advancing the kingdom of God in the ways He has told me to. —PAMELA TOUSSAINT HOWARD

FAITH STEP: *Train your mind to put Jesus first.*

TUESDAY, JULY 12

I was appointed from everlasting from the first, before the earth began. Proverbs 8:23 (GW)

THE POETRY IN PROVERBS 8, when Wisdom takes part in creation, always makes my heart soar: "When he set up the heavens, I was there. When he traced the horizon on the surface of the ocean, when he established the skies above, when he determined the currents in the ocean, when he set a limit for the sea so the waters would not overstep his command, when he traced the foundations of the earth, I was beside him as a master craftsman. I made him happy day after day, I rejoiced in front of him all the time" (verses 27–30, GW).

Some Bible scholars believe that the Holy Spirit, speaking through King Solomon, referred to Jesus in this passage. Although I'm not a Bible scholar, I am a Jesus lover and follower. That's why I agree that Jesus was God's partner at the beginning of creation. A master craftsman was rejoicing in the Father's handiwork. Who else but Jesus could have been present with God while our Creator fashioned the universe?

The major reason I hold this view is found in verse 31: "[I] found joy in his inhabited world, and delighted in the human race" (GW). Jesus is God's love personified. I find it easy to imagine Him smiling as the Father spoke every tree, ocean, and animal into being. But when God formed people—His crowning glory, made in His own image—Jesus must have cheered, applauded, and danced with joy.

Because we—you and I and every person ever created—make Him happiest. And when we believe He delights in us, our courage overflows. —JEANETTE LEVELLIE

FAITH STEP: *Think of a Jesuslike way to show your love to another human being today.*

WEDNESDAY, JULY 13

I will celebrate my weaknesses, for when I'm weak I sense more deeply the mighty power of Christ living in me. 2 Corinthians 12:9 (TPT)

WHEN I WAS ASKED TO lead a medical team to Uganda, I felt completely ill-equipped. I'm not a travel agent, and I have zero medical background. Yet the Bible is full of stories of God using unlikely leaders, such as Moses who was a poor speaker, Matthew who was a tax collector, and even Jesus—Israel expected a mighty warrior, not a baby born in a manger who died on a cross. So, I clung to these examples. Our medical missions team made it safely to Africa and had a successful ten days of providing medical services for a community of 3,500 children.

Then it was time to go home. After a ten-hour drive to catch a midnight flight, we hit a barrier. As we tried to check-in, the airline agents could not find our reservations. Panic ensued. Exhausted people started shouting at me to help. Overwhelmed, I shut down. A strong leader would have taken control, not shrunk back.

Then I silently prayed, *Jesus help!* A calm airline employee pulled me out of the fray to a quiet spot, and we arranged our flights home. I really had no explanation for this resolution other than God's intervention. This example of Jesus using me when I felt useless has reminded me of how He uses my weaknesses to show Himself strong. It takes courage to allow Jesus to use me, especially in situations where I feel inadequate, but He can use anyone. In fact, the weaker the better, because His mighty power working in me gives Him all the glory. —JEANNIE BLACKMER

FAITH STEP: *Write about a time when you experienced Jesus's strength in the midst of your weakness.*

Thursday, July 14

Surely goodness and mercy shall follow me all the days of my life.
Psalm 23:6 (KJV)

I'm chasing a one-year-old who just learned to walk. Everyone longs to see children take their first steps, but when they do, look out! This little one is curious about everything, especially anything dangerous, like electrical outlets and power cords and stairs. She's like all kids.

Escaping from my watchful eye is my granddaughter's favorite game. Because walking is so new to her, it's all the more important that I stay close to here. She's not always conscious of solid footing, tripping hazards, or maintaining a pace that will keep her upright rather than toppling toward her destination.

Because I love her, I want to protect her. But I also want to give her freedom to experience the wonders of her newly learned skill and to enjoy exploring. So I'm "on her tail," as they say, which keeps me on my toes.

Because Jesus loves me and wants to protect me, His goodness and mercy follow me all the days of my life. He knows I'm not always alert to the tripping hazards embedded in my choices. I can't always tell that where I'm planting my feet isn't solid. Sometimes I run too fast or lag behind in obeying Him, and either can hurt me more than bruised shins.

Jesus isn't on my case in a negative, condemning way. He has my back. He's always on duty, always making my safety and joy His priority because of His love.

Every time I turn around, there they are—His goodness and mercy chasing me down. How comforting to know that His love for me won't let me out of His sight. —Cynthia Ruchti

Faith Step: *Observe how diligent parents balance giving their child freedom while protecting them from danger. Thank Jesus for chasing after you.*

FRIDAY, JULY 15

Anyone who believes in me may come and drink! For the Scriptures declare, "Rivers of living water will flow from his heart." John 7:38 (NLT)

THE LITTLE TOWN WHERE I live boasts of having "The Best Water on Earth." A network of springs and streams run underneath the city. You can even view an underground stream through a giant grate in the floor of a local restaurant. The water in this region is so noted for its pristine purity that a couple of local water-bottling plants capture it for wholesale distribution. As if that's not enough, a nearby city park has the headwaters for the largest river in this state, which is 400 miles long and flows through our little town. People come from all over to fill up their five-gallon water bottles with fresh water from the headwaters.

Although it's a blessing to have ready access to pure drinking water, it doesn't compare to the true refreshment that comes from having a personal relationship with Jesus. And though I know water is necessary for my physical health so that I stay hydrated, sometimes I need to be reminded to drink some water. However, it's even more critical for my spiritual health to be drinking from the Living Water: filling up on Jesus through prayer time with Him and His Word. Yes, I'm grateful to live in a place with the best water on earth. But I know that the *really* best water in heaven and earth—from the *true* headwaters—is Jesus, the Living Water. —CASSANDRA TIERSMA

FAITH STEP: *Pour yourself a glass of water, and as you drink it, thank Jesus for the Holy Spirit, the "rivers of living water" which He promises will flow from your heart when you believe in Him.*

SATURDAY, JULY 16

But it will turn out for you as an occasion for testimony. Luke 21:13 (NKJV)

MY SOCIAL MEDIA POST WAS short: "First day. New job. A warm welcome. #thankful #newbeginnings." I added pictures of me smiling ear to ear, my new name plate, and the flowers I had received from my new colleagues.

It had been a long haul to that first day. I had endured several disappointments before I landed my new job. A parade of initial interviews by phone for various positions, followed by in-person meetings, long waits for decisions, and then the calls and emails to inform me that someone else had been chosen.

Shortly after I posted on social media, I got a direct message from a woman I had worked with years ago. "You give me hope," she wrote. "I've been out of work for a year and keep getting passed over. I was so depressed yesterday until I saw your post. I will continue to pray. Congratulations!"

I quickly responded to my former colleague, telling her I knew how she felt because I'd been there. God had provided what He had in mind for me at the right time, and it was good. "Keep hope alive," I wrote back. "The job will come. I'm a witness."

I remembered the friends who shared with me their testimonies of Jesus's faithfulness: a desired job, an amazing opportunity, or a breakthrough in a relationship. I was always encouraged by their victories after their struggles.

Now I am grateful to have a chance to share my testimony. It's what I'm supposed to do. I never know who I might be able to bless.
—BARBRANDA LUMPKINS WALLS

FAITH STEP: *We all have a testimony. What test have you faced that you can share with others?*

SUNDAY, JULY 17

Seek his will in all you do, and he will show you which path to take.
Proverbs 3:6 (NLT)

AFTER A DAY OF DOOR-TO-DOOR visits, my pastor headed back toward the temporary clinic set up by our church's mission team. Suddenly, Pastor Steve felt compelled to veer off on a side trail. His guide and translator insisted that nobody lived on that road. But just a couple hundred yards down the trail, they saw two men digging a ditch. The guide warned that the men would not want to talk while working. When Pastor Steve introduced himself, one of the men responded, "I've been expecting you." He had dreamed that a white man with a black book would visit him and that he should listen to the man's message. That afternoon on an obscure trail in Africa, two men became new followers of Jesus.

Despite my noble intentions and worthy ambitions, my personal agenda will always pale in comparison to God's plan for my life. When I make following Jesus my first priority and invite Him to direct my steps, my days become full of divine appointments. He may lead me to someone waiting to hear about Him for the first time, or to a longtime believer who needs to be strengthened and encouraged. I might encounter a person in need of practical help or friendship. Or He may direct me to someone who will fill a need of mine. Either way, my faith will grow as Jesus uses me in His work. If I stay close to Him and follow His leading, I'll never find myself on a dead-end road. —DIANNE NEAL MATTHEWS

FAITH STEP: *Ask Jesus to make you more sensitive to His guidance today. Keep alert for any unexpected path He wants you to follow. Someone may be expecting you.*

MONDAY, JULY 18

---

*Likewise, teach the older women to be reverent in the way they live,
not to be slanderers or addicted to much wine, but to teach what is good.*
Titus 2:3 (NIV)

As AN OLDER WOMAN, I used to find today's Bible verse kind of scary. I'm not a slanderer or drinker, but the idea of teaching younger women what is good is intimidating. The description in the Scripture passage makes me envision a very pious, godly woman who never makes mistakes and never fails to live up to God's standard or even her own. Oh, the freedom and power we have by grace in Christ!

Today I recognize that what I really have to offer the younger women I mentor is my real-life experience—my strength and hope in Christ. Rather than pontificating, I can share compassionate encouragement about the very real way Jesus has helped me, changed me, and continues to grow me in Him.

For instance, a young friend recently asked me if she should get engaged to her beau. I was able to share from my heart the vital steps I had failed to take before marrying my husband and the difficult problems it caused us from the onset.

I'm grateful that I can express with honesty and humility how Jesus has lovingly taught me and comforted me through my mistakes as much as through my successes. My imperfect and human real-life journey with Jesus is much more authentic, powerful, and loving than any religious sermon. Hallelujah! —ISABELLA CAMPOLATTARO

FAITH STEP: *Are you reluctant to take a mentoring role with the younger people in your life? Take time to write down how Jesus has walked with you through life experiences that you could share with others.*

TUESDAY, JULY 19

We have known and believed the love that God hath to us. God is love; and he that dwelleth in love dwelleth in God, and God in him. Herein is our love made perfect, that we may have boldness in the day of judgment: because as he is, so are we in this world. 1 John 4:16—17 (KJV)

WHEN I WAS LITTLE, THE first verses from the Bible I learned were "God is love" (1 John 4:16, NIV) and "Love one another" (John 13:34, NIV). I've lived a full forty-eight years now, been around the block a few times, and studied a lot of theology. I understand and can teach some complicated concepts. Yet I find myself returning over and over to those two simple truths.

God is love. People have many different ideas about who God is. I think there's a great temptation to create God in our image, rather than conform ourselves to His. There are Christians who focus on His power, His majesty, even His wrath. Others emphasize the grace of God—I have the tendency to do this—or His mercy and goodness. And the Bible has things to say about all of those. But John distills God's essence down to one thing: love. He seems to be saying this is the most important thing about God, the source from which everything else flows.

And when Jesus says, "Love one another," He's distilling down and clarifying the Christian life. Following Jesus is about many things, but the root is love. In and through love—that's the way Jesus wants us to relate to one another. Love is who He is and who He wants us to be in the world. —GWEN FORD FAULKENBERRY

FAITH STEP: *Search for instances of the word* love *in the Bible. Write down all of the things you find that augment your understanding of how Jesus loves you and therefore how you are to love.*

WEDNESDAY, JULY 20

If anyone comes to me and does not hate father and mother, wife and children, brothers and sisters—yes, even their own life—such a person cannot be my disciple. Luke 14:26 (NIV)

TODAY'S SCRIPTURE VERSE USED TO send me into a panic. Hate my family? I can't do that, even for Jesus. To make peace, I just set it aside as a nonissue. After all, we Western Christians don't really need to make those kinds of loaded choices. Or do we?

I've come to understand this verse differently as I've matured in my faith. My relationship with Jesus has to come first, before anything or anyone else. Placing Him and His will first will order the rest of my life rightly too (Matthew 6:33). That includes my relationships with family. What putting Jesus first looks like in real life is honoring His beliefs, His direction for my life, and His priorities, even if it's in conflict with my family's worldview.

In the midst of global turmoil, I've increasingly felt the urgency and potency of The Gospel as the antidote to all the angst and anger swirling around me. I know in my heart that Jesus is the answer for all of us, but I hate facing scorn, ridicule or rejection. Despite my sometimes overwhelming fears, I've risked sharing more vocally, even with those loved ones I know might be alienated by my boldness.

My family may not understand—or may even reject me—and that's okay. I know I'm pleasing Jesus. —ISABELLA CAMPOLATTARO

FAITH STEP: *Reflect on Luke 14:26. What place does Jesus occupy in your life?*

THURSDAY, JULY 21

Nor do they light a lamp and put it under a basket, but on a lampstand, and it gives light to all who are in the house. Matthew 5:15 (NKJV)

IN PREVIOUS EDITIONS OF *MORNINGS with Jesus,* I've shared about my crippling stage fright and fear of public speaking. Both of which have been so intense that, on occasion, they've prevented me from serving God in a full capacity. My preoccupation with avoiding the spotlight became a liability in my service to God. I wanted to avoid facing criticism, exposing my faith-filled beliefs, appearing prideful, and, in general, receiving any kind of judgment or disapproval from fellow believers or otherwise. Sometimes I mistook my behavior for humility rather than plain old fear. Still, Jesus often prodded me forward into places where I was invited to share, and I struggled.

It took a lot of prayer and seeking to help me understand that my focus was misplaced—none of this was about me. It was all about Jesus! When I gave my life to Christ, all that I am became His to use as He sees fit. I was withholding what was rightfully His. Jesus wants His light to shine through me—I'm not supposed to hide my gifts and talents. He wants me to daily hand my life back over to Him and live through Him. And He especially wants me to hand over my fears.

Today I share openly as a speaker and a writer. My audiences tell me they find my vulnerability most helpful. Only Jesus can transform our greatest fears into our most powerful ministry.
—ISABELLA CAMPOLATTARO

FAITH STEP: *Ask Jesus to liberate you from self-consciousness in any form, so His light can shine brightly through you.*

FRIDAY, JULY 22

Pray without ceasing, in everything give thanks; for this is the will of God in Christ Jesus for you. 1 Thessalonians 5:17–18 (NKJV)

I FOUND OUT THAT BEING able to pray on demand is an acquired skill. Growing up in church, we recited lovely prayers we had memorized but we never prayed using our own words. So when I found myself in a charismatic church's Bible study, holding hands with other believers in a circle and being asked to pray out loud, I marveled. Everyone seemed to be so eloquent with their prayers, as if they had rehearsed. Anxiety arose in my chest as my turn approached. I mumbled an okay prayer, I but didn't feel confident about it. I really wanted to know how these people prayed so powerfully.

As I got to know the believers at the Bible study, I found out they spent precious time in the Word of God, getting to know Jesus. Having developed intimate knowledge of Him and His character, they understood their relationship with Jesus enough to pray confidently out loud in front of others. I purposed in my heart to be able to pray like that and began studying the Word. If a verse "spoke" to me, I remembered it. Soon, I had a small arsenal of Scripture passages that I felt comfortable praying back to Jesus whenever needed. This came in handy recently when my husband had a minor medical procedure. We'd prayed before we left home, but right before he went under, he asked the nurses if some of them would pray, just to see how they'd respond. They were blindsided— no one in the room knew how! Thank Jesus, he was already covered in prayer by me. —PAMELA TOUSSAINT HOWARD

FAITH STEP: *Pick a Scripture verse you'd like to memorize and commit to do so today.*

SATURDAY, JULY 23

When Jesus had finished saying these things, the crowds were amazed at his teaching, because he taught as one who had authority, and not as their teachers of the law. Matthew 7:28–29 (NIV)

COMPLETING A MISSION TRIP OVERSEAS was one of the requirements to graduate from the Bible school I attended. We were expected to teach while on the mission trip, and to be ready to do so in season and out (meaning whenever the leader called on us, with little advance notice). Before the mission trip, we practiced at school, and we got rated and critiqued by our classmates. We were trained to teach with authority, confident in what we were sharing from the Word. School officials expected that authority to come from our own personal encounters with Jesus and the Bible, not something we'd memorized or copied verbatim from some famous preacher.

By God's grace, when we taught in two different countries, there were many salvations and a number of healings in each place! I got to experience crowds being amazed by my teaching, just as other crowds had been amazed at Jesus's teaching in today's Scripture verse. Why? It certainly wasn't because we were super dynamic speakers. Many were ordinary lovers of Jesus—bank tellers, airline reservationists, and home inspectors by day but anointed ministers by night! Our words were powerful because we believed them. We had *experienced* the Word coming alive in our own hearts, so we spoke with an authority many folks in these countries said they hadn't seen in missionaries who came before us. We were invited back everywhere we went. When we shone our light boldly for Jesus, people came out in droves to watch us burn! —PAMELA TOUSSAINT HOWARD

FAITH STEP: *Find something in the Word that you can share with someone confidently. Watch their amazement!*

SUNDAY, JULY 24

Jesus Christ is the same yesterday and today and forever. Hebrews 13:8 (NIV)

"LOOK WHAT I FOUND IN the pew where I sit on Sundays," I said, handing a greeting card to my husband, Kevin. He read in his rich baritone, "*Mom*, I don't say it enough, but I really appreciate how you love me and care for me and always put my needs before your own." Kev smiled. His mocha eyes sparkled with warmth.

"Open it and read the inside," I told him.

Twenty seconds later, Kevin's smile vanished. He sighed and handed the card back. "I'm sorry, honey." The signature inside was from my own mother.

I knew this day would come—when our roles would reverse, and I'd be mirroring the care of the sweet lady who raised me. She had exemplified Jesus in her thoughtful, generous ways. Was I happy she thought I deserved this honored title? Not particularly.

Over the last six years since Mom had been diagnosed with Alzheimer's, I've read scores of articles about dementia. I've talked to people who had been down this road with their loved ones. But no amount of expertise or advice could've prepared me for that gut-twisting moment. That wet-dishrag slap in the face—Mom calling me "Mom."

My one comfort was the knowledge that Jesus would never change. He'd walked me through a bajillion dark times: my daddy's death, job losses, the end of a close friendship. He wasn't about to give up on me now. I placed the card on top of the microwave with the ones from my actual kids. *Help me, Jesus,* I whispered, *to be a good mom to my mom.* —JEANETTE LEVELLIE

FAITH STEP: *Pray for an individual—perhaps yourself—who is wrestling with the angst of parenting her own parent.*

MONDAY, JULY 25

The God of all grace, who called you to his eternal glory in Christ, after you have suffered a little while, will himself restore you and make you strong, firm and steadfast. 1 Peter 5:10 (NIV)

WHEN WE MOVED FROM WEST Virginia to Florida, Pierce was nine and Isaac was six. Isaac, who's easygoing, made the transition overnight. Pierce, however, was miserable. West Virginia was the only home he had ever known, with his friendships forged in infancy there. Pierce was inconsolable, angry, and sad. Though a bright student, he struggled with the more demanding schoolwork. Even though I'd prayed about the move and it came together effortlessly, I wondered if I'd made an awful mistake that had irreparably damaged Pierce's psyche. I prayed for relief and urged Pierce to pray too.

Pierce, who's social and fun, made friends quickly, yet his homesickness persisted. A few months passed, and Pierce remained mildly gloomy. My heart ached. Then suddenly, the clouds parted, and Pierce emerged from his sadness. From time to time, the homesickness would flare again, then quickly subside. Soon, Pierce came to both remember West Virginia fondly and see Florida as perfect for our family, which it is.

Sometimes Jesus leads me someplace and I follow, only to find it's so hard that I fear I've made a mistake. This is when faith comes in. As the old adage says, "If He leads you to it, He will lead you through it." Believe it. —ISABELLA CAMPOLATTARO

FAITH STEP: *If you've made a prayerful decision that's proving to be much harder than expected, go back to Jesus and persist in prayer until the clouds part.*

TUESDAY, JULY 26

But Jesus Himself would often slip away to the wilderness and pray. Luke 5:16 (NASB)

I'M NOT ABOUT TO NAME names, but I've always said that between my husband, myself, and our children, we have both ends of the personality spectrum covered. Half of us have moods that bounce up and down—we're usually either excited or down in the dumps. The other half of us have calm, middle-of-the-road personalities, like a straight line forging ahead. But regardless of our personality types, everyone experiences ups and downs in life. Even Jesus, or maybe *especially* Jesus. When we consider all that He endured, we'll see He suffered more than anyone could ever imagine. But in light of the miracles He performed, which were manifestations of His divine power, He also experienced greater joy than we will know this side of heaven.

For Jesus, sometimes high and low points came close together. The people in His hometown rejected Him because they knew His family. Then Jesus heard that His cousin John the Baptist had been beheaded. After that, He miraculously fed a crowd of thousands, walked on water, and healed all the sick people in the region of Gennesaret. How did Jesus immediately come back from such a low point to minister in such amazing ways?

Jesus often slipped away to spend time in solitude and prayer. In this case, He withdrew after hearing bad news, as well as after experiencing a great spiritual victory. As I spend time alone with Jesus after all my ups and downs, my faith will grow stronger and steadier. And I'll accomplish more for Him. —DIANNE NEAL MATTHEWS

FAITH STEP: *Follow Jesus's example today. Spend time talking with Him about recent high and low points in your life. Ask for renewed strength to carry out His work.*

WEDNESDAY, JULY 27

Anyone who has seen me has seen the Father. John 14:9 (NIV)

I LINGERED LONGER THAN USUAL in John 14 during my Bible study this week. It's a familiar passage, but when my heart is open, I notice nuances more precious than the tiny raindrops clinging to the tips of pine needles after a storm.

Jesus told His disciples, "You know the way to the place where I am going" (verse 4, NIV). Thomas—naturally—doubted and shot back, "Lord, we don't know where you are going, so how can we know the way?" (verse 5, NIV). *Oh, Thomas, Thomas, Thomas.*

Jesus answered with His well-known statement: "I am the way and the truth and the life" (verse 6, NIV). Philip, who usually had a pretty level head on his shoulders, responded, "Lord, show us the Father and that will be enough for us" (verse 8, NIV).

They didn't get it, even after all that time with Jesus. So He told them again—seven times within seven verses—that if they had seen Him, then they had seen the Father. He pounded the point home.

Was His repetition just for the disciples, or for me and others who would follow Him and read that passage millennia later? It's so easy to hear the words, like those men did, but not grasp the full meaning. Research has found that the human brain needs to see or hear a statement as many as seven times (interesting connection) before it's locked into our memory banks.

I'm asking Jesus to remind me again of meaningful truths He communicated clearly but I haven't yet fully grasped them. *I'm listening, Lord.* —CYNTHIA RUCHTI

FAITH STEP: *Consider adopting the practice of repeating important biblical truths seven times to lock them in to your heart and mind. Start with "Jesus never fails."*

Thursday, July 28

Sensible people control their temper; they earn respect by overlooking wrongs. Proverbs 19:11 (NLT)

I LOVE STUDYING PLANT CATALOGS to learn about different plants and their respective personalities and idiosyncrasies. While reading a catalog of flower bulbs for commercial landscapers today, I learned something new. Having moved from a colder, bulb-loving climate, I learned that I'd have to refrigerate my bulbs before planting them in this warmer region. In addition to bulbs needing to be pre-chilled before planting, though, I learned that these bulbs must be planted *immediately*—"before they lose their cool."

Wow! I could relate to those flower bulbs. Sometimes I lose my cool too. How could I apply this horticultural wisdom to my own life, so that I can avoid losing my cool? What would this look like for me?

Flower bulbs need cool temperatures to bloom and thrive. Likewise, I need the right spiritual conditions to bloom and thrive. Spending time in the presence of Jesus has a similar, positive effect as placing bulbs in a refrigerator—Jesus's presence helps me so that I can bloom and express myself in God-honoring ways. The fact that pre-chilled bulbs must be planted immediately reminds me that in times of stress, I need to immediately plant myself in the presence of Jesus and His Word—before I lose my cool. —CASSANDRA TIERSMA

FAITH STEP: *Prepare a cold compress by placing a folded, damp washcloth into a sealable storage bag, and tuck it into your freezer. On a sticky note, write out Proverbs 19:11 and place it on your freezer door. The next time you're feeling warm, grab your cold compress, and read Proverbs 19:11, asking Jesus to give you the good sense to control your temper and overlook wrongs.*

FRIDAY, JULY 29

Then I acknowledged my sin to you and did not cover up my iniquity.
I said, "I will confess my transgressions to the LORD." And you forgave
the guilt of my sin. Psalm 32:5 (NIV)

IT WAS ONE OF THOSE days when it seemed I could do nothing right. I kept making mistakes and apologizing. "I'm sorry I misread the instructions." "Sorry, I misunderstood what you said." "I'm so sorry. I forgot to do that." I was not on top of my game and it showed. I was owning up to my mistakes and saying "I'm sorry" in rapid-fire succession. I knew I had fallen short of other people's expectations and wanted to do whatever I needed to correct my errors.

But am I just as quick to say "I'm sorry" to Jesus when I fall short of His expectations? Do I always confess when I have done something wrong or displeasing to Him? Or when I fail to follow His promptings? To be honest, my answer to those questions is "no" more often than "yes."

Scripture tells me that the Lord is willing and able to forgive. After all, Jesus died on the cross to pay for all our sins—past, present, and future. My prayer each day is that He will raise my antenna to the sin in me and around me. I want to be more aware of it and convicted to immediately repent. Just as quickly as I am to apologize to others, I want to say "I'm sorry, please forgive me" to the One who can and does cover all my transgressions. —BARBRANDA LUMPKINS WALLS

FAITH STEP: *As you go throughout the day, ask Jesus to make you more conscious of what you say and do. Confess your sins on the spot and seek His forgiveness.*

SATURDAY, JULY 30

God gave us a spirit not of fear but of power and love and self-control.
2 Timothy 1:7 (ESV)

"MOM, I NEED TO GO to the emergency room," said my son Jordan. He was pressing his hand on his bleeding forehead as he walked into the house. He'd been outside dumping a wheelbarrow of wood scraps into a large dumpster when a burst of wind blew the heavy dumpster lid into the wheelbarrow, striking him in the head. "Are you sure?" I asked. After raising three boys, I'm not quick to rush to the ER. But I also couldn't look because blood makes me dizzy. He looked at his head in the mirror and said, "Yep."

I grabbed ice and paper towels, and we jumped in the car. We'd only been on the road a few minutes when Jordan said, "I think I'm going to pass out." And he did. I kept one hand on the steering wheel and placed the other on his knee. *Jesus, help me not to panic,* I prayed. We were close to the ER, so I kept driving. A minute later, he started convulsing, then woke up with a start, disoriented. Strangely calm, I reassured Jordan that he was okay. At the ER, they stitched his forehead and diagnosed a concussion.

On the way home, Jordan said, "Mom, thanks for staying calm." In the past, my first response to scary situations was panic. But because of my growing relationship with Jesus, staying calm is now becoming my first response. I'm grateful that He hasn't given me a spirit of fear but one of power, love, and self-control. —JEANNIE BLACKMER

FAITH STEP: *Write down something that causes you to panic, and then ask Jesus to help. Place the concern in your Bible near 2 Timothy 1:7 as a reminder of His spirit in you.*

SUNDAY, JULY 31

*Therefore encourage one another and build each other up,
just as in fact you are doing.* 1 Thessalonians 5:11 (NIV)

THE WORLD HAS SEEN SOME really extraordinary challenges these last few years. Even in light of the past centuries of global trials of all kinds, what we've faced more recently does seem unprecedented. More than ever, I've had to rely on eternal truth to overcome the threat of discouragement. As a born encourager, I've taken the mandate in this verse seriously when it comes to sharing my own overcoming with others. The troubling times are also a ripe field for the gospel message, the greatest encouragement ever.

In this verse, Paul is actually urging the Thessalonian church to encourage one another in the last days, to persevere through the challenging times before Jesus's return and to maintain the eternal perspective that unbelievers lack. While the whirling threats of Armageddon have seemed more real lately, the fact is that all believers through history have believed they live in the imminence of Christ's return.

I read the crazy headlines with keener interest these days. My Christian friends and I sometimes wonder if Jesus will show up tomorrow after lunch. Wouldn't that be nice? Whatever the future holds in my own little universe or in the world at large, I want to encourage others with the promise of eternity and Jesus's triumphal return. —ISABELLA CAMPOLATTARO

FAITH STEP: *Think of someone who is grappling with fear about the future or facing an imminent threat of any kind and write them a note of encouragement, citing a Scripture passage to support your message.*

Monday, August 1

Each of you should use whatever gift you have received to serve others, as faithful stewards of God's grace in its various forms. 1 Peter 4:10 (NIV)

Every evening, around six o'clock, I hear three dreaded words: *What's for supper?* My family turns up regularly to eat. Sadly, I don't enjoy cooking. Neither did my mother. My kids say I have six dishes in my repertoire. They are the same six dishes my mother prepared for us when I was growing up. I might be inspired to cook if my family enjoyed interesting foods, but no, they are strictly meat-and-potatoes folks. And really picky too!

I wonder if Jesus had any worries when He set out to feed five thousand hungry people with five loaves and two fish? I'll bet those people didn't complain about the lack of variety or whether the food was the right temperature. Matthew 14:20 tells us, "They all ate and were satisfied" (NIV). Not a picky eater in the bunch.

One day recently, I was stuck on what to cook for supper. I had some ground beef thawed and spotted a jar of spaghetti sauce in the pantry. That would be quick and easy. I added a spinach salad and a wheat roll. My husband, Jeff, devoured his meal. He announced "Pat, this is the best thing I've ever tasted." His joy because of the food he was eating made me ashamed of my lack of joy while preparing it. Serving my husband, and others, should be my delight.
—Pat Butler Dyson

Faith Step: *Ask Jesus to show you new ways to find joy in serving.*

TUESDAY, AUGUST 2

---

*Let us therefore come boldly unto the throne of grace, that we may obtain
mercy, and find grace to help in time of need.* Hebrews 4:16 (KJV)

IMAGINE THE FOLLOWING SCENE. A starving man collapses at the
gate of a castle. Guards try to shoo him away, but he begs, "Please,
I must see the queen. It's a matter of life and death." They let him
pass, snickering behind his back. *He'll never get in there.*

Sure enough, when he knocks on the castle door, the butler
answers, but seeing the man's tattered clothes, worn shoes, and dirty
hands, the butler slams the door in his face. He musters the strength
to knock again. The butler yells, "Go away!" and calls for guards to
dispose of the man, who has become a nuisance. As the guards are
dragging him away, the prince rides up on his trusty white steed.
"Stop!" the prince calls. He is resplendent in his royal riding gear,
and the man looks down at his rags, then back at the prince. "Is that
you?" the prince asks, staring into his eyes. "It is you! We've been
looking forward to your visit!"

The prince slides off the horse as the guards release the man in
astonishment. The prince says, "Come with me." Together, they
walk up the path and through the door of the castle. The man
hesitates at the entry to the throne room. His heart hammers in
his chest. He says, "I can't. I can't face her like this." But it's too
late. The queen has already seen him. She jumps from the throne,
gathering her robes, and runs toward him. "Come in! Come in!"
she calls, taking his hand and pulling him forward. She asks, "How
can I help you today?" —GWEN FORD FAULKENBERRY

FAITH STEP: *Draw a picture of yourself as the man and put God in place of the
queen. What would you ask for if you weren't afraid?*

WEDNESDAY, AUGUST 3

But don't be so concerned about perishable things like food. Spend your energy seeking the eternal life that the Son of Man can give you. For God the Father has given me the seal of his approval. John 6:27 (NLT)

WIDOWED IN 2008, MY MOTHER cooks for one and eats meals alone. This has been difficult for her because, during my growing up years, she found much joy in serving others the food she'd prepared. I'll always remember the aroma of freshly baked buns, fruit pies with flaky crusts, cinnamon rolls, and soups of every sort. She prepared every meal or dessert with love.

My presence in her home for ten days gave Mom the opportunity to cook for two and enjoy company at the table. Every morning as we washed the breakfast dishes, she looked at me and asked what I wanted to eat for lunch. "Soup," I said. She smiled and said, "Me too. What type?" The conversation continued as we decided which soup to cook and what we'd have for a side. A similar conversation took place after lunch as we pondered what to prepare for dinner and then what to eat for a bedtime snack. We followed this pattern, and on the fourth day, we both burst into laughter. We'd consumed a lot of good food together, but food had also consumed us.

Food is a gift given for our enjoyment and sustenance, but there's so much more to life than what we eat and drink. Jesus encourages us to invest more energy in His kingdom and less on what will not last for eternity. Food falls into that category. Enjoy it but keep it in the right perspective. —GRACE FOX

FAITH STEP: *Focus on Jesus, the Bread of Life, and you will never be hungry again.*

THURSDAY, AUGUST 4

This is my Son, whom I love; with him I am well pleased.
Listen to him! Matthew 17:5 (NIV)

MY OLDEST GRANDCHILD TEXTED TO let me know she and her roommate had made a gluten-free lemon poppy seed cake for me and wanted to bring it over. I didn't get the message because I rarely have my notifications turned on.

When I finally discovered the message, my husband and I weren't even close to home but somehow I could almost smell that cake from miles away. The thoughtfulness of those young people was even more satisfying than eating the cake would have been.

They'd looked up a recipe online, shopped for the proper ingredients, and pulled off what I discovered the next day was more luscious than I had imagined it could be. I almost missed it and the opportunity to bless those young people in return because I hadn't been tuned in to the messages coming my way.

I can almost see Jesus nodding His head over the similarities to the messages He sends me. He's speaking—through His Word and the impressions on my heart and those little nudges that I sometimes blame on my conscience—but I don't always pick up on His signals. *Oh, You want me specifically, not just people in general, to be slow to anger? The inclination to make conversation with the woman behind me in the grocery line—that was You? I guess I missed it.*

Although I'm not intentionally ignoring Him, if I don't remember to leave my "notifications" on, I risk missing a sweet connection with Him. —CYNTHIA RUCHTI

FAITH STEP: *When your phone or other device pings today to let you know someone is trying to reach you, pause long enough to check your connection with the messages Jesus is sending.*

Friday, August 5

With that he breathed on them and said,
"Receive the Holy Spirit." John 20:22 (NIV)

Kerry, my beloved mother figure, is an avid scuba diver. At seventy, she's still going strong, having logged five hundred hours of dive time. So when I wanted to do a special one-on-one activity with my young teen son Pierce, scuba diving seemed like a great choice because we could also share it with Granny. I signed us up.

I knew I'd have to face some fears to scuba dive, but I believed that in Christ I could do all things (Philippians 4:13). Among other fears, I experience severe claustrophobia when breathing deep underwater, loaded down with tanks and gear. Fear isn't just a mere distraction when scuba diving. It can lead to panic and in turn, life-threatening disaster. So I was highly motivated to combat it with supernatural might. I often use Jesus's name as a simple meditative prayer when fear strikes. I wouldn't be able to do that with a regulator in my mouth. But what I could do was breathe deeply with my mind focused on Jesus.

Pierce and I passed our checkout dives with flying colors and have already made a few trips with Kerry. I now find scuba diving is a special time to commune with Jesus. Breathing deeply, enjoying soothing weightlessness in the water, and beholding creation in quiet splendor is time with Jesus I've come to savor.
—Isabella Campolattaro

Faith Step: *Is fear holding you back from something you'd love to try? Trust in the name of Jesus to enable you to do it, and then give it a try.*

SATURDAY, AUGUST 6

For exaltation comes neither from the east nor from the west nor from the south. But God is the Judge: He puts down one, and exalts another. Psalm 75:6–7 (NKJV)

WHEN I WAS TRYING TO further my career in media, I had to do a lot of praying. I lived in New York City, the largest media market in the country, and jobs in the industry were coveted by many who had journalism degrees just like mine. I applied for a position at a well-known nonprofit organization, and I felt in my spirit that the job was mine. I heard back from them pretty quickly, and after two interviews, they narrowed it down to me and another candidate. I waited to hear from them, but a week went by and they didn't call. I phoned the manager I had interviewed with, but I could tell right away from her tone that it was going to be no.

Needless to say, I was disappointed—but thankfully I was also "prayed up." I had committed my job search to Jesus and knew He would come through. I asked Him for a job that paid well, but also one I would enjoy. So I sat with the rejection and waited on the Lord. Two weeks later my phone rang. It was the same manager, but she had a bounce in her voice. She explained that the person she hired had quit abruptly and that I was the only other candidate she wanted. She humbly asked, "Would you still consider us?" I knew this was Jesus, so I said yes *and* asked for a salary increase—it was approved immediately. As they say in church here in the South, "God's favor just ain't fair!" —PAMELA TOUSSAINT HOWARD

FAITH STEP: *Remember who promotes you and maintains your peace.*

SUNDAY, AUGUST 7

But as for me, I know that my Redeemer lives, and he will stand upon the earth at last. Job 19:25 (NLT)

I OPENED THE SMALL BLACK box Aunt Joyce had mailed me and gasped. "Honey, look at this," I said to my husband, Kevin. The pendant I held up to the light was crafted in two different colors of gold and was shaped like an angel in flight. "What a lovely gift!"

Aunt Joyce had recently been cleaning out her jewelry box and came across the angel. It was a uniquely fashioned gift from a friend many years before. She told me, "Since you're my angel, I feel you should have it."

I wiped away happy tears as I thought of the miracle this gift represented. When I was fourteen, I lived with Aunt Joyce and Uncle Dwayne. They gave me a stable home during a rough patch in our broken nuclear family. At first Joyce, Dwayne, and I lived in harmony. But my teenage insecurities and my aunt's ways soon clashed. When I returned home to my parents after only seven months, the feelings between Aunt Joyce and me were anything but angelic.

Over the decades, Jesus changed both our hearts. I grew up and acknowledged the world didn't spin to please me, and Aunt Joyce softened. We became friends—good enough friends that she considered me her angel. *Wow.*

My favorite quality of Jesus is how He loves to take the broken places of our lives and fix them. But He doesn't simply repair wounded souls. He mends and heals and makes them better than before. I believe the word for that is *redeemer.* —JEANETTE LEVELLIE

FAITH STEP: *Find a drawing or painting of an angel. Thank Jesus that His power to redeem your brokenness is greater than every angelic force in the universe.*

MONDAY, AUGUST 8

---

*You will keep in perfect peace all who trust in you, all whose
thoughts are fixed on you! Isaiah 26:3 (NLT)*

DURING A LONG VISIT AT my daughter's house, it was hard to find
time to connect every day with my husband back home while I was
around my active grandkids with their busy schedules. One evening,
Richard and I FaceTimed as I lounged with my granddaughters on
the guest bed. Suddenly, my new laptop went crazy. Files opened on
their own, one after another. The cursor darted all over the screen.
I quickly ended the conversation and closed the laptop. My mind
reeled with questions: *Who had hacked into my computer and gained
control of it? Would I lose valuable files? Could the culprit access financial information?* Then my teenage granddaughter explained that
her little sister had grabbed my mouse out of the nightstand drawer
and started playing with it.

Sometimes people can really mess with our minds, even when
they aren't trying. So can circumstances and emotions. On some
days, watching the world news is enough to give me the impres-
sion that events are spinning out of control. I may have moments
when I'm tempted to question who is in ultimate control, but then
I always remember the answer.

Day by day, moment by moment, I choose what or who I allow
to shape my thinking. If I focus on what I see or what I feel, life
may seem chaotic. But when I concentrate on Who I know and His
power, then my mind can be at peace. —DIANNE NEAL MATTHEWS

FAITH STEP: *Write a list of the guidelines for evaluating our thought life, which
are found in Philippians 4:8. For the next few days, meditate on how one of the
attributes listed points us to Jesus. Ask Him to help you keep your mind fixed on
Him all day long.*

TUESDAY, AUGUST 9

Don't let your hearts be troubled. Trust in God, and trust also in me. John 14:1 (NLT)

IF YOU'RE LIKE ME, YOU might page through your Bible, looking for a nugget, in place of a more serious time of study and reflection. Sometimes a single word rises off the page. Or a note I wrote in the margin long ago catches my eye, and my heart returns to when that Scripture verse intersected with my life.

The header prior to John 14 in my study Bible reads, "Jesus Comforts His Disciples." I paused for a moment before continuing to read. Jesus—the teacher, the healer, the Messiah—spoke to the disciples with the express purpose of comforting them.

Today's Scripture passage assures me that He's preparing a place for me in heaven. In Scripture, it appears immediately following His announcement that despite Peter's claim that he would lay down his life for Jesus, Peter would in fact deny Him three times before the next morning.

Jesus sees denial, betrayal, pain, and death ahead. But He takes time to tell His followers and us, "Don't let your hearts be troubled. Trust."

I can be troubled by what's happening around me—or I can trust. One negates the other. If I'm troubled, I'm not trusting. If I'm trusting, I won't be troubled.

Jesus communicated the truth His disciples most needed before everything would seem to fall apart. He anticipated the depth of their concern and responded with a simple comfort that could be paraphrased, "Don't *let* your hearts be troubled. There is another option. Trust Me."

This is the comfort I need too. —CYNTHIA RUCHTI

FAITH STEP: *What troubles you most today? Imagine the word* TRUST *stamped over that concern in big, bloodred letters.*

WEDNESDAY, AUGUST 10

Now we really live, since you are standing firm in the
Lord. 1 Thessalonians 3:8 (NIV)

I'M A CHICKASAW INDIAN, AND before I met Jesus, I wanted to experience a traditional vision quest—spending time in nature on a mountain, alone with God. So, taking no food or supplies other than a tarp, I spent three days and two nights alone on a mountain, seeking God as I offered up my songs, prayers, and tears.

During my vision quest, a weird thing happened. I lost a favorite smooth, flat stone that I'd been wearing in a medicine bag pouch on a leather cord around my neck. When preparing to end my vision quest, I found the missing stone in the strangest place—pressed against my leg! It was pressed flat into the side of my leg.

Back at base camp, I told Grandfather (a Christian minister in the Native American Church) what had happened. He responded by speaking of the disciple Peter whose name means "rock," and how Jesus is the Rock upon which God's church is built. Grandfather then gave me a Chickasaw Indian name, which means "One Who Stands on the Faith of the Rock." That prophetic name came true for me a few years later, when I received Jesus as my Lord and Savior.

I've always been attracted to rocks. River rocks, smooth stones, even pebbles. I even attend a rock church, hand-built over a century ago out of local stone. But the rock which I now have the deepest appreciation for is Jesus. For I now know what it means to stand on the faith of Him, the Rock. —CASSANDRA TIERSMA

FAITH STEP: *Go outside and find a special stone to display in your home as a daily reminder to put your faith in Jesus, the Rock upon which we stand.*

THURSDAY, AUGUST 11

For we are God's masterpiece. He has created us anew in Christ Jesus, so we can do the good things he planned for us long ago. Ephesians 2:10 *(NLT)*

I'M AN UNABASHED FOOD NETWORK junkie. I enjoy watching everyone, from the Pioneer Woman to the Barefoot Contessa, whip up mouthwatering dishes. But the show I absolutely love is *Chopped*. The contestants take a basketful of four mystery ingredients and create an appetizer, entrée, or dessert—usually in thirty minutes or less—to impress a panel of judges. One by one, the chefs with the least successful dishes in each round are "chopped" from the competition.

I am always amazed by the chefs' skills and creativity. How could quail eggs, white asparagus, hibiscus flowers in syrup, and spiced ham in a can come together in an edible appetizer? Sometimes the contestants are stumped, but after their creative juices kick in, they are able to make something wonderful.

When I look back over the past couple years, I see Jesus as the master chef in my life. What appeared to be a jumble of decisions—some good, some not so good—about jobs, finances, family, and how I spend my time turned out to be key ingredients to shore up my faith in Him. Jesus took my messes and successes and put me on the road that would accomplish His plans.

Although sometimes I feel as if I'm on the chopping block, I've learned that Jesus will eventually set me straight and see me through. Mistakes are just part of the delicious stew that help me nourish and encourage someone else along the way.
—BARBRANDA LUMPKINS WALLS

FAITH STEP: *Recall how Jesus turned around a tough situation for you. Share that experience with someone going through a challenge to encourage them.*

FRIDAY, AUGUST 12

Be gentle with one another, sensitive. Forgive one another as quickly and thoroughly as God in Christ forgave you. Ephesians 4:32 (MSG)

MY FRIEND CAROL WENT TO the grocery store and faced a long checkout line. Another checker opened her register and asked for the next in line. A man behind Carol started to force his way to the front and she spoke up, "Excuse me, sir,"—but before she could finish, he spun around and cursed at her. Then he let her go in front of him. The angry man stood behind her in line. She braved a glance at him and noticed his hands were shaking. Suddenly, she was overcome with compassion and forgiveness rather than anger, which in her past had been her first response. She touched his forearm lightly and said, "I'm sorry I upset you." Instantly, she saw a change in him as he looked her in the eye and said, "I'm sorry too."

Carol has more control over her anger now than she used to, thanks to Jesus, His complete forgiveness, and His transformational spirit inside her. With Jesus in her heart, old behaviors have fallen away, and she's adopting Christlike actions. She's more sensitive and quick to forgive those who are irrationally unpleasant to her. Carol has inspired me not to fight for my rights when someone is unjustly unkind to me, but to instead forgive quickly, respond with kindness, and offer the love and forgiveness that Jesus gave His life to give me. —JEANNIE BLACKMER

FAITH STEP: *What action can you take today to express Christlike kindness and move quickly to forgive someone who's been unkind to you recently?*

SATURDAY, AUGUST 13

And I tell you that you are Peter, and on this rock I will build my church,
and the gates of Hades will not overcome it. Matthew 16:18 (NIV)

I AM FOREVER ENCOURAGED BY Peter, the passionate, hotheaded apostle who denied Jesus three times. Not only did Peter's weakness not disqualify Him from serving Jesus, Peter became the rock on which Jesus built His church.

I used to feel woefully unqualified to serve Jesus in almost any capacity, and today I still squirm sometimes at the thought of being viewed as a teacher or leader. I thought I had too much baggage and wasn't good enough, healthy enough, improved enough, or perfect enough to have such a role. Yet Peter, and all the apostles really, are God's gracious proof that He actually prefers to use cracked pots.

I've come to believe this, because our strength is made perfect in our weakness (2 Corinthians 12:9). My brokenness also helps keep me humble and hanging onto Jesus even while it helps me connect to others too.

I see the evidence in the messages I receive from readers. Being transparent about my struggles comforts and encourage others as they deal with their struggles. So, what qualifies me to help someone else is less about my competence, and more about how Jesus helps me cope with my brokenness. More to the point, God uses broken people like me because we're all broken in one way or another (Romans 3:10). —ISABELLA CAMPOLATTARO

FAITH STEP: *List all the reasons you don't feel qualified to be used by Jesus. Say a prayer, offering all of it to Jesus to use as He wills.*

SUNDAY, AUGUST 14

Let your speech always be gracious, seasoned with salt, so that you may know how you ought to answer each person. Colossians 4:6 (ESV)

WHEN MY LOCAL VITAMIN WORLD closed, I decided to drive to another location at a mall twenty miles away. When I shopped there, a knowledgeable young man who was cheerful and helpful provided such a pleasant experience that I knew I'd return. On my next visit, however, the nice young man was absent. In his place was a sour-faced woman whose greeting was "Need something?" I was extra kind, asked her opinion, complimented her expertise, but despite all that, she was rude and unhelpful. She even had the nerve to correct my pronunciation of *turmeric*. And she refused one of my coupons!

Jesus had His share of encounters with difficult people. Those annoying Pharisees were always popping up and harassing Him for working on the Sabbath. The Canaanite woman accosted Him, demanding He heal her daughter. And so-called friends and neighbors from His hometown of Nazareth wanted to throw Him off a cliff!

By the time I left the store, I was fuming. Despite my graciousness to the salesperson, she'd remained impolite and hostile, making me regret my visit. As I got in my car and drove away, a nudge from Jesus made me pause. *Do you have any idea what that woman may be coping with in her life?* I did not. As much as I like to think of myself as a pleasant, positive person, I have my off days. I asked Jesus to help the woman deal with whatever might be troubling her.

—PAT BUTLER DYSON

FAITH STEP: *Ask Jesus to help you maintain an attitude of kindness toward others, even if that kindness isn't reciprocated.*

MONDAY, AUGUST 15

---

*We may boldly say, The Lord is my helper, and I will not fear
what man shall do unto me. Hebrews 13:6 (KJV)*

WHEN I WAS A KID in school, I was always trying out for something.
I won sometimes, and I lost a lot. The older I got, the more sense I
acquired, at least in that department, and it's been a long time since
I've made myself vulnerable to the approval of others on any large
scale. Maybe that's why I was reluctant to enter a local political
contest and why the race itself is so terrifying. Every single day I ask
myself what in the world I've gotten myself into.

The job, if I get it, will be difficult. But it's not the job right now
that keeps me up at night. It's the knowledge that if I'm not elected
by the people in my district, I still have to live here because it's my
home. And I'm not sure I want to know if I'm not my neighbors'
choice. The thought of that hurts. And no matter how many advisors tell me this stuff isn't personal, it feels personal. I don't know
how to get that feeling to change by the time of the election.

What I do know how to do is boldly declare that Jesus is my
helper, and I will not fear what people do or don't do. When I
prayed about the decision to run, He never promised I'd win. Jesus
promised to be with me. Seems like that's what it always gets back
to. Because Jesus holds my hand, I can walk through this—and
every other situation—fearless. —GWEN FORD FAULKENBERRY

FAITH STEP: *What is really important to you right now, and what if it doesn't
work out? Sit with that for a minute. Then insert Jesus right there in the middle
of it all, holding your hand. Visualize this truth every day, and you'll be ready to
face anything.*

TUESDAY, AUGUST 16

Hallelujah! For our Lord God Almighty reigns. Let us rejoice and be glad and give him glory! For the wedding of the Lamb has come, and his bride has made herself ready. Revelation 19:6–7 (NIV)

BROWSING MY DAUGHTER KIM'S WEDDING photo album brought a rush of memories. I recalled the day we booked the venue—a private acreage owned by an event planner who hosted numerous weddings every summer. Venue secured, we then focused on other details: the caterer, menu, flowers, and photographer.

On her wedding day, Kim and her attendants prepared in a spacious en suite bedroom room built especially for bridal parties. A stylist swept Kim's hair into an updo and secured her veil. Her future mother-in-law applied her makeup. I helped her don her wedding gown and fastened the satin-covered buttons decorating its back. We marveled at the fit, grateful for the skilled seamstress who altered it from a size 10 to a size 2.

Kim slipped her sandals on, studied herself in the full-length antique mirror, and smiled. So did everyone in the room. She was a radiant bride, ready and excited to marry the man she loved.

As you read this, preparations are being made for the grandest wedding ever. Jesus is the groom, and we are His bride. When every detail is ready, our Beloved will come for us. In the meantime, I want to prepare my heart, looking forward to that special moment with joy and anticipation. What an incredible celebration that will be! —GRACE FOX

FAITH STEP: *Think about the upcoming wedding of eternity. Have you left any detail unfinished? If so, take time to tend to it so you can be fully prepared when Jesus comes.*

WEDNESDAY, AUGUST 17

When you are brought before synagogues, rulers and authorities, do not worry about how you will defend yourselves or what you will say, for the Holy Spirit will teach you at that time what you should say. Luke 12:11–12 (NIV)

I USED TO HAVE A terrible fear of public speaking. The kind of fear that causes knee-knocking, voice-quaking sweats. It's kind of ironic because I've always been a talker and, most would say, quite articulate. I have many thoughts and opinions, but they used to evaporate with terror as I stepped up to a podium.

In this verse, Jesus is encouraging His disciples not to worry about what to say if they were arrested or otherwise confronted. The stakes were a lot higher for the disciples than for me to share my testimony or an inspirational message. But the simple and powerful truth found in today's verses—that Jesus's Spirit will speak through me and that I shouldn't worry—was what helped me finally overcome my fear of public speaking.

Now, before a speaking engagement, I pray for Jesus to give me the words to speak, and then I let go peacefully. Many times, people will tell me that I've touched them deeply and I'm altogether oblivious as to what I said—which underscores the truth of today's Scripture. My words have much greater impact when I get out of Jesus's way. —ISABELLA CAMPOLATTARO

FAITH STEP: *Are there situations in which you struggle for the words to say? Remember today's verses as both inspiration and prayer, and let the Holy Spirit speak for you.*

THURSDAY, AUGUST 18

We know that in all things God works for the good of those who love him, who have been called according to his purpose. Romans 8:28 *(NIV)*

HERE'S WHAT I WANTED TO know: Who is Katelyn Masters and why is she friending me? We didn't have any Facebook friends in common. As a rule, I don't accept friend requests from people I haven't met, but I felt a little nudge to accept this one. Moments later, Messenger pinged. Kate was from West Virginia, where I used to live, and wanted to buy my house there. The house I'd lost...

Kate had Googled my name and learned all about me. She had some questions, but also...gulp...she had a little girl with Down syndrome. She asked if we could talk. My eyes welled up. How like Jesus to take a challenge and turn it into something beautiful.

MightyTykes was inspired by my son Isaac, who has Down syndrome. I'd lost the house and abandoned the MightyTykes brand due to a prolonged legal battle with my prior investors. It hurt at the time, but it was also so tainted with negativity that I was ready to let it go, trusting God. Now, months later, Jesus redeemed a painful loss to bless me and to bless someone else richly, making connections way beyond my human hands.

I shared information with her about the house, the community, and resources for her precious daughter, Elsa. Kate and her husband made an offer on the house. Only God. —ISABELLA CAMPOLATTARO

FAITH STEP: *Are you grieving a loss or hesitating to let something go? Ponder this story and ask Jesus what He would have you do.*

FRIDAY, AUGUST 19

How sweet are your words to my taste, sweeter than honey to my mouth!
Psalm 119:103 (NIV)

WHEN MY DAUGHTER, KIM, AND her husband relocated to northern British Columbia, they discovered hummingbirds living in the trees near their apartment balcony. These feathered miniatures whizzed over, under, and between branches like wee fighter jets. They provided such entertainment that Kim bought a hummingbird feeder to hang near the balcony railing, hoping to entice them closer. She boiled one quarter cup of sugar in one cup of water, let the juice cool, and filled the feeder.

The first visitor arrived within minutes. He sipped the syrup and then zipped to a tree perch. Several seconds later he returned for a second helping. When another hummingbird approached, the first chased the other away and then returned immediately for thirds. The sweet drink obviously pleased his palate. He enjoyed it so much that he couldn't get enough.

In today's verse, the psalmist described Jesus's words as sweet to the taste, and I find this description true. His words feed me. They satisfy my soul's need for nourishment. You might even say that I'm jealous for them. Distractions appear and try to needle their way into my time of feeding on the Word, but I purposefully chase them away. The more I savor Jesus's words, the more I crave them. They keep me coming back day after day after day. I can't get enough.
—GRACE FOX

FAITH STEP: *On YouTube, find a video of a hummingbird sipping sugar water from a feeder. Ask Jesus to make His words sweet to your soul and to give you a craving so that you keep coming back for more.*

SATURDAY, AUGUST 20

For I am persuaded that neither death nor life, nor angels nor principalities nor powers, nor things present nor things to come, nor height nor depth, nor any other created thing, shall be able to separate us from the love of God which is in Christ Jesus our Lord. Romans 8:38–39 (NKJV)

AS MY BELOVED MOM WAS dying in my arms, today's Scripture passage came to my heart, and I spoke it in her ear. I wanted her to go to Jesus knowing that no sickness could ever separate her from Him. In the ensuing weeks and months after her passing, I was the one who needed to be reminded of that Scripture. Though I was confident my mom was safe with Jesus, I felt lost, discouraged, and discombobulated. Everything I had envisioned for my future in some way included her. She had been there for all of my life's achievements, and I had looked forward to her meeting my future husband, helping me wedding plan, decorate a new home, hold my long-awaited first child. What now? Jesus assured me that all would be well, that He would not—could not—leave me alone (Hebrews 13:5). The devil tried his best to plant contrary thoughts in my mind, but I held on to Jesus like my life depended on it (it did!). He told me He would actually bring life out of death, joy out of sadness. It didn't all happen instantly. There were many obstacles to overcome, and a lot of emotional healing needed to take place in several areas of my life. But I can say with confidence that I was never separated from Jesus's love and that He restored great joy to the painful areas in my life. —PAMELA TOUSSAINT HOWARD

FAITH STEP: *No matter what comes against you, know that you are loved.*

SUNDAY, AUGUST 21

There are also many other things which Jesus did, the which, if they should be written every one, I suppose that even the world itself could not contain the books that should be written. Amen. John 21:25 (KJV)

A YOUNG MOM SIGHED LOUD enough that I heard. I didn't have to wonder why. Her small child had spent twenty minutes or more telling a circuitous story with as much fantasy and as many grandiose ideas as the little one could cram into one very long sentence. I sympathized. One of my children could also turn a ten-second sentence into a half-hour proclamation that was devoid of punctuation and breaths. He practiced the skill *every day.*

I leaned toward the exasperated mom and whispered, "You'll have to listen to a lot of that in order to be standing near when your child says something that you won't want to miss." She smiled and nodded. I hope she remembers that little piece of advice for decades, just as I still remember it, years after it was first spoken to me.

Jesus didn't spend a minute of His earthly life talking nonsense. Not one word was wasted or unnecessary or without meaning. Not every word He uttered or every story He told is recorded in the Bible; He did and said so much more, according to today's Scripture verse.

Rather than sighing when Jesus spoke, His mother, Mary, in essence, encouraged the servants at the wedding of Cana to listen to Him. She said, "Do whatever he tells you" (John 2:5, NIV). Our best option is to remain near to Jesus, because we don't want to miss anything He says. —CYNTHIA RUCHTI

FAITH STEP: *Of the words Jesus spoke that are recorded in the Bible, what are your favorite ones? Focus on those words today and note how they influence your approach to challenges.*

MONDAY, AUGUST 22

So God said to Noah, "The rainbow is a sign of the agreement that I made with all living things on earth." Genesis 9:17 (NCV)

RAINBOWS HAVE ALWAYS ENCHANTED ME. Biblically, they're an uplifting sign of great reassurance, a promise from God that He will never again destroy all life on earth with a flood. To me, rainbows symbolize colorful, creative expression. Early in my creative journey, while working as a young artist in a school, I felt like a rolled-up rainbow. I painted a picture of that image, and scribbled, "When it stops raining, I'll come out." Praise Jesus, He's since blessed me with ample opportunities for creative expression in multiple artistic endeavors, throughout different seasons of my life.

I'm happiest and most fulfilled when Jesus provides a creative outlet through which I can express my God-given gifts and talents. Some seasons, though, we might feel like that rolled-up rainbow, waiting for the rain to stop, so that our creativity can come out of hibernation. But just as rain never lasts forever, seasons of creative drought also don't.

Some people claim they just aren't creative. But, that's not true, because we're made in the image and likeness of the Creator God, whose very nature is creative. So, the question is never "How creative are you?" But rather, "*How* are you creative?" Just as God paints His rainbow signature across the heavens, reassuring us that He will never again flood the entire planet, He also paints His colorful signature of creativity into each and every one of us. This creativity is to be used for His glory—in our homes, churches, and communities. —CASSANDRA TIERSMA

FAITH STEP: *Ask Jesus to show you how to use your creativity to bless your family, church, or community. Thank Him for both the seasons of rain and the seasons of drought in your life.*

TUESDAY, AUGUST 23

Remember the days of old; consider the generations long past. Ask your father and he will tell you, your elders, and they will explain to you.
Deuteronomy 32:7 (NIV)

I'M NOT FOND OF CLEANING my house, but there's one chore I don't mind: dusting the old piano. When my daughters began taking lessons, I searched for a piano for our home. Not able to afford a new one, I found a perfect used piano at the local music store—a beauty in dark maple, with gently curving lines and graceful legs. "Good choice!" said the store owner. "This Acrosonic is over fifty years old and belonged to the Women's Poetry Society at Lamar University."

My girls have grown and moved out, but the piano stayed with me. Occasionally, I pick out the one tune I know, "Silent Night," and sometimes my granddaughter Ana plays for me. But mostly, I dust the old Acrosonic and daydream of Violette Newton, the poet laureate of Texas, reading her poems to the Poetry Society members: Charlotte, Gwendolyn, Elizabeth, Marian, and Olive. When Marian plays "Eine kleine Nachtmusik," I can almost hear the melody.

Jesus had great respect for His elders and for things of the past. I share that love for old things. I've inherited several lovely antiques, but my most cherished possession is my grandmother Memie's old Bible. Housed in an ornate box that has an image of Jesus with the woman at the well, this King James Version was published in 1946. Inside it is an inscription in Memie's hand, "Presented to Vivian Jarvis Butler by her husband O. D. Butler, December 23, 1948." Less than a year later, my grandfather died of a heart attack, leaving Memie with her Bible and her memories. —PAT BUTLER DYSON

FAITH STEP: *Is there an old Bible in your family? Open it and read your favorite Scripture passages.*

WEDNESDAY, AUGUST 24

Carry each other's burdens, and in this way you will fulfill the law of Christ. Galatians 6:2 (NIV)

DURING THE COVID-19 QUARANTINE, a dear friend went to heaven after a nine-year battle with cancer. Our heartbroken community felt helpless and unable to console the family because large gatherings were not allowed. Then some of her closest friends came up with a plan, and asked everyone to drive by the family's home at an appointed time and toss lemons onto the yard, because the woman who had passed away loved iced tea with lemon. At the designated time, we drove to their home—more than 150 cars were doing the same. The family sat in lawn chairs, collected lemons, smiled, cried, and waved at all of us for at least an hour. This experience of collective grieving was a powerful and important moment. No matter the circumstances, we can find creative ways to support one another through sorrow.

Jesus knew the importance of carrying one another through heartache. While He was dying on the cross, some of His last words were a reminder to care for one another. When Jesus saw His mother and His disciple, John, standing together, He said they were now each other's family (John 19:26–27). John cared for Mary the rest of his life. In Brené Brown's book *Braving the Wilderness,* she writes about the importance of collective pain: "The collective pain (and sometimes joy) we experience when gathering in any way to celebrate the end of a life is perhaps one of the most powerful experiences of inextricable connection." Grieving together is a profound way of carrying one another's burdens. —JEANNIE BLACKMER

FAITH STEP: *Is someone you know grieving? Express your shared sorrow and then do something tangible to help. (Take a meal, make them iced tea . . .)*

THURSDAY, AUGUST 25

Cast all your anxiety on him because he cares for you. 1 Peter 5:7 *(NIV)*

MY MOM WAS CHARMING, LOVING, beautiful, brilliant and...a paranoid schizophrenic. Her mental illness made it painful to love her. Even so, I adored her and treasured the times when she took her medication and was at her best.

For many years she lived in group homes. Some were nicer than others. When I got married, I invited her to move in with me and my husband. Four of those five years were the best times of our relationship, and we forged precious memories. Eventually, though, she stopped taking her medication, and her behavior became erratic again. By then I had my two-year-old son Pierce. I didn't want him to have the scary, chaotic childhood I'd had. But I couldn't just abandon her. I didn't know what to do.

In my despair, I slipped away alone with my Bible and begged God to help me. After hours of prayers and tears, a deep calm came over me, and I heard Jesus's gentle voice speak to my heart, *You can let her go. I've got her.*

Within a few months my mom had a breakdown. She was hospitalized and then moved into a lovely assisted living facility where she was required to take her medication. She lived another five years in safety, and I was able to love her freely until she died in 2014.
—ISABELLA CAMPOLATTARO

FAITH STEP: *Who do you need to let go? Write Jesus a letter, asking for help and entrusting the situation to Him.*

FRIDAY, AUGUST 26

Give to him who asks you, and from him who wants to borrow from you do not turn away. Matthew 5:42 (NKJV)

THE LITTLE BOY LOOKED ABOUT nine years old, near the age of my grandson Winston. He was intently studying cans of cat food, looking each one over carefully and then putting it back, unconsciously blocking me from reaching the cat food I needed. As I tried to squeeze by him, he said, "Ma'am, can you help me find the best cat food for kittens?" He'd found two kittens near his house, and he knew they were hungry. He told me he needed to find good food for them, but he didn't have much money.

We chatted about the merits of dry food versus wet, and I showed him a special food for kittens. He listened intently and respectfully. I took a ten-dollar bill from my wallet and advised him to try a variety of foods, wet and dry, and some specifically for kittens. He thanked me profusely and even after I'd selected my cat food, he remained in the aisle, deciding what to buy.

When I shared the story with a friend, she said, "Boy, he saw *you* coming! I'll bet he didn't spend that money on cat food." That thought had never occurred to me. I was pretty sure what Jesus would have done under the circumstances. If the boy had expressed his need to Jesus, I don't think He would have turned away. The boy hadn't really asked me for money. He was doing a good deed by adopting stray kittens. I trusted that his heart was in the right place. Cynicism has no place in Jesus's world. —PAT BUTLER DYSON

FAITH STEP: *When in doubt, ask yourself what Jesus would do.*

SATURDAY, AUGUST 27

Now faith is confidence in what we hope for and assurance about what we do not see. Hebrews 11:1 (NIV)

AFTER SHOPPING IN STORES THAT line an oceanfront, I returned to my third-floor room at the inn. The view that morning had been incredible, and I looked forward to relaxing on the balcony while my skin drank in the sunshine. Instead, a wall of fog, dense as a winter blanket, rolled in. I couldn't see the waves tumbling and tossing their crowns or people-watch the tourists strolling along the shore. My heart sank.

Though I prayed for the skies to clear, Jesus had different plans. Seated there, my eyes still closed, He offered blessings I'd have missed had I continued relying on my vision. I heard the haunting cry of seagulls, the crashing of waves. I smelled the brisk bite of salty air and felt the tickle of mist on my cheeks. Hidden from my sight, the sea remained, its magnificence undiminished by my blindness.

Sometimes challenges steamroll into my world, blinding me to life's goodness. But when I slow down and turn my focus to things unseen, I find Jesus working sublime peace into the situation. Whether He's calming my heart through loving friends or whispering His reassurances on the breeze, I sense His presence. My "fog" lifts.

I can trust tomorrow will be brighter because Jesus helps me see and hear and feel beyond my troubles and into eternity. "So we fix our eyes not on what is seen, but on what is unseen, since what is seen is temporary, but what is unseen is eternal" (2 Corinthians 4:18, NIV). —HEIDI GAUL

FAITH STEP: *Have trials clouded your vision? Take a moment to close your eyes and breathe deeply. Let Jesus reveal eternity's unseen, magnificent peace to you.*

SUNDAY, AUGUST 28

That I may open my mouth boldly, to make known the mystery of the gospel, for which I am an ambassador in bonds: that therein I may speak boldly, as I ought to speak. Ephesians 6:19–20 (KJV)

I TEACH LITERATURE AT A local university, and one of the poems my class discusses is about a young girl who measures her worth by society's standards. Instead of getting her value from internal—or eternal—sources, she lets the world's definition of beauty and what a girl should be define her existence. There's a line that has always stuck with me more than the others, which basically says that she went around apologizing all of the time.

I've tried to teach my children—and myself—not to do that. And I've noticed that it's hard, especially for my daughters. I think sometimes we get the idea that girls should be quiet and soft-spoken and seen more than they're heard. I also think that's a stereotype of a Christian. We're to be gentle and kind with our words. Our deeds are what's most important.

But as today's Scripture verse illustrates, we ought to speak *boldly*. Paul uses the word *boldly* twice in that small space to get the point across. Bold doesn't have to mean loud, but it does mean fearless. We are to open our mouths boldly—without fear—to make Jesus known. —GWEN FORD FAULKENBERRY

FAITH STEP: *Think of a specific person who makes you want to shrink back instead of being bold. What would it look like if you made the gospel of Jesus known to that person? Write a journal entry in which you plan how you can approach the subject with boldness the next time you get the chance.*

MONDAY, AUGUST 29

I love you, LORD, my strength. Psalm 18:1 (NIV)

SEVERAL YEARS AGO, I BECAME intentional about doing workouts and taking long walks for exercise. Now I've ramped up my efforts to include jogging. I'll be honest, I managed only a few seconds the first time I tried. I slowed my pace to a walk for several minutes to catch my breath, and then I tried again.

One day I read about another woman's fitness journey. She built up her jogging stamina by incorporating two things into her exercise routine. The first was a prayer: *Make me strong.* The second was changing the way she viewed her jogging route. Looking far down the road made her feel overwhelmed but looking from one landmark to the next and then the next made her efforts feel doable.

I've incorporated this woman's methods. *Jesus, make me strong,* I pray. I set my sights on a particular park bench and jog to it. Then, without stopping, I set my sights on a tree several hundred feet farther down the path and run to it. I repeat until I need to take a break. My stamina is slowly increasing.

The same method has proven effective for me when tackling challenges of a different sort. Looking at a problem in its entirety seems overwhelming, especially in my own strength. Praying for and then receiving Jesus's strength rejuvenates me. As does viewing the challenge through a different lens. Rather than focusing on it as a whole, I take one action toward resolution. Then I take another and another. Taking one step at a time in Jesus's strength always helps me through it. —GRACE FOX

FAITH STEP: *Take a short walk today if you're able. Make it a prayer walk by interceding for the people you see. Recite today's verse as you go.*

TUESDAY, AUGUST 30

Be strong and courageous. Do not be afraid; do not be discouraged, for the LORD your God will be with you wherever you go. Joshua 1:9 (NIV)

FOOTBALL IS A BIG DEAL in a small town like Ozark. Our high school mascot is the Hillbilly, my husband is the coach, and my son, Harper, is the quarterback of the team.

Last year the team lost one game in the regular season. Harper's greatest strength is running. I spent my time in the stands screaming for him to run, run, *run*—always on the edge of my seat. It felt like a miracle every game when I took him home unscathed. But in the first round of the state playoffs, Harper went down.

What first seemed to be a simple fracture turned out to be a complicated break and torn ankle ligaments that required surgery. His sister Grace gave him a journal with Joshua 1:9 on the cover. He took it with him to the hospital, and he let that verse sink in deep.

Harper said he knew Jesus was with him. "When I walked into the hospital, He was there. In the operating room, He was there. I knew—and I know—Jesus is with me. That gives me strength and courage."

Through it all, Jesus was right there. I watched my child learn what it means that Jesus is with us, no matter what. I hope Harper never has to go through anything like that again. But it was a beautiful thing to see a verse on the front of a book become his experience. And whatever happens in the future, I know Harper knows the Lord is always there. —GWEN FORD FAULKENBERRY

FAITH STEP: *Write Joshua 1:9 on a notecard. Replace the words "wherever you go," with your own circumstances.*

WEDNESDAY, AUGUST 31

Do not despise these small beginnings, for the LORD rejoices to see the work begin, to see the plumb line in Zerubbabel's hand. Zechariah 4:10 (NLT)

MY HUSBAND AND I WERE learning the importance of speaking the Word over ourselves, and Andrew suggested we pray Psalm 91 together each night, out loud. We immediately saw how it lifted the atmosphere in our home and focused our hearts on Jesus rather than the news reports. We included the kids and had them speak Psalm 91 each night also. You could hear their confidence grow each time they read it. We encouraged them to make the psalm personal, using *I* and *me* in place of *those* and *they*. After a few weeks, Andrew had a great idea for the kids to each choose one relative and read the psalm to them, and they did. Our daughter read to her uncle Jake, who was battling throat cancer and who had lost his hearing many years before as a result. To everyone's shock, after reading the psalm to her uncle a few times, he began to hear—without his hearing aid! The smile on his face was priceless, she reported. And her aunt called the whole family and told them her husband had started hearing—after hearing the Word from his young niece!

What started as a small beginning to encourage my husband and me in Jesus became a tool for growing godliness in two teenagers and seeing physical healing. It produced a celebration among many family members, shining a bright, bold light for Him in the midst of a dark time. —PAMELA TOUSSAINT HOWARD

FAITH STEP: *Take a small step of obedience toward Jesus; it could ultimately bless many.*

THURSDAY, SEPTEMBER 1

They said to him, "Lord, let our eyes be opened." Matthew 20:33 (ESV)

WHENEVER PEOPLE ASKED HOW THEY could pray for me, my requests were usually about minor issues, such as clarity about a decision or how to use my time wisely. Not that those aren't important—I believe God cares deeply about my daily desires, big or small. But I sensed Him encouraging me to start praying boldly and sharing my bold requests.

Then I read the Bible story about the two blind men in Matthew 20. Who knows how long they sat on the roadside begging for money and food to sustain them? But when they heard Jesus was near, they shouted. Some in the crowd tried to hush them, but that only made them more determined to attract Jesus's attention, so they yelled louder. Then Jesus stopped and asked them a question: "What do you want me to do for you?" (verse 32, ESV). They boldly asked for the impossible: "Lord, let our eyes be opened" (verse 33, ESV). So Jesus touched the blind men's eyes, and immediately they could see.

This story changed my prayer life. Now when I have my personal prayer time, I imagine Jesus asking me, "What do you want me to do for you?" I still have my everyday desires, but I've incorporated big bold, seemingly impossible requests too. I pray I'll see revival in our world. I pray for peace to reign on earth. I pray for those I love to have their eyes opened to see Jesus and follow Him.

Now, when friends ask what I need prayer for, along with my heartfelt personal requests, I always add one big bold prayer request too. —JEANNIE BLACKMER

FAITH STEP: *Write down your bold answer to Jesus's question, "What do you want me to do for you?"*

FRIDAY, SEPTEMBER 2

All your words are true; all your righteous laws are eternal. Psalm 119:160 *(NIV)*

MANY YEARS AGO, I CHECKED out a library book about God's grace. After all this time, I still remember turning the page to read the writer's assertion that the crucifixion was an accident and that Jesus did not need to die for our sins. I thought about how much of the Bible, including John 3:16, this author had to ignore or deny in order to make that claim.

In Matthew 16:21–28, Jesus told His disciples that He must go to Jerusalem, suffer terribly, be killed, and rise again the third day. Peter pulled Jesus aside and corrected Him, insisting that such things could not possibly happen to Him. Peter reprimanded Jesus—think about that! Jesus, the One whom Peter had watched perform miracles and raise the dead. The One who had allowed him to walk on water. Jesus responded by speaking directly to Satan, who was trying to use Peter as his instrument. Then Jesus told Peter he was thinking from his own point of view, not God's. Although Peter had just proclaimed Jesus as the Son of the living God, he couldn't understand the idea of the Messiah having to die, so he denied the possibility.

Many people want to disregard or deny parts of the Bible they don't like, even direct statements from Jesus. I need to guard my mind to make sure I read the Bible from the right point of view, not based on my human ideas and preferences. If I call Jesus my Savior, why wouldn't I trust every word that He speaks?
—DIANNE NEAL MATTHEWS

FAITH STEP: *Write down the nonnegotiable truths about Jesus that you believe. Keep the list and add supporting Scripture references whenever you come across them.*

246 | MORNINGS WITH JESUS 2022

*Flee the evil desires of youth and pursue righteousness, faith, love
and peace, along with those who call on the Lord out of a pure heart.*
2 *Timothy* 2:22 *(NIV)*

ON A RECENT SURVIVAL-TYPE TELEVISION show where contestants
are completely and utterly alone in a hostile environment, one
contestant woke to find his small shelter surrounded by wolves.
The animals came within three yards of the man. By my estimate,
that's three hundred miles too close.

I've wondered how I would react if my path crossed that of an animal that was bigger, stronger, fiercer, faster, and hungrier than me.
One of the black bears that occasionally wanders into our yard. A
bobcat that doesn't just cross the highway in front of my car but is
on my walking trail. One of the wolves that howls at night in our
wooded neighborhood. My natural instincts are to freeze or flee.

The Bible says there are times when the right thing to do is flee
(Jeremiah 48:6). Run! Run for my life.

I long ago surpassed the youth category that 2 Timothy 2:22
talks about, but I don't have any trouble remembering what youthful desires and pursuits are like. That part of my memory is well
intact. When I'm surrounded by the *wolves* of immaturity or foolish choices that would take me away from the path that Jesus calls
me to, there's really only one option. Run! "Run, [insert your name
here], run!" —CYNTHIA RUCHTI

FAITH STEP: *Keeping your secret weapon—God's Word—always handy will
ensure your mind and heart are prepared to flee the scene when evil desires or
unholy thoughts prowl.*

SUNDAY, SEPTEMBER 4

But small is the gate and narrow the road that leads to life, and only a few find it. Matthew 7:14 (NIV)

A LONG, NARROW ROAD RUNS through my town. It's a mountain railway that carries eighteen trains a day. Living in a historic railroad town is nostalgic, with the lonesome call of train whistles, clanging bells, and the high-pitched sound of steel wheels squealing on the rails. (Even as I write this, I'm enjoying the sound of train whistles calling in the distance.) I especially love gospel train songs that compare railroads to the road to heaven—songs about getting on trains bound for glory.

Narrow paths—railroad tracks in my case—have featured repeatedly in my life. As a child living next door to a track, I'd hear the train going by during the night. When I had small children of my own, we took a camping trip in the Pacific Northwest. Heavy rain forced us out of our tent into a motel in town. It wasn't until the middle of the night that we realized a train trestle was right behind that old two-story motel—making for a very loud, clattering stay. Eventually, I took my children on annual summer vacations at a small log cabin by a lake, where on the railroad track behind it, a train would rumble by early every morning.

Now my children are grown, and they sometimes ride the train to visit me here in the small town I call home. Though they can find their way here, today I'm praying that they'll all find the narrow road that leads to life through faith in Jesus Christ.
—CASSANDRA TIERSMA

FAITH STEP: *Are you praying for loved ones to find the narrow road that leads to eternal life through Christ? Ask Jesus to show them the Way.*

LABOR DAY, MONDAY, SEPTEMBER 5

. . . fixing our eyes on Jesus, the pioneer and perfecter of faith. For the joy set before him he endured the cross, scorning its shame, and sat down at the right hand of the throne of God. Hebrews 12:2 (NIV)

I GREW UP IN COLUMBIA, Maryland, a tidy, affluent suburb conceived by visionary developer James Rouse. A model of urban planning with everything carefully placed, Columbia had strictly enforced codes, too. You'd hear about lawns that hadn't been mowed.

Later, I moved to the charming arts hamlet of Berkeley Springs, West Virginia, where there was little if any zoning. Our ranch-style home was on four acres of beautiful parklike land, with lots of shrubs and trees. Doesn't that sound great? Well, it was, but I couldn't see the park because of the shrubs. For a few years, I was fixated on achieving the highly manicured landscapes of my childhood, so I pruned and waged war on weeds. This was a frustrating and futile battle for perfection, when the luxuriously natural landscape was lovely. My pursuit of perfection prevented me from fully enjoying it.

I liken this to my painful pursuit of spiritual perfection by my own hand. I've tried so hard and failed, when Jesus never expected me to be perfect in the first place. In fact, my striving prevented me from enjoying the lush freedom I have in Him! He is both the author and perfecter of my faith. —ISABELLA CAMPOLATTARO

FAITH STEP: *Is your pursuit of perfection making you miserable? Rejoice in your freedom to be in Jesus!*

TUESDAY, SEPTEMBER 6

Then, because so many people were coming and going that they did not even have a chance to eat, he said to them, "Come with me by yourselves to a quiet place and get some rest." Mark 6:31 (NIV)

THE NUMBER OF MISSIONARIES WITHIN our international nonprofit ministry is growing. That means God is doing a good work, and for that I'm excited and grateful. The gospel is spreading, more disciples are being made, and more people are practicing generosity toward God's kingdom. That's all good. But growth also means more behind-the-scenes administrative work, additional staff care, more volunteer recruitment and training, and so forth. I'm often away from home for a total of three to four months every year. When I'm on North American turf, I'm either writing or spending time with my family, all whom live far from Vancouver.

Nothing thrills me more than serving Jesus, and this ministry is what He's called me to do. I marvel at the health and strength He gives me day by day. However, I can learn much from His encouragement to administer self-care.

The disciples had just returned from a short-term mission trip (Mark 6:30–32). Jesus knew they'd poured out their lives to teach and perform miracles, and He knew they needed to refill. He invited them to a quiet place, a guilt-free retreat to rest and debrief. "So they went away by themselves in a boat to a solitary place" (verse 32, NIV).

Jesus has blessed me with the means to follow His example literally. I can sail away to a quiet cove for rest—and I do. It works! What can you do for self-care? Remember it's guilt-free and for your good. —GRACE FOX

FAITH STEP: *Schedule a day to rest your body and renew your soul.*

WEDNESDAY, SEPTEMBER 7

I can do all this through him who gives me strength. Philippians 4:13 (NIV)

I WAS A SCHOOL MENTOR for several years. Once a week, I'd have lunch with an at-risk young girl and informally talk to her about academics, friendships, and dreams. I enjoyed it and I think the girls did too. My second year, I was assigned a nine-year-old named Serenity who was anything but serene. I knew she had a very troubled family life. Serenity was unpredictably angry, often contrary, and sometimes utterly defiant. I was lost.

Serenity didn't respond to my love, humor, or my other usual ways of connecting with kids. She loved thoughtful gifts but always wanted more. She liked crafts but was downright mean when she needed help. We often played games, but she cheated and gloated about winning.

I knew intellectually these were all defenses she was using, so I knew not to take them personally, but it was hard. Several months passed. I was at the end of my rope, about to give up. I prayed for Jesus to show me the way. And that's when the miracle happened. Serenity didn't change. I did. I was able to lavish love on Serenity without wanting or needing her to be different in any way.

The difference was Jesus. I'd been trying hard in my own strength and with my own flawed human motives to be Serenity's friend. Only through Christ could I love her freely and without conditions.
—ISABELLA CAMPOLATTARO

FAITH STEP: *Are you handling something in your own strength and failing miserably? Get on your knees to exchange your helplessness for Jesus's infinite strength.*

Thursday, September 8

Indeed, the very hairs of your head are all numbered. Don't be afraid;
you are worth more than many sparrows. Luke 12:7 (NIV)

RIDING MY BIKE EARLY THAT morning, I spotted him slowly making his way across the road. I knew he might not make it. Should I stop and help him? Ugh, no. I tolerated turtles at a distance, but I sure didn't want to touch one. Besides, he carried germs for salmonella. Yet I'd seen too many turtles smashed in the road. *He's one of your creatures, Jesus.* I knew what I needed to do. I rode home as fast as I could, grabbed an old towel to pick him up, got in my car, and drove to where I last saw him.

I couldn't have been gone more than five minutes, but the turtle was nowhere in sight. I pulled the car over and searched the grass surrounding the pond where I'd planned to place him. Not a trace. Where could he have gone?

That turtle. So slow and ugly and covered with slimy seaweed. Would anyone have wanted him for a pet? I doubted it. There could be no other explanation than that Jesus saw to it that His creature made it to safety. One turtle more or less in this world might not make a difference to most people, but it did matter to Jesus.

How much more important am I to Jesus than that turtle? Lately I'd been feeling distant from Jesus, as if He wasn't concerned about me and my problems and heartaches. But if Jesus cared enough to rescue a lowly turtle, that should convince me that He cares about me. —PAT BUTLER DYSON

FAITH STEP: *Never ever doubt that Jesus cares for you.*

FRIDAY, SEPTEMBER 9

Grace be with all those who love our Lord Jesus
Christ in sincerity. Ephesians 6:24 *(NKJV)*

THE OTHER DAY ON TWITTER, I noticed someone posted, "I highly recommend loving Jesus." It struck me as interesting, probably because it was one of the few things on there that was positive, sweet, and, at least in my feed, not controversial. I kept thinking about it and agreed that I, too, could highly recommend loving Jesus.

The biggest reason is in today's Bible verse: grace. Loving Jesus means I walk around in an atmosphere of grace. I inhale grace and exhale it. I'm bathed in it, sheltered by it, fed by it, and led by it. Grace holds my hand. I pull it over me like a blanket for comfort. I put it on like clothes to meet the day. Grace is the lens through which I see people and life. It looks back at me in the mirror. Grace is there to celebrate when things go well and to pick me up off the ground when I fall. Grace bolsters me when I'm afraid. It makes me strong when I feel weak. It opens my eyes to beauty. Grace corrects me when I'm wrong. Like Paul writes elsewhere, grace is sufficient. As long as I have Jesus, I have grace, and it is never lacking.

Jesus is the embodiment of grace: the unmerited favor of God. I didn't—and don't—do anything to make Him love me. But He does. It's His life in me that empowers me to love, even showing love to people whom I think might not deserve it. There's nothing else like it, just like there is no one else like Jesus. —GWEN FORD FAULKENBERRY

FAITH STEP: *Do you highly recommend loving Jesus? Make a list of your top ten reasons why, and share it with someone in your family.*

SATURDAY, SEPTEMBER 10

"The LORD who rescued me from the paw of the lion and the paw of the bear will rescue me from the hand of this Philistine." Saul said to David, "Go, and the LORD be with you." 1 Samuel 17:37 (NIV)

I'VE COME TO REALIZE THAT it's good to regularly rehearse the triumphs Jesus has orchestrated in my life. When bigger obstacles come, remembering past victories and rescues help me overcome the new ones. Just as David thought about the lion and bear he'd already fought, when he had to face the giant problem named Goliath (1 Samuel 17:34–36).

In my life, one of the giant areas has been finances. When I decided to freelance, it was often difficult to believe Jesus would provide for me long-term. If I was hired to write a book, I hoarded the advance money due to fear that there might not be another deal anytime soon. Even one year when I had a salaried job, I lived meagerly on one paycheck a month—and banked the rest like the world was ending!

A turning point in my faith came when 9/11 devastated New York City's economy. At that time, my mom and I had a catering business that regularly serviced restaurants. In an instant, orders completely ceased. This went on for months. We didn't know how we would pay back our large business loan with no customers. The two of us knelt on our living room carpet and believed in Jesus's mercy. It came! Our loan was reduced to a fraction of what was owed. Now when I face financial challenges, the Holy Spirit reminds me of how Jesus came through for us back then, and my confidence builds that He will surely do it again. —PAMELA TOUSSAINT HOWARD

FAITH STEP: *Keep a log of Jesus's faithfulness in specific circumstances so that you can look back and be encouraged like David was.*

GRANDPARENTS' DAY, SUNDAY, SEPTEMBER 11

Do not be interested only in your own life, but be interested in the lives of others. Philippians 2:4 (NCV)

MISS SOPHIE, AN ACTIVE MEMBER of my childhood church, was deaf. Her husband didn't share her faith. She never had children of her own. But those things never stopped Miss Sophie from living a full and joyful life. Her secret? Motivated by love for Christ, she was always keenly interested in other people—everyone around her, as a matter of fact.

She loved on me during my teenage passive-aggressive years. When I brought my boyfriend to church on weekend visits from college, she'd tease us, calling us "the lovebirds." When I moved away as a young wife, she sent letters filled with expressions of love and her *Guideposts* magazine from the previous month. Whenever we went back to visit family, I always managed a visit with Miss Sophie so she could gush over my kids. This precious lady passed away just days shy of her hundredth birthday.

God created us with a need for family. Even if we didn't have a single living biological relative, we would still be surrounded by spiritual family—those who have accepted the gift of grace extended by Jesus. As a young, transplanted mom, I appreciated any interest that older members of our church showed my children. Now I'm a senior adult living away from family members, and I try to be alert to similar needs that I can fill.

During His earthly ministry, Jesus valued people at every stage of life, from babies to elderly widows. If I follow His example, I'll discover the mutual blessings that come from adding to my family by reaching across generational lines. —DIANNE NEAL MATTHEWS

FAITH STEP: *Look around and ask Jesus to show you which new "family members" He wants you to adopt.*

Monday, September 12

Because of the increase of wickedness, the love of most will grow cold, but the one who stands firm to the end will be saved. Matthew 24:12–13 (NIV)

A FRIEND RECENTLY MOVED HERE to Minnesota from Hawaii—just in time for a record cold November. I asked if her family had enough winter clothes. "We're getting there," she said. I joked about how hard it must be to endure our climate when her body is used to Hawaii. She laughed and said, "Yeah, but I'm noticing that when it's really cold, everyone feels it. Even folks who have lived in Minnesota all their lives."

She's right. No matter how many years I've lived through the cold seasons, there are days that a winter morning can still shock me with its harshness. Thankfully, I can dig out my long johns, warmest sweaters, a hat with ear flaps, and cozy boots. I have ways to keep the freezing temperature from chilling my bones.

Jesus warns about a whole different sort of coldness. As many in the world escalate their rejection of Him, I may face disdain and mockery for my faith. Even persecution. Faced with that, I may feel scared, overwhelmed, or even angry. And if I'm not mindful, such emotions can make my own heart grow cold toward those who need His love.

I wouldn't venture into a Minnesota blizzard without plenty of protection. As I daily venture out into the world, I also need the protection only Jesus can provide. As I see people through His eyes, the warmth of His love will kindle in my heart and keep it from growing cold. —SHARON HINCK

FAITH STEP: *As you grab a jacket or sweater on a cold day, ask Jesus to keep your heart warm toward Him and others.*

TUESDAY, SEPTEMBER 13

The second is this, "You shall love your neighbor as yourself." There is no other commandment greater than these. Mark 12:31 (NRSV)

WHEN I READ TODAY'S SCRIPTURE verse, it would be natural to think, *Okay, how I can do something nice for a neighbor?* (That's a good start.) In fact, my husband, Andrew, and I bless a couple of widows in our neighborhood with gifts in their mailboxes on various holidays, just to let them know they are valuable to our community. But when I *meditate* on this verse, what sticks out is the "as yourself" part. How can I go a step further and show love to people in a way that's more meaningful to them—the way I myself like to be loved? Since charity (love) begins at home, I try to show this kind of thoughtful love in simple ways. For example, not clanging pots or dishes when my husband is watching sports, leaving the last one of anything for someone else to enjoy (especially that last cookie or K-Cup!), laundering my family's favorite clothing with extra care, listening instead of talking—which includes holding my tongue when I'm tempted to criticize.

Andrew and I took this thoughtful love up a notch when we sent his stepmom a Mother's Day gift from a popular Atlanta cake shop. We chose flavors we knew she liked, packed it nicely, and mailed it express. We also added sparkly red streamers and a handwritten note. When the present arrived, she cried—she had never felt so appreciated! Her heartfelt comments were about all the specific, little touches we added to make it special *to her*—just the way Jesus loves me. —PAMELA TOUSSAINT HOWARD

FAITH STEP: *Do something extra for someone to exercise your new understanding of loving them as you love yourself.*

Wednesday, September 14

Follow God's example, therefore, as dearly loved children. Ephesians 5:1 (NIV)

The unmistakable sound of claws on metal interrupted my devotions. I stood up from the loveseat, flung my hands in the air, and whined, "Again?"

My eighteen-pound cat, Wally, stood on the back porch, gazing up at me. His emerald eyes held an angelic look. When I opened the door on a bright September day, Wally rushed to the counter where six pouches of cat treats stood. Each a different flavor.

A year before, when Wally was a kitten, I began the unwise habit of rewarding him with treats each time he was outside and returned home. Now he went outdoors at every opportunity. He knew those treats awaited him on his return.

I opened a yellow pouch and set a couple treats in front of Wally. Then I gave my other three cats the same reward. "Everybody gets treats!" I sang out. It seemed only fair to give the other "fur children" equal prizes, so they didn't feel left out. Or think Wally was my favorite.

Jesus tells a story in Matthew 20:1–16 about a landowner— representative of God—who paid all his workers equal wages, although some worked all day and others only an hour. The all-day helpers were angry at what they considered unfair treatment. But the landowner said, "Are you envious because I'm generous?" Ouch.

When I feel jealous of blessings God showers on new believers, I need to remind myself that God loves all His children with the same measure of love, no matter how long they've been His children.

It's also a comfort to think that when I spoil my kitties, I'm imitating God. —Jeanette Levellie

Faith Step: *Find a way to show generosity today. Then thank God for His huge heart.*

THURSDAY, SEPTEMBER 15

All the believers were united in heart and mind. And they felt that whut they owned was not their own, so they shared everything they had. Acts 4:32 (NLT)

TWO OF MY COUSINS LIVE in economically depressed southern Italy. Jobs are scarce and corruption is rampant, a painful contrast to the area's physical beauty and warm people. My cousin Desiree lives in a two-bedroom apartment with her husband, two teenagers, and my ailing, elderly aunt, Zia Marisa. Life is very hard, but Desiree has a sweet and sunny disposition. But after a series of recent challenges, I could hear the weariness in her voice. An ocean away, there was little I could do. Or was there?

Even though we were going through a tough time financially, my finances were flush by comparison, and I knew it was by grace. I also knew that my parents moving to America fifty years ago meant I have opportunities my cousin and her family would never have. I sent her a sizable check. The money wasn't life-changing, but the loving gesture of caring solidarity touched her deeply and had a lasting impact.

Jesus lived simply, often relying on others for basic needs. Early Christians shared everything because they thought what they had wasn't theirs (Acts 4:32–35). And so it was with me. What I did wasn't so much sharing sacrificially but simply sharing what I have by grace. How very different the world would be if I, and all of us, lived this way every day. —ISABELLA CAMPOLATTARO

FAITH STEP: *Ask Jesus whom you can bless by sharing what you have by grace.*

FRIDAY, SEPTEMBER 16

Wait on the LORD; be of good courage, and He shall strengthen your heart; wait, I say, on the LORD! Psalm 27:14 (NKJV)

BEFORE I MARRIED A FOOTBALL coach, I had no idea the game was such a science. In the early days of our marriage, when it was just us, I learned this by watching recordings with him, breaking it down play by play, and taking note of what each player did in order to strategize. Little did I know this skill would serve me well one day as the mom of a quarterback. Most of the time, though not all the time, I now have at least a clue what's going on when a certain play is called.

One of the most interesting things about football, I think, is the waiting. When both teams are on the scrimmage line, they're waiting for my son, Harper, to give the snap count. If someone can't wait and jumps offside, that person's team gets a penalty. So Harper acts sneakily sometimes and tries to make them jump by using a different cadence for the snap count. It takes intense concentration for the teams to wait for the perfect timing. Sometimes a penalty makes the difference between winning and losing the game.

Unfortunately, the culture we live in discourages waiting. Fast food, video-on-demand, overnight shipping—these are our way of life. Yet the Bible seems to suggest it's in the waiting that I reap the best. Often that's when Jesus comes to me, as He came to Anna and Simeon, and the people of Capernaum. And as He will come in clouds of glory when He returns. —GWEN FORD FAULKENBERRY

FAITH STEP: *Instead of pining for the thing you want, set your heart today to look for Jesus as you wait.*

SATURDAY, SEPTEMBER 17

Let us not neglect our meeting together, as some people do, but encourage one another, especially now that the day of his return is drawing near. Hebrews 10:25 (NLT)

DURING A WOMEN'S BIBLE STUDY on the topic of spiritual gifts, we realized there's one important spiritual work and ministry that is seldom acknowledged: the gift or ministry of showing up—of participation. We agreed that the ministry of showing up is vital and discussed how much we appreciate it when a sister in Christ gives of herself by making it a priority to show up to spend time in fellowship with the family of God. Whether it's for a worship service, Bible study group, church potluck, or prayer night.

The Greek word *koinonia*, which is used several times in the Bible, relates to the ministry of showing up. *Koinonia* refers to fellowship, participation, community, and togetherness. I may not always be in a place in my life where I can be active in church leadership, administration, teaching, evangelism, or even hospitality. But I can always at least show up to participate in fellowship, community, and togetherness with the body of Christ. I'm so grateful for the blessings that I receive when I make the effort to show up, even when I'm tired or uninspired. When I do, I always come away feeling encouraged and am glad for the time spent with other believers and Jesus.
—CASSANDRA TIERSMA

FAITH STEP: *Ask Jesus to show you how you can exercise the ministry of showing up. Where and when will you show up this week to participate in fellowship with other followers of Jesus? Is there someone you can encourage to show up too?*

SUNDAY, SEPTEMBER 18

Therefore God also has highly exalted Him and given Him the name which is above every name. Philippians 2:9 (NKJV)

DURING MY YEARS OF SINGLENESS, I served in my church and stayed in fellowship with believers, but I still often felt alone and unloved. I was mopey and sad at times, and it was sometimes hard to worship Jesus. That empty seat next to me on Sunday mornings would mock me, saying, "If you're so loved, why are you alone?" But as I meditated on this Scripture verse, I pictured the Lord smiling down on me, just as He smiled down on His beloved Son Jesus in Matthew 17:5—not because of Jesus's accomplishments as the dutiful Son but just because Jesus was His Son. I treasured that vision because I was already middle-aged and had just ended a relationship with a man at the Lord's direction, and my mom, Gloria, had gone home to be with the Lord a few months earlier.

As I mourned, I developed a habit of bursting into tears at the drop of a hat—but that's when I experienced Jesus as my "Consolation" (Luke 2:25, NKJV). During those dark times, Jesus was always available to me, telling me that He understood and reminding me that He still had great new plans for my life. Only His supernatural consolation helped me keep it together. He has shown Himself fantastically faithful.

As David said in Psalm 30:11–12 (CEV) when he envisioned the fulfillment of God's promise to build the temple: *He has turned my sorrow into joyful dancing. No longer am I sad and wearing sackcloth. I thank you from my heart, and I will never stop singing your praises..."*
—PAMELA TOUSSAINT HOWARD

FAITH STEP: *Get to know Jesus in a new way by looking up some of His biblical names.*

MONDAY, SEPTEMBER 19

Wait patiently for the LORD. Be brave and courageous. Yes, wait patiently for the LORD. Psalm 27:14 (NLT)

WAITING PATIENTLY IS NOT A strength of mine, but I'm working on it. After our last dog passed away I wanted a new dog—soon. My husband, Zane, didn't. I kept showing him adorable puppy photos and explained why we should adopt a new dog. Finally, I convinced him. But he wasn't as excited as I was, and the first few months were rough. A puppy is demanding, and Zane didn't relish the responsibility.

First Samuel 24 provides an inspiring example of a time when David waited well and didn't take matters into his own hands. David was on the run from King Saul, who was trying to kill him. At one point, David hid in a cave and had the chance to kill Saul and immediately become king, but he didn't. Instead, David waited for God's timing and became king later, which we can read about in 2 Samuel 5:3–4.

I'm thankful for our new sweet puppy, Ody, and the valuable life lesson that has shown me what happens when I rush my will rather than wait patiently for God's timing. Fortunately, I learned this from a puppy rather than a bigger decision that could have significantly derailed my life. I'm also grateful that Zane's fallen for Ody too. Most of all, I'm more aware of my tendency to succumb to impatience. In the future, I want to look back on my times of waiting and say I waited well. —JEANNIE BLACKMER

FAITH STEP: *Are you tempted to make a rash decision today? Ask Jesus to help you wait well and postpone the decision for a few days.*

TUESDAY, SEPTEMBER 20

We are God's handiwork, created in Christ Jesus to do good works, which God prepared in advance for us to do. Ephesians 2:10 (NIV)

AFTER A LONG SEASON OF various struggles, I was spending a rare quiet morning in prayer. I was interrupted by the sound of a snare drum in the park across the street. I peered out the window and saw a few high school students gathering. More cars pulled up and more drummers emerged. Soon an entire drum corps began an amazing rehearsal. And then—even better—they marched down the sidewalk and all the way around our block.

Neighbors emerged and applauded. My spirits lifted at the drummers' musical skills and impressive coordination as they twirled drumsticks and marched in step. Their strong rhythms stirred courage in my heart, as if in answer to my earlier prayers. While I waited for them to come back around, I chatted with my next-door neighbor, whom I hadn't caught up with in many weeks.

Those students lightened the load of everyone on our block. Celebrating them together brought fellowship to neighbors. A gift of art—whether music, theater, dance, ceramics, fabrics, culinary, painting—has the ability to bring change. No wonder we followers of Jesus are compared to works of art. As we serve Him, we become a vehicle for Him to lift hearts and create unity. Our daily lives can do what that drum corps did for my neighborhood.

I sometimes feel as if I'm an out-of-step drummer who keeps missing the beat. Yet I can trust that in Jesus, I am His handiwork who will unfold His good works. —SHARON HINCK

FAITH STEP: *As a reminder that you are a work of art, create something to share with a friend today in whatever art form you enjoy most.*

WEDNESDAY, SEPTEMBER 21

You will again have compassion on us; you will tread our sins underfoot and hurl all our iniquities into the depths of the sea. Micah 7:19 (NIV)

MY HUSBAND, GENE, AND I live on a boat. Just for fun, we keep a list of items that have fallen overboard. The list includes three pairs of cheap reading glasses, a baseball cap, a screwdriver, and a winch handle. The latter disappeared while our boat was tied to the dock. It slipped into the murky water and vanished, sinking to the river bottom in seconds. Thankfully, Gene was able to retrieve it, but the other things are long gone, never to be seen again.

Their fate is a good visual of what happens to our sin when Jesus forgives us. Figuratively speaking, He takes our sin and hurls it into the sea. This description blesses me big-time. You see, Scripture doesn't say He accidentally drops our sin overboard and later retrieves it. It doesn't say He tosses our sin onto the waves so the tide can eventually carry it back to shore. Neither does He plop our transgressions into an inch-deep tide pool for all to see.

Scripture teaches that Jesus forgives completely and forever when we confess our transgression. He takes our sin and hurls it—throwing it with great force—into the deep sea. Its weight drags it to the bottom. Down it goes, drifting into inky blackness. It settles in a space where no one can fetch it.

When the devil taunts me with doubts about whether Jesus has truly forgiven my sin, perhaps I ought to respond by telling the devil to go jump in the lake where he belongs. —GRACE FOX

FAITH STEP: *Fill a glass with water. Drop a small stone into it and watch it sink. Thank Jesus for hurling your transgressions into the ocean depths.*

THURSDAY, SEPTEMBER 22

Am I now trying to win the approval of human beings, or of God?
Or am I trying to please people? If I were still trying to please people,
I would not be a servant of Christ. Galatians 1:10 (NIV)

I BIT MY LIP AND clicked the attachment. My publisher had forwarded a journal review of my newest novel. A good review in a literary journal can open doors for libraries to order the book and bookstores to stock it. I squinted at the screen, scared to read the opinion of a story I'd labored over.

Then I grinned and shouted a prayer of thanks. The description of the novel was beautiful. I floated the rest of the day, buoyed by the approval of someone I didn't know. The next day I saw a post from a friend whose book had garnered a terrific review in a more prestigious journal. My joy deflated. I suddenly felt second rate.

Ashamed of myself, I asked Jesus to forgive my attitude and change my heart to one of gratitude. I celebrated with my friend's success and thanked Jesus for my own path. But the experience reminded me that chasing accolades is a never-ending and futile pursuit.

As a servant of Christ, I fly off course quickly when I focus on pleasing people or when I compare myself to others. Human measures of success rarely line up to the servant heart that Jesus has called me to emulate. What a relief to cast aside that burden of people pleasing. It can be an endless and fruitless chase. But seeking to please Jesus is a fulfilling joy. —SHARON HINCK

FAITH STEP: *Whose approval are you chasing? Lay that burden down at Jesus's feet today, and seek only to please Him.*

FRIDAY, SEPTEMBER 23

It shone with the glory of God and sparkled like a precious stone—
like jasper as clear as crystal. Revelation 21:11 (NLT)

CRYSTALS ARE A BIG DEAL in a town near my home. Crystal shops abound. As a self-avowed "rock puppy" with an appreciation for minerals and stones, I can understand the attraction. However, for some, the crystal allure is akin to a religion. These people consider crystal shops as spiritual, almost holy places. In fact, that town's slogan is "Where heaven meets earth."

A long time ago, before I was walking with Jesus, I used to be drawn to such places. Now looking back, I recognize my folly. I can still appreciate the natural appeal of quartz crystals and other rocks as God's workmanship. But I no longer view them as spiritual or magical. Because I now know the truth of Jesus, I no longer believe them to be endowed with any kind of mystical powers. What blessed relief—and how freeing—to be liberated from those old false beliefs and to be able to rest in the One who created the gems, minerals, and crystals.

Whenever I read the verse in the book of Revelation about the Holy City of Jerusalem shining and radiant like a precious stone that's as clear as crystal, I look forward to that day when we will truly see what heaven's like—when heaven really does meet earth. In the meantime, I can keep a lighthearted sense of humor about life here, where the bumper stickers say, "We're all here because we're not all there!" —CASSANDRA TIERSMA

FAITH STEP: *Has Jesus freed you from any old false beliefs? Thank Him for delivering you from that and for providing all the crystal clear guidance you need to live life for His glory.*

Saturday, September 24

Make every effort to add to your faith goodness; and to goodness, knowledge; and to knowledge, self-control; and to self-control, perseverance; and to perseverance, godliness; and to godliness, mutual affection; and to mutual affection, love. 2 Peter 1:5–7 (NIV)

I'M GLARING AT MY HAND weights. Bright orange eight-pound hand weights sit three feet away from me when I'm at my desk. Why am I glaring? They've been sitting in that same spot for months, and I am not one bit stronger than I was when I bought them.

It's too late now to get my money back. And they do make great paperweights. But my wrists are still weak from daily keyboard tasks, and my biceps are nothing to brag about. My forearm muscles aren't straining to be noticed through the skin covering them. And my posture hasn't improved a bit from their presence in my office.

Too often I apply the same rationale to growing in strength and courage in my walk (or my *sit*) with Jesus. There He is. Right there. Not even an inch away from me. But my anti-fear muscles are still flabby. My courage needs the boost He can give. What He teaches me can change my endurance. But nothing will change if I'm not spiritually exercising with Him.

"Let's take your patience out for a walk," He might say.

But I'll reply, "Not today, Jesus. Full calendar."

I grow my faith, patience, love, fearlessness, stamina, and strength through exercise. Faith, patience, love and such are nice theories, but Jesus intends they be put to use. It's the only way I'll see improvement in my spiritual muscles. —CYNTHIA RUCHTI

FAITH STEP: *As an athlete or wellness coach might look at strengthening physical muscles, consider the challenges that stretch your spiritual muscles—and even the sweat and straining, which are evidence that you're growing in that area.*

SUNDAY, SEPTEMBER 25

God shows his love for us in that while we were still sinners,
Christ died for us. Romans 5:8 (ESV)

THIS MORNING, A PHONE CALL informed me that I owed a debt—a debt I didn't know I had! I needed to get the necessary information so I could pay my debt. But before I could find out more, a ringing telephone jarred me from a deep sleep. I realized then that I'd been dreaming. But once awake, that distressful phone call in my dream still haunted me... *A debt I didn't know I had?! How could that be? What could that mean?*

While pondering that, Jesus revealed to me what my dream meant, reminding me that, when He died on the cross for my sins, His death paid the debt for my sins—a debt I didn't even know I had.

Before accepting Jesus as my Lord and Savior, I was oblivious to the fact that my sin separated me from Him and that the cost of my sin was death. I know I'm responsible for paying my own debts in this world. But there's one debt—a debt I didn't know I had—which I never could've paid. I'm relieved this morning's phone call was just a dream and that I don't actually have an unknown outstanding debt in the physical world. But I'm overjoyed that Jesus paid the price for my sins—a debt I didn't know I had. —CASSANDRA TIERSMA

FAITH STEP: *Do you have a bill that needs to be paid? If you're able to, make that payment today. Thank Jesus for paying the debt, which only He could pay, by dying for us while we were still sinners.*

Monday, September 26

Let thy mercy, O Lord, be upon us, according as we hope in thee.
Psalm 33:22 (KJV)

My brother is the superintendent of schools for our little country district, and he deals with situations that seem impossible but must be dealt with anyway. Whatever the situation, he's the one ultimately responsible for our kids.

I've seen him with dark circles under his eyes more than once. When he comes home from the office, he stays up late poring over data and planning. And then he has to make the call.

Some situations do have a rational solution. But sometimes leadership takes you deep into shades of gray. After all, if big problems were easy to solve, they usually seem that big to start with. But a wise person does her homework, exhausts all resources, tries her best, and makes a decision. Then she throws herself on the mercy of God.

Trusting Jesus is not a cop-out. It's an act of will that takes tenacity and strength. Hope is not a passive thing but an active choice. Colossians 1:27 says, "This mystery . . . is Christ in you, the hope of glory" (KJV). Jesus in me means I can trust that I'll see God manifest His glory—His power, majesty, wisdom, beauty, and amazing love—in my life. Sometimes through me and sometimes despite me. I work hard, as unto Him, and then throw myself onto His mercy. I trust and wait because Jesus is my hope. —Gwen Ford Faulkenberry

Faith Step: *If there's a problem you are laboring over, do your best to solve it. When you know you've done what you can do, throw yourself upon His mercy. Make yourself stay there waiting and hoping. The glory will come.*

TUESDAY, SEPTEMBER 27

But he said to me, "My grace is sufficient for you, for my power is made perfect in weakness." 2 Corinthians 12:9 (NIV)

LAST YEAR, MY FRIEND ANGIE was diagnosed with a fast-growing breast cancer. Practically overnight, she was undergoing very aggressive chemo, fighting for her life. This was especially troubling because she was just forty-four years old and had a twelve-year-old—my son Pierce's good buddy—at home. Up until her illness, we'd just been casual friends, moms who made small talk at baseball games. That changed.

I stepped up to organize meals, and Angie, knowing I was a passionate Christian, started reaching out to me more and more. We're like-minded: analytical, practical—thinkers with a philosophical bent. Suddenly, Angie and I are connecting on a very deep level, and truth be told, she's helped me every bit as much as I've helped her, if not more so.

While wondering if she will live or die, Angie has simple faith. Yes, she does a lot of Bible reading, and we have had some very intense conversations, but ultimately, she finds the simple peace that surpasses understanding in Christ Jesus (Philippians 4:7).

Angie's experience reminds me of my own journey. I've encountered Jesus's sufficiency most deeply during the most crushing crises—when I was weakest. Jesus and His grace are all we need.
—ISABELLA CAMPOLATTARO

FAITH STEP: *Are you facing a challenge that is (or seems) life and death? Ask Jesus to help you experience His utter sufficiency and peace.*

WEDNESDAY, SEPTEMBER 28

Whatever I tell you in the dark, speak in the light; and what you hear in the ear, preach on the housetops. Matthew 10:27 *(NKJV)*

I USED TO BE AFRAID of the dark. When I was a girl in my parents' house, I loved it when I went to bed and they were still up. I could hear the soft, muffled sound of the TV, and light from where my mom was grading papers would drift down the hall, lending just the right amount of luminescence to my room.

I also used to be afraid of dark times in life. If I'm honest, I still am. But I have learned there are treasures to be discovered in the dark that aren't visible in the light. Like stars. And sounds. In the dark, we have to rely a lot more on our other senses, such as hearing, and we listen better than we would otherwise. That's probably why I seem to hear Jesus's voice the best in the darkest times of my life.

When He speaks words of wisdom or comfort or whatever I need, it feels as if it is just for me. But the beautiful thing about Jesus's voice is that it reverberates. He gives me these treasures—and they are just for me in the dark moment. But later, when I come into the light, I can share them with others who need to hear, who may be dealing with their own darkness. This is a part of the hope I have— that it all works together for good—and that gives me courage. Even in the dark. —GWEN FORD FAULKENBERRY

FAITH STEP: *After sunset, go outside. Take a loved one with you if you can, and lie down on a quilt. Look up at the stars and thank Jesus for being the light that shines in darkness.*

THURSDAY, SEPTEMBER 29

Two are better than one, because they have a good return for their labor:
if either of them falls down, one can help the other up. But pity anyone who
falls and has no one to help them up. Ecclesiastes 4:9–10 (NIV)

I'D NEVER FELT SO ALONE. My husband, Jeff, was away in Dallas and floodwaters from a tropical storm were encroaching on our house. The power had gone out, and darkness engulfed me. When I wandered outside to see how much the water had risen, I spotted a shadowy figure walking under an umbrella. "Pat, is that you?" yelled my neighbor Virginia, who was newly widowed and alone. We hollered back and forth a few times and then promised we'd call and check on each other. Virginia hadn't lived across from us for long, and I didn't know her well, but here we were—just the two of us.

Fear gripped me as I contemplated what I would do if the water came in the house. We'd come close with past hurricanes, and other houses in our neighborhood had flooded, but blessedly we'd been spared thus far. *Jesus, give Virginia and me strength and courage to face this challenge.* While praying and agonizing and watching the weather over the next twelve hours, Virginia and I were constantly in touch by phone. It gave both of us great comfort to know that one other human being was nearby and doing all right.

Finally, the rain let up, and the floodwaters stopped just short of my front door. Virginia, too, was spared. The two of us had withstood the storm, relying on Jesus and on each other—the *three* of us—standing firm against the peril. —PAT BUTLER DYSON

FAITH STEP: *Remember you are never alone because Jesus is always with you.*

FRIDAY, SEPTEMBER 30

But Jesus, knowing their thoughts, said, "Why do you think evil in your hearts?" Matthew 9:4 (NKJV)

THE OTHER DAY I WAS wrestling with a hard issue. I felt embarrassed for not being stronger, for not handling it well, for not knowing one hundred percent what to do. I turned the problem over and over in my mind like a gemstone under a light, trying to see it from every angle and identify the flaws. I suspected where things had gone wrong, but I couldn't see how to fix it. And for some reason I didn't want to pray. It was like when your friend asks if you want to talk about something and you don't. You'd rather do anything else. Yet I knew I couldn't figure out the matter on my own.

Today's verse from Matthew came across my radar, and instead of the emphasis being on Jesus's words, as it usually is, what resonated most was the first part: "Jesus, knowing their thoughts." I remembered I was not alone in my head even though I hadn't prayed, and I realized that just because I don't engage the Lord doesn't mean He hasn't engaged with me. He knows my thoughts. So, I might as well not try to hide them or edit them.

It's funny how I was helped by this. Instead of feeling caught, I felt comforted. It was as if Jesus said to me, *It's okay. I am with you, even here. You are not alone.* I still haven't solved the problem, but I have confidence the answer will come. I probably need to talk to Jesus about it some more, and then I need to listen.
—GWEN FORD FAULKENBERRY

FAITH STEP: *If there's something you need to get out of your head, write a letter telling Jesus all about it. Then listen for His still small voice.*

SATURDAY, OCTOBER 1

You are the salt of the earth. But if the salt loses its saltiness, how can it be made salty again? It is no longer good for anything, except to be thrown out and trampled underfoot. Matthew 5:13 (NIV)

IN AN EFFORT TO STAY healthy, I have started eating salads at lunch. I am incorporating all the colors of the rainbow: green spinach, cucumbers, and peas; purple beets and onions; red tomatoes; orange sweet potatoes. I am getting hungry just thinking about it. But the thing is, even with all of those delicious veggies, something is missing. It needs that little extra something to push it over the top—salt. If there isn't that hint of salt, the veggies taste bland. There is nothing worse than going to the trouble of preparing a delicious meal and then having it fall flat. That small sprinkle of goodness brings out the fullness of the flavors.

Jesus says that I'm the salt of the earth. My life is supposed to bring out the fullness of His purpose in this world. My presence should always yield a hearty helping of mercy and grace. My words should offer a taste of encouragement, bringing hope and light to every conversation. My actions should be anchored in a sense of gratitude and joy, allowing others around me to see the goodness of Jesus at work. Being salt in this world is no small thing. Sometimes it's daunting to think that only I can bring that saltiness to the people and situations in my life. But in the Spirit of Jesus, I want to be as salty as I can. —SUSANNA FOTH AUGHTMON

FAITH STEP: *Your life reflects the life of Jesus to those around you. Sprinkle your conversations with the sense of His hope, love, and encouragement today.*

Sunday, October 2

The eyes of the Lord are on those who fear him, on those whose hope is in his unfailing love. Psalm 33:18 (NIV)

In Mark 12:41–44, Jesus watched people drop money into the temple's collection box. With so many rich people putting in large amounts, many bystanders would have failed to notice the poor, elderly widow who quietly slipped in two copper coins. But Jesus saw her, and He knew her heart. He told His disciples that her gift was worth more than the bigger offerings because she gave all she had to live on.

When Jesus walked on the earth, He noticed the poor, the elderly, the lepers, the grieving, the demon possessed. He hasn't changed. He doesn't only pay attention to famous singers, speakers, television preachers, or church leaders. He also sees the young mom struggling to meet the demands of a growing family, the lonely resident in a nursing home, the troubled adult who wants to turn his life around but doesn't know how. For each one of us, Jesus wants to be our Savior, our source of comfort, strength, wisdom, and joy. Whatever we truly need, Jesus wants to provide it.

When Jesus looks at me, He sees *into* me. He knows my heart better than I do. He understands the hurts and longings I've never spoken aloud. The fears and temptations I struggle with daily. Regardless of how insignificant I may sometimes feel, Jesus sees me, loves me, and values me. And He wants me to keep my eyes on Him so I can learn to see into His heart too. —Dianne Neal Matthews

Faith Step: *As you go about your normal activities today, stop occasionally to picture Jesus watching you with eyes filled with love. Don't forget to smile back at Him.*

MONDAY, OCTOBER 3

*He is sitting in the place of honor at God's right hand,
pleading for us. Romans 8:34 (NLT)*

WHEN MY FRIEND JACKIE BREATHED her last of almost ninety years' worth of breaths, I lost a prayer partner like no other. I mourned not having my friend with me after forty years of friendship, serving in ministry side by side, sharing Jesus through the everyday and the exceptional. But I also mourned the loss of her prayers for me.

Beyond a friend's traditional prayers for family concerns, health, and financial needs, Jackie devoted herself to pray for my writing and book launches and travels for speaking.

Days ahead of time, she'd sit with her Bible and collection of favorite quotes to create specially tailored encouragement regarding whatever I faced. Before I loaded up the car or packed my luggage for a flight, she'd call to share that biblical encouragement. We'd pray together, her words a sweet blessing over me. She'd want to know the exact time I'd be speaking and in what time zone, so she could figuratively, if not literally, be on her knees for me at that moment. Her faithfulness mirrored the unfailing faithfulness of Jesus.

When she moved from earth to glory, I instantly felt the loss of her encouragement.

But Jesus did not ignore my need. He never ignores needs. A stranger picked up the baton. For reasons only Jesus knows, a woman I'd just met at a conference devoted herself to stand in the gap. Every week without fail, she emails me a special encouragement from God's Word and prays for me. She doesn't need to know specifics. Jesus does. And He gives good gifts of encouragement. —CYNTHIA RUCHTI

FAITH STEP: *Consider carefully who might need the encouragement of your words or prayers today.*

TUESDAY, OCTOBER 4

In the same way, even though we are many individuals, Christ makes us one body and individuals who are connected to each other. Romans 12:5 (GW)

I WAS STARTLED TO OVERHEAR a disgruntled volunteer in the church snap, saying, "I'm not just a warm body!" The remark surprised me, as I thought to myself, *What's wrong with being a warm body? I'm a warm body. We're all "just warm bodies" doing various acts of volunteer service as unto the Lord.*

Though I said nothing, that heated comment stayed with me. It caused me to reflect on all the warm bodies in our congregation who serve without thought of accolades or recognition. Warm bodies who pray, encourage, prepare lessons, teach classes, arrange and rehearse music, make coffee, wash dishes, change diapers, buy toilet paper and tissue and paper cups, clean the church, weed the flower bed, paint the walls, make repairs, print the bulletins, attend planning meetings, visit shut-ins, make phone calls for the prayer chain, arrange flowers, launder tablecloths, prepare food, decorate the church, take out the trash...the list goes on and on.

We're all so grateful for each other and the countless acts of service performed by one another in our church family. Each one is doing his or her part to serve the Lord and the church body. It's my prayer that I never make anyone feel like just a warm body but always remember to express my gratitude for each person's contributions to the upkeep and service of our church. —CASSANDRA TIERSMA

FAITH STEP: *Are you a warm body serving in your congregation? If not, ask Jesus how He would like you to be connecting with the body of Christ. Thank Him for making us to be one body of individuals connected to one another.*

WEDNESDAY, OCTOBER 5

*God demonstrates his own love for us in this: While we were
still sinners, Christ died for us.* Romans 5:8 *(NIV)*

I STARTED A NEW JOB recently, one that I had prayed for while waiting
for several years. A successful interview, as well as my education,
previous work experience, and references all helped me snag the
position, but I still felt I needed to prove my worth after I arrived at
the office. I also knew that I would be evaluated by my supervisor
every thirty days for the first three months of my employment. So,
I made sure that I arrived on time, met deadlines, turned in quality
work, and presented myself as a pleasant and reliable colleague. I
didn't want anyone to regret the decision to hire me.

What a relief that I don't have to prove myself to Jesus! He knows
all my sins and shortcomings, yet He still loves me. That's pretty
amazing. The Lord sacrificed His life for me—and all sinners—
despite my unworthiness. It's a good thing that I don't have to stand
before Him every thirty days to see if He'll keep me around or boot
me off the island. It's only by His grace that I am saved.

I am so thankful that Jesus loves me and is always with me
(Matthew 28:20). And because I believe in Him, there's nothing
I can do that will make Him fire me. As I do work for my boss, I
also want to offer Jesus my best and hear Him say, "Job well done."
—BARBRANDA LUMPKINS WALLS

FAITH STEP: *Pause today to think about what it means to be saved from sin.
How will you give thanks to Jesus for accepting you as you are?*

THURSDAY, OCTOBER 6

The thief comes only to steal and kill and destroy. I came that they may have life and have it abundantly. John 10:10 (ESV)

MY HUSBAND, ZANE, AND I are opposites in many ways. He's competitive and I'm not. I obsessively clean and he doesn't mind clutter. I'm a planner and he's spontaneous. Unfortunately, we've fallen into a trap of arguing with each other about ridiculous little things, such as which drawer to use to store the toothpaste. During our engagement, our premarital counselor warned us of the detrimental pattern of silly arguments. He told us to remember that we're on the same team and we're not each other's enemies. Although our personalities are so different, I never thought we'd become a couple who argued all the time.

I asked my group of close friends to pray for us. Turns out, they too sometime struggled with senseless arguments in their marriages. Then, one of the girls showed us a video of two gazelles with antlers locked and fighting. In the background, a lion was sprinting toward them. The two gazelles were so engrossed in their conflict that they didn't see their enemy coming. Then the lion pounced and killed one of the gazelles. What a powerful image of how Satan, the thief, comes to steal, kill, and destroy. When I argue with Zane, one or both of us can be hurt and our relationship damaged. Jesus said He came to give us abundant life. Arguing with my loved ones is not living life abundantly. So I'm trying—not always successfully—to avoid silly arguments and experience the abundant life and relationships Jesus came to give us. And to remember who my true enemy is. —JEANNIE BLACKMER

FAITH STEP: *Post an image of a lion somewhere as a reminder that those you love are not your enemies and that Jesus came to give you abundant life.*

FRIDAY, OCTOBER 7

I pray that Christ may live in your hearts by faith. I pray that you will be filled with love. I pray that you will be able to understand how wide and how long and how high and how deep His love is. Ephesians 3:17–18 (NLV)

MINNIE WAS A COWORKER IN a jobs program for disadvantaged youth. Minnie was hilarious, many times without even trying to be. Everyone in the office adored Minnie.

One day Minnie came to work looking glum. When I asked her what was wrong, she said, "I feel so unnecessary." The way she rolled her eyes when she said it made me laugh. *So Minnie!* But when I thought about her statement, it was anything but funny.

In our frantic, impersonal world today, how many of us feel unloved, unwanted, or unimportant? I know I've felt that way. I need to reassure myself that Jesus's love is constant and unwavering. Whether I deem myself good, bad, or somewhere in between, Jesus loves me just the same. His love is eternal and perfect, no matter the circumstances.

I've been guilty of looking at myself through another person's eyes and frequently falling short. Seeking approval from others is a losing proposition. My value comes from Jesus, who thought highly enough of me to die for me.

I went over to Minnie, gave her a big hug, and told her, "Oh, Minnie, you're *totally* necessary to me and to everyone in this office." She gave me a smile, then went to her desk and got to work. We all need to be reminded that we are valuable, especially to Jesus.
—PAT BUTLER DYSON

FAITH STEP: *Make a list of things that make you valuable to Jesus.*

SATURDAY, OCTOBER 8

Neither death nor life, nor angels nor principalities nor powers, nor things present nor things to come, nor height nor depth, nor any other created thing, shall be able to separate us from the love of God which is in Christ Jesus our Lord. Romans 8:38–39 (NKJV)

A FEW DAYS AGO, THE darkness seemed suffocating as I laid blurry-eyed and sleepless. I felt as if I was choking on grief. Surely, all believers have been there—crying out in agony to the God of the universe, demanding some kind of explanation, desperate for that peace that surpasses all understanding, though it seems to have passed by us.

But isn't it arrogant to believe I am somehow out of Jesus's reach? I was reminded of this when I am cuddled up with my family watching one of our all-time favorites, *Anne of Green Gables*. Anne tells Marilla that she is in the depths of despair, asking for sympathy, only to be hushed by Marilla's stern reply: "I have never been in the depths of despair. To despair is to turn one's back on God."

In that same way, when I weep, I must remember that I am not alone. Jesus is there crying with me, holding me together when everything falls apart, bottling up my tears (Psalm 56:8; Psalm 147:3). There is nothing stronger than our Savior and His love for me. And at the end of the day, that's really all I have to hold onto, a truth that cannot be shaken or taken away. —GWEN FORD FAULKENBERRY

FAITH STEP: *In prayer, give Jesus everything, and rest in the peace of knowing He has good plans for you, plans to make all things beautiful in His time. Reflect on all the goodness and mercy you have received, and give thanks.*

SUNDAY, OCTOBER 9

Because the gatekeeper knows who he is, he opens the gate to let him in. And the sheep recognize the voice of the true Shepherd, for he calls his own by name and leads them out, for they belong to him. John 10:3 *(TPT)*

MY HUSBAND, KEVIN, IS NOT only a pastor but also a composer. He began writing songs while attending college and has now composed over two thousand.

When Kev wrote his first hundred songs during the eighties, every reference to Jesus was "He" or "The Man" and included titles like "Surely He Is Lord" and "Behold the Man." But as Kevin grew to know Jesus better, his lyrics cast Jesus not as an unknowable creator, but as a lovable, personal shepherd.

Driving to work last week, I sang "Hallelujah! Jesus Is King"—a snappy tune Kev wrote for Vacation Bible School. I could almost feel Jesus's smile and hug as I serenaded Him. Then it hit me: *Jesus craves our fellowship more than we long for His.* That thought led to a fresh perspective on how I relate to Him.

If Jesus corrects my stinky attitude by squeezing my heart with conviction, His goal is to let more of His love flow through me. If He leads me to do something I'd rather not do, I know He's setting me up for a huge blessing. And if He whispers, "I'm proud of you, honey," I don't reject His applause.

Not only have I grown to know Jesus by name. He knows my name too. Jesus's voice calls me to a life brimming with sweetness.

—JEANETTE LEVELLIE

FAITH STEP: *Envision Jesus walking into the room where you are right now. What secret would you like to tell Him? How will He respond to you?*

NATIONAL MENTAL HEALTH DAY, MONDAY, OCTOBER 10

About three in the afternoon Jesus cried out in a loud voice, "Eli, Eli, lema sabachthani?" (which means "My God, my God, why have you forsaken me?"). Matthew 27:46 (NIV)

A WOMAN I'VE KNOWN FOR years struggles with mental health issues. This complicates our relationship. I've weathered numerous bouts of her hurtful accusations and behaviors. Recently she said I didn't care about her and returned the unopened birthday card I'd mailed, telling me she wanted no further contact.

It's so complicated. My efforts to show support and my attempts to be her friend have failed. Some days I feel so sad for her, for us. I understand that her mental health issues are largely responsible for her behavior, but it still hurts to be mistreated by someone you love.

Jesus knows all about it. He handpicked twelve men to train as ministry leaders. He invested time and energy in them. He poured wisdom into them. He put up with their foibles and immaturity. On the night before His arrest, He took them to the Mount of Olives and told them to pray. Then He stepped a stone's throw away and knelt down to do the same. When He returned, He found them asleep.

It must have hurt deeply to not have His friends' support when He needed it most (Luke 22:39–46), when Peter denied Him three times (Luke 22:54–62), and when Judas betrayed Him (Matthew 26:15). But the greatest pain must have come as He hung on the cross and His Father turned away from Him (Matthew 27:46).

Being mistreated by a loved one hurts the heart, and there are no easy answers. But Jesus knows all about it, and He feels our pain.
—GRACE FOX

FAITH STEP: *Draw a heart. Write "it hurts" on it. Thank Jesus for understanding your pain.*

TUESDAY, OCTOBER 11

I will never leave you; I will never abandon you. Hebrews 13:5 (NCV)

I CRINGE WHENEVER SOMEONE REMINISCES about being accidentally left behind at a restaurant or gas station on a childhood trip. Sure, they laugh about it now, but until recently I had no idea how it must have felt. I never dreamed it would happen to me, especially in my sixties.

During a visit from our son Kevin, I loaded the car with water and snacks for a day trip and climbed in the back seat. My husband, Richard, was moving his truck out of the way, and Kevin was still in the house, so I went back inside to grab a book. I returned to find the car gone and the garage door shut. *I'd better call before they get too far!* I thought. Then I remembered that my cell phone was in the car. Since we don't have a landline, there was nothing I could do but wait. Later, I learned that they'd left the subdivision before Kevin smiled and asked, "Dad, did you forget something?"

People are not infallible. We make mistakes and let each other down. Even those who love us may sometimes forget about us or ignore our needs. But the One who loves us the most will never do that. Jesus knows exactly where we are at any given moment. He also knows what we're going through. Jesus is right there with us, seeing us through trials and circumstances in ways that even well-intentioned loved ones can't.

Being left at my own home wasn't scary, but it *was* disappointing. What a wonderful feeling to know that I have Someone who never forgets me. —DIANNE NEAL MATTHEWS

FAITH STEP: *When you feel abandoned, forgotten, ignored, or left out, recite Hebrews 13:5 as a reminder during those times.*

WEDNESDAY, OCTOBER 12

Finally, be strong in the Lord and in his mighty power. Ephesians 6:10 (NIV)

HIGHER ON A LADDER THAN was comfortable, I shouldered one end of a support beam while my husband, nine feet away, shouldered the other end. We worked and sweated to hoist the beam into place overhead. No big deal. It was only going to hold up the entire second story of our house. What could go wrong?

Our first attempt failed. The beam was just a smidge too long for the opening we'd created when we removed a wall separating the kitchen and dining room. We climbed down from our perches, balancing the beam by sheer determination.

A saw stroke or two later, we climbed up again. My end of the beam slid into place. I held it snug, grunting, groaning, and pretending I had enough strength while my husband maneuvered what he called the heavy end.

"Can you hold it while I secure it with screws?" he asked.

Did I have any other choice?

Project completed, we marveled that the two of us had accomplished what we probably should have hired a professional to do. The key was to focus on believing I had more strength than I assumed. I acted as if the strength I needed was already mine.

I imagined what would happen if I applied that to all challenges in life: resisting temptation, staying strong through trials that seem never-ending, holding my tongue when my nature wants to lash out, obeying what Jesus asks of me even when it feels beyond my ability. What if I acted as if the power Jesus promised was already mine? —CYNTHIA RUCHTI

FAITH STEP: *What are you facing today that seems too high, too hard, or too long? Hold steady and lean on the truth that you are strong in Him.*

THURSDAY, OCTOBER 13

People can make all kinds of plans, but only the LORD's plan will happen. Proverbs 19:21 (NCV)

SOME MINISTRIES ARE ACCIDENTAL. WHENEVER I run into anyone from my old church, the comment is always the same: "We miss your laugh!" I never planned to have a "ministry of laughter." It was an accident. I love humor and a good joke. I did wonder what people thought when I was the only one laughing out loud when the pastor told a funny joke. But, as more and more people thanked me for my laughter, I became comfortable with my accidental ministry of laughter.

After relocating to another state, I'd planned to start a worship dance ministry. (Dance was my background, and I'd trained for leading worship dance ministry.) But the Lord had other plans. The Holy Spirit put a comedic monologue on my heart, addressing a touchy subject within our church in a humorous way. I wrote it out, read it over the phone to the pastor, then performed the comedy sketch for both services. The tongue-in-cheek skit brought to light the unspoken arguments and grievances in everyone's hearts and minds regarding a decision on which the church would vote the next day. Getting it all out in the open through comedy had a healing effect within the congregation that had become divided over this controversial issue.

More comedy followed, including a one-act play for a women's retreat, a monologue called "Little Red Riding in the Hood" for a recovery ministry, and an annotated, musical rendition of Proverbs 31. A worship dance ministry would've been pleasing to me. But instead, Jesus gave me a ministry of laughter that's pleasing to Him.
—CASSANDRA TIERSMA

FAITH STEP: *Listen to a Christian comedian online. Thank Jesus for the gift of laughter.*

FRIDAY, OCTOBER 14

For God is a God not of disorder but of peace. 1 Corinthians 14:33 *(NRSV)*

WHEN I PRAYED ABOUT MY "word of the year" last fall, Jesus's voice in my heart was unmistakable: *Simplify.*

I wasn't upset by the prospect of decluttering. For years I'd wanted to make my environment—and my life—less complicated. But then the Lord shocked me with His next idea: *Start with the cards on your closet doors.*

Over the last twenty years, I'd taped and tacked my favorite thank-you cards onto the closet doors in our bedroom. One, which had two bunnies in a smiling embrace, was from my husband, Kevin. One, which had colorful balloons, was from my daughter after her baby shower. And another precious one was from a student I'd given a Bible to.

Oh, Lord, I whined, *These cards remind me to keep a thankful heart. As I pace around the bedroom when I pray every morning, they help me remember how good You are.* There was no answer from above. And I couldn't shake the conviction that Jesus wanted me to start my year with bare closet doors. Sigh.

Slowly, in shifts, I obeyed. Over the course of a week, I lovingly pulled each card down, tucking them into a bedside drawer dedicated to keepsakes. I comforted myself with the thought that I wasn't throwing them away. But the bedroom seemed so stark and empty.

The next morning as I prayed, my focus and concentration were sharp. *Wow, Lord. I realize now what a distraction all those cards had become. No wonder You wanted them gone.* I thanked my loving Shepherd that, as always, He knew best how to help me love Him.
—JEANETTE LEVELLIE

FAITH STEP: *Ask Jesus if there are any distractions in your life that keep you from focusing on Him.*

SATURDAY, OCTOBER 15

She was deeply distressed and prayed to the LORD and wept
bitterly. 1 Samuel 1:10 (ESV)

RECENTLY, I WATCHED *THE CROWN,* a Netflix drama about the life of Queen Elizabeth. She's portrayed as a woman who suppresses her emotions, especially as she ages. I watched uncomfortably as I saw myself in her and wondered if this was due to my English heritage and my upbringing in a family who rarely expressed their emotions openly.

Because God made us emotional beings, I decided to do some research. Some articles suggested that suppressing emotions can cause increased blood pressure, negativity, and impaired memory. So it's important to express our emotions. But it's interesting to note that emotions are freely expressed throughout Scripture. Hannah prayed to the Lord and wept bitterly in front of Eli, the priest, because she had no children. Hannah was so overcome with sadness that Eli thought she was drunk. David got angry, danced with joy, felt lonely and jealous, and expressed a multitude of emotions in his psalms. Jesus wept, overturned tables with righteous anger, and pleaded with God to take His cup of suffering away.

I have work to do to comfortably express my emotions, but on this journey of self-discovery, I've received one gift: realizing I can take all my feelings to Jesus. He understands. He is not repelled. He can handle whatever I bring to Him. I believe He welcomes my emotions, and as Paul writes to the Philippians, He will meet *all* my needs, even my emotional needs, according to His glorious riches (Philippians 4:19). He's given us emotions, and thankfully we can freely express them to Him. —JEANNIE BLACKMER

FAITH STEP: *What emotions are you experiencing today? Journal about them until you sense Jesus's presence in the emotions with you.*

SUNDAY, OCTOBER 16

Even the darkness is not dark to you; the night is bright as the day,
for darkness is as light with you. Psalm 139:12 (ESV)

MY DAUGHTER GRACE IS STRONG, beautiful, brilliant, and kind. This year, she started college with a full scholarship and hopes to finish her undergraduate and law degrees in five years. She also started having night terrors. Her university allows her to live at home, but still she found little rest.

We tried melatonin, sleepy teas, and reading before bed, but there were many tearful nights. Sometimes, there is no logic behind anxiety—it just is. So the amount of soothing I gave or telling her all the reasons she was safe didn't matter. My baby couldn't sleep. Eventually some combination of snuggles from our Boston terriers and her younger sisters eased her into slumber. But of course, life happens, and sometimes the sisters were smooshed or the dogs were dirty, and she needed to be able to sleep alone. Somehow, she did.

I asked what changed, and she told me that after staring at her walls for hours, hearing every little creak of our wooden floors and every creature stirring in the woods around our house, she flipped her Bible open to the book of Psalms. Little tears of joy rolled down her sweet face as she showed me her "love letter from Jesus" that she had read over and over until she drifted off: "Even the darkness is not dark to [Me]; the night is bright as the day, for darkness is as light with [Me]." —GWEN FORD FAULKENBERRY

FAITH STEP: *Read these verses and know how very much Jesus loves you. Deuteronomy 31:6; Psalm 23; Psalm 139:1–18; and Romans 8:31–39; Philippians 4:6–7. Let your heart find rest and healing in His everlasting arms.*

MONDAY, OCTOBER 17

Submit yourselves, then, to God. Resist the devil,
and he will flee from you. James 4:7 (NIV)

TWO-YEAR-OLD LUKE STUDIED THE OPEN Styrofoam container sitting before him at a fast-food restaurant. One half had held chicken nuggets, which he'd promptly devoured. The other half held a few straggling fries.

Luke looked from one side to the other. Then, in an effort to close the container, he raised the half with the fries. As he inched it higher, he realized the fries would fall. He stopped, shook his head, returned that half to its original position on the table and said, "Don't do dat." He then raised the empty half, closed it on the fries, and grinned. Victory.

From the mouth of a child, right? Luke's simple but profound wisdom comes to mind when temptation strikes. His three words help me resist the devil. When the evil one suggests that I participate in a juicy conversation or embellish stories about my latest adventure or procrastinate on a task to which I'd committed, I think, *Don't do dat.* There's no point in arguing or reasoning with the devil. The less engagement I allow, the more likely I'm able to resist him.

Jesus resisted the devil too. He did so by quoting the Word. Then He told Satan to go away because God alone deserved worship. The devil departed, and angels came to minister to Jesus (Matthew 4:1–11).

The enemy is bent on my destruction, but I don't need to let him intimidate me. As a believer, I have the authority to say no to him. He can't stand against the power of God at work in me.
—GRACE FOX

FAITH STEP: *Write "Don't do that" on paper and post it in the room where temptation strikes most often.*

TUESDAY, OCTOBER 18

Whoever wants to be great among you must be your servant. And whoever wants to be greatest of all must be the slave of all. For even I, the Messiah, am not here to be served, but to help others, and to give my life as a ransom for many. Mark 10:43–45 (TLB)

WHILE VISITING A ZOO, I passed a grandmother standing with her preteen granddaughter. She called the girl by name and said emphatically, "You are the greatest person in the world." Her words startled me. Later, they made me more determined than ever to help foster a healthy, Christ-centered self-esteem in my own grand-children. I grab every opportunity to praise them and make them feel special and dearly loved, because they are. But I also want to help them grow up to be sensitive to the needs of others. I want them to be like Jesus.

Human nature tends toward self-centeredness. Even after walking with Jesus a few years, His twelve disciples argued over which of them was the greatest. The mother of James and John asked Jesus to let her sons sit at His right and left in His kingdom. Jesus explained in words what He had been living out in front of them: to be great in God's kingdom means becoming a servant of others.

The only way I and my grandchildren can develop healthy self-esteem is to know Jesus and His love and to follow His teachings. As we imitate Him by serving those around us, we won't think about being a great person. We'll just know it's a great way to live.
—DIANNE NEAL MATTHEWS

FAITH STEP: *Take a moment to evaluate the basis of your self-esteem. If it's something other than your relationship with Jesus, ask Him to help you change your priorities.*

WEDNESDAY, OCTOBER 19

Don't have anything to do with foolish and stupid arguments, because you know they produce quarrels. And the Lord's servant must not be quarrelsome but must be kind to everyone, able to teach, not resentful.
2 *Timothy* 2:23–24 (NIV)

WHEN YOU HEAR RACCOONS FIGHTING, you don't wonder, *What's that animal out there in the dark?* Their distinct, whiny screech—a possessive "give-me-that" sound—is easily recognizable even if a person is tucked into bed two stories above the deck on which the raccoons are partying.

My husband and I removed anything they might find worth fighting over—sunflower seeds in the bird feeder and high-quality potting soil (which they'd apparently deemed snack worthy). It didn't matter. They still regularly visit the deck and make a ruckus around 11 p.m. Destructive little critters.

Jesus's followers sometimes act like critters. We whine at one another even if we have to invent something to complain about. Decades ago, the standard church joke was that every Sunday noon meal was "Roast of Pastor." Everything from his choice of ties to his lack of vocal modulation during the sermon to whether or not he made eye contact during the sermon's key point was fair game for discussion.

We've matured, haven't we? Or have we? Are we done with fussing and fighting? Moved past that? Or are we like raccoons arguing over rights to a single sunflower seed, snarling about the rant of the day, because of or despite the necktie?

Jesus teaches us to respect each other and those who shepherd us. Will we? —CYNTHIA RUCHTI

FAITH STEP: *What guard can you set up to prevent what the Bible calls foolish arguments? Perhaps a simple morning prayer—Lord, keep me from being quarrelsome today?*

THURSDAY, OCTOBER 20

Regardless of what else you put on, wear love. It's your basic, all-purpose garment. Never be without it. Colossians 3:14 (MSG)

A TINY THROW PILLOW IN my house makes me smile every time I see it. It says, "You're never fully dressed without cat hair." So true, if you're a cat lover. But what constitutes being fully dressed varies according to different camps of thought.

The little orphan Annie may have sung, "You're never fully dressed without a smile," but personally, I'm never "fully dressed" without lipstick, earrings, and a bra! However, even those essentials are considered inconsequential compared to other concerns.

For example, during a couples' game night with friends, this question was posed to the wives: "What single beauty item could you not live without?" To everyone's surprise, one honest woman blurted, "Tweezers!"

Whether or not I've plucked my eyebrows or am wearing a bra, lipstick, earrings, and cat hair, there really *is* something else, without which I might as well consider myself unclothed and not fully dressed. The most important part of my beauty regimen needs to be, first and foremost, putting on the love of Jesus. Without that, nothing else matters. —CASSANDRA TIERSMA

FAITH STEP: *Go through your makeup stash, and discard anything you don't really use. Write out Colossians 3:14 on a sticky note and put it on your bathroom mirror. Thank Jesus for clothing you in His love.*

FRIDAY, OCTOBER 21

Create in me a clean heart, O God, and renew a right spirit within me. Psalm 51:10 (ESV)

WE RECENTLY BOUGHT A NEW home and inherited a ninety-gallon fish tank. I knew nothing about aquariums and didn't have the desire to learn. It seemed like too much work. Within a few months, the water was murky, the live plants were overgrown, and algae covered the top. I did a quick clean with a net and skimmed the algae off, pulled out the overgrown plants, and added water. It didn't take long before it looked filthy again. One of my sons was home and he decided to help. After hours of research, he found a fish called a bristlenose plecostomus that would clean the tank. It looks like a little orange catfish.

As he was on the phone ordering this tank cleaner, I thought about the fourth and fifth steps of the twelve-step program. The fourth step involves doing a fearless moral inventory of yourself, and the fifth is admitting to God, yourself, and another person what you discover. Just as a bristlenose pleco cleans a fish tank, a moral inventory is a soul-cleansing practice. It demands time and courage to fearlessly search yourself for character qualities you no longer want. I was lazy about cleaning the fish tank and had also become lazy about regularly cleansing my soul. So I set aside some time that afternoon and prayed for Jesus to create a clean heart in me and show me how to live more like Him. Next step, I called a trusted friend and shared. —JEANNIE BLACKMER

FAITH STEP: *Spend time with Jesus today and write down qualities you believe you need to change to cleanse your soul. Call a friend and share two of these with her.*

SATURDAY, OCTOBER 22

I am the LORD, the God of all living things! Is anything too hard for me? Jeremiah 32:27 (CEB)

ISN'T IT FRUSTRATING THAT WE can't be God? What I wouldn't give to snap my fingers and fix difficult situations! Sometimes I wish I could just be good enough and do enough to make it all better, to never make mistakes, and to heal all the hurts that stretch so wide and deep in the world. But alas, I cannot. I never could.

Ann Voskamp wrote words that comfort me in this: "You aren't the one who got it all wrong…you aren't the one…left ashamed, you aren't the one who isn't enough…you aren't the one who is XY, or whatever terrible Z you whisper at yourself at 3 am." She also wrote, "Your core identity is that you are the disciple whom Jesus lavishly loves right through to the core."

When I come to the end of myself, I remind myself that Jesus is my core. He measured the waters with His hands (Isaiah 40:12) and poured out Himself as the only holy offering that could atone for my sins (Matthew 26:28). All I have to do is come to the cross, submit my heart, and yield my life to my loving Savior. He is in control. —GWEN FORD FAULKENBERRY

FAITH STEP: *Is there anything you are holding back from God? What would it look like for you to trust Him completely, with every aspect of your heart and life? What do you need to surrender today? Pray this prayer:* Jesus, I relinquish full control. I trust that You have a plan for me and that even now You are working to create new life in me and in _____ . Your grace is so much more than enough. Your love is everything I need. Thank You for choosing me over and over, and chasing me forever with Your relentless, redeeming love.

SUNDAY, OCTOBER 23

Praise be to the God and Father of our Lord Jesus Christ, the Father of compassion and the God of all comfort, who comforts us in all our troubles, so that we can comfort those in any trouble with the comfort we ourselves receive from God. 2 Corinthians 1:3–4 (NIV)

I GOT SICK AT THE very beginning of the pandemic of 2020 and was urged to quarantine even though I didn't meet the requirements for COVID-19 testing. Being in quarantine turned out to be an amazing gift. Shut away alone for two weeks, I spent more time praying, reading, journaling, and writing than ever before. I was full of the inexplicable peace and joy only Jesus can provide. Because I knew many people were struggling terribly, I asked Jesus how I could help. The inspiration came instantly: a daily time of reflection and prayer on Facebook Live.

My dear friend Barbara had written something she dubbed the *4 O'Clock Prayer*, which inspired my daily *4 O'Clock Faith*. So began my thirty-four messages, broadcasted daily, six days a week. Some were ten minutes, others thirty minutes, all with a message of encouragement and comfort. I can hardly believe that God provided so much inspiration. What's more, He enabled me to face and overcome the discomfort I have with "putting myself out there."

4 O'Clock Faith garnered a nice little following of people, who said it helped them get through a difficult time, and it led to my weekly program *Unfiltered*. Sharing how Jesus has helped me through trials and triumphs blesses me and others. —ISABELLA CAMPOLATTARO

FAITH STEP: *Pray about whom you can comfort with the comfort Jesus has given you. Take a minute to write or call them today.*

MONDAY, OCTOBER 24

Gracious words are a honeycomb, sweet to the soul and
healing to the bones. Proverbs 16:24 (NIV)

MOVING ONTO A SAILBOAT MEANT purging almost all our earthly belongings. One exception was a box containing the letters my husband and I wrote to each other during our long-distance engagement and my collection of Mother's Day and birthday cards from my kids. I could not bring myself to throw them away. I treasured these words. They make me feel wanted and loved.

That's how Jesus's words made people feel. On one occasion, He spoke to a woman whose medical condition made her untouchable (Luke 8:43–48). With no human options left for healing, she sneaked through a crowd and touched the hem of His garment. Jesus could have scolded her for being so bold, for presuming upon His kindness. He could have rebuked her for contaminating Him. Instead, He focused His attention on her and said, "Daughter, your faith has healed you. Go in peace" (verse 48, NIV).

Imagine how Jesus's words, spoken within the crowd's earshot, must have made her feel. While everyone around her considered her unclean, Jesus called her "daughter." This implied a term of endearment, equal to "my little one." He pronounced healing to her body and blessed her with shalom peace.

Jesus's words made the woman feel valued and whole. They breathed life and hope into the deepest recesses of her heart. How do the words I speak compare? Do they make others feel wanted and loved? I want to always follow His example and speak words that are sweet to the soul and healing to the bones. —GRACE FOX

FAITH STEP: *Write an encouraging note to someone expressing appreciation for a particular characteristic you see in her.*

TUESDAY, OCTOBER 25

The LORD All-Powerful says, "I will send my messenger, who will prepare the way for me." Malachi 3:1 (NCV)

MY SON'S GIRLFRIEND WAS A recent contestant on a national singing-competition TV show. Her schtick was that she's always the opening act for bands doing gigs in the city where she lives. They dubbed her the Universal Opener. The opener paves the way and gets everyone warmed up and ready for the big-name headliner. It's a pretty important gig, but with none of the glory.

Similarly, John the Baptist paved the way, getting the people ready for Jesus's public ministry. His job was preparing the way for the Lord. John's ministry was foundational for introducing Jesus's public ministry to the audience of that day. Yet there was no glory in it for John. It wasn't about him. His purpose was merely to point people to Jesus.

In a sense, we all have a similar calling: to point people to Jesus—not for His public ministry on earth (which He already completed) but for when He returns. Sometimes I get stage fright at the prospect of telling people about the big-name headliner—my Lord and Savior, Jesus, who is coming again. But, like my son's girlfriend, the Universal Opener, and like John the Baptist, I have an important gig. And like the Universal Opener and John the Baptist, it's not about me; it's for Jesus's glory. —CASSANDRA TIERSMA

FAITH STEP: *Are you prepared for Jesus's return? Ask Him how you can be a messenger to prepare the way for His return.*

WEDNESDAY, OCTOBER 26

Search me, God, and know my heart; test me and know my anxious thoughts. See if there is any offensive way in me, and lead me in the way everlasting. Psalm 139:23–24 (NIV)

MY MIDDLE SON, WILL, IS prepping to get his driver's license. After taking driver's ed and completing behind-the-wheel training, he has taken on the open road, with either Scott or me in the passenger seat. He is very confident in his newly acquired driving abilities. I am, too, until he comes up too quickly to the rear of another car approaching a stop sign. Then my foot slams into the imaginary brake pedal on the passenger floorboard, and I find myself clutching the handle above the door. I also tense up when he is merging with oncoming traffic. I call out things like "Watch your blind spot" and "Slow down" and sometimes "Jesus, help us!" He has told me that slamming on the imaginary brakes or calling on Jesus's name doesn't actually help him a whole lot. Instead, he wants me to offer calm direction. I've promised to do my best.

Jesus is the best guide on this journey of life. He designed it. No matter how many behind-the-wheel hours I have, I desperately need His instruction. My first move should always be to turn to Him and ask for direction and to only proceed when I hear His voice. When I take time to pray and read His Word, Jesus's truth bring clarity and peace, even when the path I am on seems difficult and confusing. He is leading me in the way everlasting. —SUSANNA FOTH AUGHTMON

FAITH STEP: *Jesus offers us guidance through His Word and His Holy Spirit. Ask Him for direction as you head into all that awaits you today.*

THURSDAY, OCTOBER 27

*Jesus replied, "Anyone who loves me will obey my teaching.
My Father will love them, and we will come to them and make
our home with them." John 14:23 (NIV)*

HOME, SWEET HOME.

Perhaps you grew up in a sweet home. Maybe you did not. Nonetheless, today's verse contains a concept of home that is perfect, and it's not a place I ever leave because Jesus never leaves me. He promises that if I love Him, I'll obey Him, and then He and the Father will come to me. They'll make Their Home in me wherever I am.

But what does this mean? I'm sure I can't conclusively capture it, but here are some things it means to me. It means a father who provides for me, a brother who's always in my corner, and a mother who gathers me in her arms like a hen with her chicks. It means safety, and security, and a place where I can hide. It means joy. It means I am known with all my warts—and loved anyway. It means forgiveness. It means I'm fed. It's a place I can rest, a place to find comfort when I'm sad, and a place for celebrations when things go well.

The home that Jesus provides for me is where every day starts and every day ends. It's the comfort I take with me wherever I go that keeps me grounded. His home reminds me who I am. Because Jesus makes His home in me, I'm accepted as well as challenged and disciplined as well as tenderly loved. —GWEN FORD FAULKENBERRY

FAITH STEP: *Draw a picture of what home looks like to you. Furnish it with all the things Jesus brings when He comes to make His home with you.*

FRIDAY, OCTOBER 28

Let us not become weary in doing good, for at the proper time we will reap a harvest if we do not give up. Galatians 6:9 (NIV)

MY HUSBAND, JEFF, AND I had been working in the yard all day, and it was too late to start supper, so we decided to pick up burgers at a drive-through. When it was time to pay, the worker told us, "No charge. The people in front of you paid for your meal." What a lovely surprise! To pay it forward, we picked up the check of the person behind us in line. I craned my neck to get a look at the lucky soul who'd benefitted from our kindness. Would she wave, throw a kiss, honk? Disappointingly, she didn't acknowledge our gift.

Why hadn't I expended such effort to see the person who'd *bought* our meal? Easy. Rather than wanting to *offer* gratitude, I expected to *receive* it. It's fortunate that Jesus didn't expect gratitude for all the good He did. The blind, the lame, and the lepers appreciated His healing, but most of them were too excited to hang around and thank Him. Individuals in the crowds who may have been touched and awed by Jesus's words didn't thank Him, although many were changed forever. How often do I remember to thank Jesus for His ultimate sacrifice so that I can enjoy eternal life?

If I expect gratitude for the good I do, then I'm sure to be disappointed. It's never a good idea to keep score. Jesus didn't. Doing good and loving others should be its own reward. —PAT BUTLER DYSON

FAITH STEP: *Ask Jesus to remind you not to expect gratitude for your good deeds. If He is pleased with you, that is thanks enough.*

SATURDAY, OCTOBER 29

The LORD your God will be with you wherever you go. Joshua 1:9 (NIV)

MY FRIEND AND I HAD been invited to a reading event two hours from our homes. My friend came from the southern part of the state, and I drove from the west.

The setting was everything you'd want in a reading event. A charming coffee shop with warm lighting, a stone fireplace, hardwood floors, good food, and great ambiance. Holding a microphone and reading to the crowd gathered for that purpose stirred no uneasiness and no fear. It was a comfortable setting with attentive listeners.

The discomfort came later.

We'd left one of our cars at the hotel where we'd stay the night. After the event, we assumed we'd find our way back with little trouble. But unfamiliar surroundings and my phone's slow-to-respond navigation system meant "I think it's this way" turned out to be "It's not this way."

Getting lost made us panic briefly. But after a few moments of unease, we switched to having a sense of adventure. Why? Because we remembered that Jesus has our back in every situation—large or small. He goes before us, behind us, and beside us. All need for fear evaporates when He's the backseat driver (or when He "takes the wheel").

Our unexpected route took us along a beautiful lake, just as the sun was saying its brilliant, colorful goodbyes for the day. Longer and slower, the backroad was just what our souls needed.

Sometimes Jesus gives us courage by standing between us and danger. Sometimes it's His still small voice from the backseat saying, "It'll be okay. Let's have an adventure." —CYNTHIA RUCHTI

FAITH STEP: *Take an unexpected route today. Note the wonders you may have missed if you hadn't detoured. Thank Jesus for accompanying you wherever you go.*

SUNDAY, OCTOBER 30

Anyone who lives on milk, being still an infant, is not acquainted with the teaching about righteousness. But solid food is for the mature, who by constant use have trained themselves to distinguish good from evil. Hebrews 5:13–14 (NIV)

SPENDING TWO WEEKS WITH MY youngest granddaughter, Lexi, gave me an opportunity to know her better. During that time, I watched her learn several new skills. She graduated from taking two or three consecutive steps to walking six or eight. She learned to blow kisses and identify her nose. She began folding her hands when we asked the blessing on our meals, and she learned to play "This Little Piggy" with her toes. Her parents, her grandpa, and I clapped and cheered for her each time she practiced those skills. She clapped for herself, and flashed a toothy grin.

We celebrated Lexi's first birthday during that visit, and I recalled the day she was born teeny, pink, and utterly helpless. Seeing the difference one year made in this baby's development left me amazed. It also left me grateful because her growth evidenced good health.

As a believer, I had much to learn when I first placed my faith in Jesus. I started with basic knowledge about His love for me. Taking baby steps, I learned how to grow in my relationship with Him. My spiritual understanding has deepened and grown over time and through experience.

Lexi's growth delights her greatest fans. I suspect my spiritual development delights Jesus as He watches me mature into the woman He created me to be. —GRACE FOX

FAITH STEP: *Our spiritual growth continues as long as we're alive. Identify one step you can take to grow your faith at this time.*

MONDAY, OCTOBER 31

Examine yourselves to see whether you are in the faith;
test yourselves. Do you not realize that Christ Jesus is in you—
unless, of course, you fail the test? 2 Corinthians 13:5 (NIV)

THE NEW BATTERY IN MY daughter's car kept draining, needing a jump start. An auto mechanic ran a diagnostic test, discovering a problematic AC reactor. Once the necessary part was ordered, it was an easy fix.

When I'm emotionally drained, or haven't been spending enough time in the Word, I need a spiritual jump start. Today, when my "reactor" kept overreacting to minor frustrations, I needed a spiritual diagnostic test.

The word *auto* comes from the Greek *autos*, which means "self." Apostle Paul said to perform a self-diagnostic test, to see if we're being true to our faith. He said to check ourselves, to see if we're living as Christ-filled believers. I performed my own self-diagnostic test today, troubleshooting possible causes for my less than ideal reactions. I'd gotten enough sleep, and I'd read the Bible today. However, I'd become hangry (hungry to the point of anger.) Consequently, my reactions to minor frustrations weren't very Christlike. I feel as if I'd "failed the test" today.

We needed a qualified mechanic to do the auto repairs on my daughter's car. But I need Jesus to help me have more Christlike "auto" responses to irritating frustrations of day-to-day living. I'm grateful to that auto mechanic for the good work he did in solving my daughter's car problem. But most of all, I'm grateful to Jesus for the good work He began in me, which He'll bring to completion upon His return (Philippians 1:6). —CASSANDRA TIERSMA

FAITH STEP: *Test your faith: Is Jesus in you? If not, ask Him to jump-start your faith. Thank Him for the good work He began in you.*

TUESDAY, NOVEMBER 1

I pray that you, being rooted and established in love, may have power, together with all the Lord's holy people, to grasp how wide and long and high and deep is the love of Christ, and to know this love that surpasses knowledge—that you may be filled to the measure of all the fullness of God. Ephesians 3:17–19 (NIV)

MY SON ADDISON JUST TURNED fourteen. He is our youngest and tallest son. He has passed everyone in the family and is very proud of that fact. He is also very proud that he just passed the six-foot mark. We have a wall where we measure each of our boys. The growth has been fun to watch. My husband, Scott, who has been passed by all three sons, has told them that whoever is the shortest son is his favorite. None of them want to be his favorite. They want to be as tall as possible. It is not just their bodies that are growing; their personalities, hearts, and minds are still in the process of reaching their full potential too. But then that is true of me too.

As long as I am alive, Jesus will continue to work in my personality, my heart, and my mind. There is so much room for growth. Jesus wants me to reach my full potential. The more I grow in Him, the greater capacity I have to fill up with His love and pour it out on those around me. I never want to stop growing.
—SUSANNA FOTH AUGHTMON

FAITH STEP: *Are you filled to the measure of the fullness of God? Ask Jesus to fill you to overflowing today, so that as you encounter others, they might sense the overwhelming power of His love for them.*

WEDNESDAY, NOVEMBER 2

He will be like a tree firmly planted [and fed] by streams of water, which yields its fruit in its season; its leaf does not wither; and in whatever he does, he prospers [and comes to maturity]. Psalm 1:3 (AMP)

WHEN I MEDITATE ON TODAY'S Scripture verse, I always envision the tree. I imagine myself becoming a mature, strong tree with lots of fruit and flowers, standing by a gently rolling stream. Since this tree is planted near Living Water (Jesus), it is always well fed and in bloom. As I grew older, I imagined people coming to sit under this tree, comforted by my shade as they eat good fruit from my full, green branches.

But how? I have invested years in Bible study, Christian service, Bible college, and Christian writing, but I felt that I should be doing more to influence others for Christ personally. As I pondered this (admittedly feeling inadequate), I met an old college roommate in the mall unexpectedly. We hugged and talked, and best of all, she shared that she had received Jesus some years before! She was also battling cancer. As I encouraged her, she smiled and said, "Well, you always used to say, 'We walk by faith, not by sight!'" I was blown away that she remembered something I had said thirty years ago! Shortly after this, another old friend shared that when the group leader at a local women's prayer group asked the ladies to name one person who'd significantly affected their walk with Jesus—three of the six women wrote my name down! Selah. Thanks to Jesus, I am more of a shade tree than I thought! —PAMELA TOUSSAINT HOWARD

FAITH STEP: *Ask Jesus to show you someone with whom you can share what you know about walking with Jesus.*

THURSDAY, NOVEMBER 3

We have this hope as an anchor for the soul, firm and secure. Hebrews 6:19 (NIV)

GENE AND I HAD MOTORED up the river to a fuel dock to fill our sailboat's tanks with diesel. Task complete, we found a nearby cove in which to anchor for the afternoon.

Our anchor hangs off the bow with a sturdy chain and weighs about eighty pounds. We step on a switch on the deck to release and lower it. Down, down, down it goes. The goal is to set it (positioning it) on the sea bottom so it holds fast. If it doesn't set, the boat will drift and likely suffer or cause damage. In this cove, we set it firmly in the mud on the sea floor. A gentle breeze blew, waves lapped, and the tide's current flowed. Despite nature's combined forces, our vessel remained secure.

Things don't always work so well. We've discovered that an anchor set in a kelp bed provides no security. A friend once thought he'd set his anchor on a sandy sea floor. When the boat began to drift, he discovered that the anchor had caught in a bag of garbage.

A boat anchor is an essential piece of nautical safety equipment just as hope is a spiritual anchor essential to my soul. R. C. Sproul said, "Hope is called the anchor of the soul because it gives stability to the Christian life…. It is that which latches on to the certainty of the promises of the future that God has made."

My future is secure solely because of Jesus's death and resurrection. Setting my hope on anything less will send my soul adrift.
—GRACE FOX

FAITH STEP: *Memorize Psalm 62:5: "Yes, my soul, find rest in God; my hope comes from him" (NIV).*

FRIDAY, NOVEMBER 4

Out of his fullness we have all received grace in place of grace already given. John 1:16 (NIV)

WHILE ON VACATION, MY HUSBAND, Jeff, and I had just picked up our to-go dinners when we received simultaneous emergency text messages from our daughter Brooke. Figuring it was a mistake, I called Brooke. When she didn't respond, I called her boyfriend, Matt. "Brooke's been in a wreck!" he said breathlessly. Panicked, I asked if she was okay. Matt answered, "I don't know!" At that moment, I heard Brooke crying in the background. She was alive! *Thank you, Jesus! Grace.*

Jeff and I rushed back to the condo, packed our things, and headed for the trauma center where Brooke had been taken. It was an hour away. All the way, I prayed over and over, *Jesus, Jesus, Jesus.* As we drove, Matt reported in, telling us Brooke had been hit by a drunk driver, her leg crushed. She was being stabilized in the ER before surgery.

When we arrived at the hospital and located Brooke, I was horrified to see the bone protruding from her leg. She'd been taken to the premier trauma center in the area, staffed with outstanding surgeons. It could have been so much worse. *Grace.*

Matt had tried to call Brooke on his way to her house but had gotten no answer. Hearing sirens, he'd approached an area cordoned off to traffic. Led by an inner voice, he pulled his car over and ran all the way to the accident site, arriving just as Brooke was being loaded into the ambulance. He was able to ride with her to the hospital, holding her and comforting her. *Grace.* —PAT BUTLER DYSON

FAITH STEP: *When life feels desperate, look for signs of Jesus's grace.*

SATURDAY, NOVEMBER 5

In my distress I cried to the LORD, and He heard me. Psalm 120:1 (NKJV)

THERE'S NO WORSE PLACE TO be on a Saturday night than in an emergency room. Yet here I was, in Houston's Memorial Hermann hospital, waiting and watching over my daughter Brooke, who'd been seriously injured in a car wreck. In a treatment room, doctors and nurses hovered over her, tending to her badly shattered ankle. Brave though she tried to be, I could see Brooke was in great pain. As one of the nurses dashed off to get Brooke pain medicine, we heard, "Gunshot wound, clear the area." In a flash, another nurse scooted Brooke out into the hall, next to other patients on stretchers.

I wish I could unsee some of the things I witnessed that night: gunshot wounds, heart attacks, overdoses, car accidents—the mass of hurting humanity overwhelmed me. Brooke moaned in pain. I looked for her nurse but didn't see her. Hospital personnel were running around, dealing with each new crisis. Now Brooke was crying, "Mom, help me!" I didn't want to cause a scene, but I was feeling desperate. We needed help immediately!

Jesus, I prayed, *please send someone to help Brooke with this pain.* How many times I prayed that prayer, I do not know. The agony on Brooke's face and her sobs tore me apart. I'd never felt so helpless. Finally, I caught the eye of a nurse running past. She nodded, and in a few minutes, she injected some pain medicine into Brooke's IV. I thanked her—but not before I thanked Jesus for answering a mother's desperate plea. —PAT BUTLER DYSON

FAITH STEP: *When you need help, cry out to Jesus!*

SUNDAY, NOVEMBER 6

Being strengthened with all power according to his glorious might so that you may have great endurance and patience. Colossians 1:11 (NIV)

"I'M SORRY, BROOKE, I KNOW you were counting on getting a cast, but it's too soon."

My daughter's face crumbled when she heard the surgeon's words. Weeks before, she had been hit by a drunk driver. Her ankle was shattered, and all the ligaments were torn from her tibia. She had endured two surgeries and was facing another. With her leg encased in bandages, surrounded by a Frankenstein-like cage of rods and pins, she used a walker to get around.

"In six months," the doctor continued cheerfully, "you'll be good as new."

When the doctor left, Brooke burst into tears, and it was all I could do to keep from joining her. Six months is an eternity to an active twenty-six-year-old high school teacher and soccer coach. Brooke would need strength, courage, and patience to endure this trial. And I had to help her. *Jesus, guide me.*

Jesus, of all people, understood suffering. Brooke's situation was nothing compared to the agony He withstood. Still, I knew Jesus cared about Brooke and all she was facing. I felt Him whisper, *I'll be there.*

I took Brooke home with me, nestled her in the cozy guest room, and fed her the food she liked best. During the long days, I listened to her worry about missing school—her students falling behind, her team losing games, her sick leave running out. I sympathized when she cried about the unfairness of her situation, the misery of being cooped up, and the loss of her new car. And every night, I thanked Jesus for His strength. —PAT BUTLER DYSON

FAITH STEP: *Lean on Jesus for support when you must endure trials.*

MONDAY, NOVEMBER 7

On the day I called to you, you answered me. You made me
strong and brave. Psalm 138:3 (NCV)

AS AN AMATEUR GREEN THUMB, I'm reading about tough plants for tough places. Plants are like people. Some are happier in warmer climates. Some can go longer than others without a drink of water. Some thrive in sunlight; whereas others sunburn easily, requiring shade. And some enjoy a robust four-season climate, gladly withstanding snow and freezing temperatures.

Tough plants can endure adverse garden conditions, such as drought, shade, heavy clay soil, or dry rocky soil. Likewise, tough people can endure adversity and hardship yet persevere and still thrive. Spiritually, I want to be like a "tough plant for tough places"—able to endure adversity and still bloom and thrive—despite tough situations in life.

But I'll need help. God, the master gardener, creates both plants and people, giving each unique attributes and characteristics. Deep-rooted spiritual strength, stability, security, and resilience come from Jesus—from abiding in Him by staying planted in His Word.

Psalm 138:3 confirms that Jesus will make me strong and brave if I call out to Him. So, rather than wonder if I'm the right type of "toughness," I'm asking Jesus to make me spiritually tough—so I can survive and thrive—despite whatever adverse conditions I may face in the garden of life. —CASSANDRA TIERSMA

FAITH STEP: *Spiritually, are you a tender annual, hardy perennial, or a tough person for a tough place? As a reminder that it's Jesus who gives strength and courage, visit a local plant nursery to find a tough plant for a tough place (i.e., drought tolerant, not fussy about soil type) for your home or garden. Ask Jesus to make you strong and brave for the tough situations in life.*

TUESDAY, NOVEMBER 8

When the cares of my heart are many, your consolations cheer my soul. Psalm 94:19 (ESV)

I WAS JOGGING DOWN THE street when two dogs, a yellow hound and a small bulldog, ran up to me. I kept moving. I'd heard it's a bad idea to meet a dog's eyes, so I didn't, but I was alarmed by the yellow dog's snarling and the fact that every hair on his back stood up. Suddenly, the dog jumped on me, growling and baring his teeth. I didn't even have time to call out to Jesus! I yelled for the dog to stop and about that time, his owner appeared and she hollered for her dogs to come. The dog continued to menace, barking and snapping, but finally headed toward his mistress. "I'm so sorry," she said. "They never do this." I muttered, "Okay," but I was badly shaken.

After I got home, I checked out the pain in my leg and discovered the dog had bitten me. I didn't know the owner, but I wanted to make sure the dog had been vaccinated. When I found the neighbor's phone number and called, she apologized and assured me the dog was up to date on shots.

That night I couldn't sleep. I obsessed about what I might have done differently. I agonized about what might have occurred if I'd had one of my grandchildren with me. *Why had this happened to me?* The longer I fretted, the more agitated I got. Finally, I asked Jesus to take away my burdens, and He soothed my soul. What had happened was an unfortunate incident in my life, but Jesus had been with me all along. —PAT BUTLER DYSON

FAITH STEP: *No matter how dire the circumstances, remember Jesus is in control.*

WEDNESDAY, NOVEMBER 9

You were all called to travel on the same road and in the same direction, so stay together, both outwardly and inwardly. You have one Master, one faith, one baptism. Ephesians 4:4–5 (MSG)

WHEN MY BIBLE STUDY COORDINATOR assigned Carla to my table, she told me that Carla was new in town. *A kindred spirit,* I thought. *We'll become good friends.* Later, I learned that Carla had moved only an hour away from her old home and now lived next to her daughter's family. Nothing like my situation—four different states in ten years, family members all scattered six to nine hundred miles away. I kept looking for something that Carla and I might have in common.

One day after Bible study, Carla and I chatted. I gasped when my eyes fell on her unique pendant: a silver square embellished with gold leafy branches and the Hebrew words *El Shaddai*. I'd only seen a pendant like that once before. I pulled my necklace from underneath my sweater where it had slipped. We let out identical squeals. I said, "Mine came from Israel!" She said, "So did mine!" I said, "But I've never been there!" She said, "Neither have I!" Carla and I had bought our pendants from different sources, but both could be traced back to jewelers who were Jewish followers of Jesus.

What could be a more solid foundation for a relationship than a shared faith in Jesus? To experience the same forgiveness, to follow the same Shepherd, and to live with the same hope for the future. I might discover that I'm surrounded by kindred spirits when I pay less attention to what seems different and focus on the Savior we have in common. —DIANNE NEAL MATTHEWS

FAITH STEP: *Initiate a new friendship that's based on your shared faith in Christ.*

THURSDAY, NOVEMBER 10

We are hard pressed on every side, but not crushed; perplexed,
but not in despair; persecuted, but not abandoned; struck down,
but not destroyed. 2 Corinthians 4:8–9 (NIV)

MY MOTHER RECENTLY FELL FLAT on her face and split open her lip. The nurses at her assisted living home called the EMT squad, which whisked her away to the hospital. Doctors kept Mom for several days to make sure she had not suffered any other injuries and to see what may have caused her to fall.

My octogenarian mother was finally released, and she was virtually unscathed, except for a few facial bruises. Throughout her hospital stay, her spunk was evident to everyone. What might have taken out others her age was merely a blip on the screen for her.

Although she looked a bit battered and bruised, Mom had survived the fall. I thought about some of the falls that I, too, have survived. Losing a job that I *knew* I would retire from. Having financial struggles that caused sleepless nights. Being disappointed when a ministry program didn't work out the way I had envisioned. Enduring a painful health condition.

Of course, my challenges were nothing compared to what the apostle Paul faced as a sold-out follower of Christ. Yet he told the Corinthians that despite being hard pressed, perplexed, persecuted, and struck down, he was not crushed, in despair, abandoned, or destroyed. Paul kept his eyes on Jesus and his mission to spread the gospel, and he knew he would receive his reward in the end.

Jesus gives me power to endure life's struggles. When I fall down, He always helps me get back up. —BARBRANDA LUMPKINS WALLS

FAITH STEP: *What has knocked you down? How did Jesus get you back on your feet?*

VETERAN'S DAY, FRIDAY, NOVEMBER 11

Only be strong and very courageous. Joshua 1:7 (ESV)

WHEN I WAS A STUDENT, one of my favorite books was *The Red Badge of Courage*. The author, Stephen Crane, created a character who was self-shamed for his cowardice and believed that the only thing that would erase the shame and legitimize him as a soldier was a war wound—a bloodred badge of courage.

The character's internal struggle forms the framework of the entire novel. He faced numerous opportunities to do the courageous thing, but crippled by fear, he opted for cowardice...until the pivotal moment when he chose bravery above comfort.

Many Scripture verses' instructions to "be strong and take courage" first referenced God's people facing war battles. But if I apply those verses to internal warfare—the battles in our minds and emotions about choosing the comfortable thing versus the courageous option—those Scripture verses take on a whole new meaning. When does a day pass when I *don't* face a choice between personal comfort or the greater good, between self-satisfaction and selflessness, between Jesus's way and human nature's way?

My red badge of courage isn't my own war wound but the wounds Jesus bore. The blood He shed as He walked bravely into harm's way for me. The scars He bore, visible even after His resurrection, are evidence that our shame is gone.

The foundation of any bravery I need was secured for me by Jesus's love and sacrifice, His unsurpassed badge of courage.
—CYNTHIA RUCHTI

FAITH STEP: *Conduct an internet search for how often the word* courage *appears in the Bible. If it's one of the Bible's favorite themes, shouldn't it be ours as well?*

SATURDAY, NOVEMBER 12

So when they continued asking him, he lifted up himself, and said unto them, He that is without sin among you, let him first cast a stone at her. John 8:7 (KJV)

WHEN I ENCOUNTER PEOPLE WHO are struggling with drugs, abusive relationships, and repeated crimes, I have to be careful to remember that it could've been me. And I remember the first time my friends introduced me to cigarettes, drinking, and drugs. I wasn't so saintly in those situations.

In seventh grade, my best friend and I decided to try smoking in a back alley near our homes. It looked cool when my father smoked. He had a way of holding his imported Du Maurier cigarettes in his fingers just a certain way. But when I tried it myself, I coughed so much I knew it wasn't for me. My best friend, however, became a lifelong smoker.

In college, the pressure to get drunk on the weekends was immense. I would go out to bars occasionally, mainly to socialize with my classmates. Before I knew it, there would be three or four drinks lined up in front of me, and friends would dare me to drink them all. I got drunk once and vomited violently. I had a headache for days.

Also during that time, I attended a house party where just about everyone was doing drugs. I didn't partake, and I tried to act as if I was enjoying myself, but I followed a strong urge to ditch my friends (and my ride!) and run. The police raided one of those parties later that year, and students I knew were arrested. What's the difference between me and them? Only Jesus's mercy. —PAMELA TOUSSAINT HOWARD

FAITH STEP: *Today, show love to someone who may be struggling with addiction issues, or is in recovery and having a tough time.*

SUNDAY, NOVEMBER 13

Who is to condemn? It is Christ Jesus, who died, yes, who was raised, who is at the right hand of God, who indeed intercedes for us. Romans 8:34 (NRSV)

WHEN YOU HEAR THE NAME Jesus, what image comes to your mind? Depending on the season, it might be a sweet baby sleeping on a hay-filled manger or a bleeding Savior wearing a crown of thorns and hanging on a cross. Or maybe you envision a man with kind eyes teaching crowds and healing the sick. If you grew up with a picture of Jesus in your home, you might visualize Him seated at a table with His disciples during the Last Supper or visualize Him ascending into the clouds as His followers look up.

All these images of Jesus relate to His life on earth. Revelation 19 paints a picture of Him returning in the future as a fierce warrior to wage war against evil. But what is Jesus doing right now? We know that Jesus lives inside us, because we were given the Holy Spirit at salvation. But several Scriptures say that Jesus now sits at God's right hand, interceding for us. While that doesn't conjure up a specific mental image, it certainly fills me with hope and joy.

How comforting to know that Jesus is serving as my advocate in heaven. He comes against anything and anyone who tries to condemn me. He stands ready to mediate on my behalf in every detail of my life. Knowing that the One who loves me most intercedes for me in heaven gives me courage to face anything that happens on the earth. —DIANNE NEAL MATTHEWS

FAITH STEP: *How do you need Jesus to intercede on your behalf right now? Tell Him what it means to know that He is your advocate.*

MONDAY, NOVEMBER 14

Have nothing to do with irreverent, silly myths. Rather train yourself for godliness. 1 Timothy 4:7 (ESV)

MY ITALIAN MOTHER WAS VERY superstitious. Some superstitions were familiar, while others had an obscure Italian angle. I remember someone once broke a mirror, and the whole family made a pilgrimage down to the nearest lake to ceremonially dispose the broken pieces into a large body of water. Hats and purses on the bed were a big no-no, and there were others I can't recall. If we violated one of these warnings, there would be dreadful consequences. Superstition is all about fear.

Throughout Scripture, including Paul's letter to young Timothy, we're discouraged from dabbling in anything that smacks of the occult. But in the past, I've been superstitious about routine spiritual practices. When and how long I pray, what time I go to church, and even where I sit. If I didn't do it just so, I felt a little anxious. I was so fixated on the method that I was missing the forest for the trees. Jesus picked this bone with the Pharisees pretty regularly.

As the adage says, "It's about relationship, not rules." In Christ, we're free. We take on His cloak of true godliness, even as we grow spiritually. Religious practices can be blessings that foster our relationship with God or they can be empty, pious superstitions that lead to no good. I want the former. —ISABELLA CAMPOLATTARO

FAITH STEP: *Take inventory of your spiritual practices and flag anything that smacks of superstition. Ask Jesus to help you see and be free.*

Tuesday, November 15

Be strong and take heart, all you who hope in the Lord. Psalm 31:24 (NIV)

"You're the strongest person I know." "What doesn't kill you makes you stronger." "Stay strong."

We throw the word *strong* around as if we know what it means, just like the word *hope.*

"I hope things work out." "Hope you have a good day." "She has high hopes."

Both *strong* and *hope* are kind of vogue. They are nice concepts that make us feel good. But what is hope? And what does it have to do with strength?

When I worked at DaySpring Cards, I had a mentor named Roy. We were talking about addiction one day, and he said, "I'd like to challenge you to use the word *hope* instead of *wish.* A wish is a nice thought, but there's no power in wishing. But hope—hope is grounded in Jesus. We hope people get well. We hope they are comforted. We hope their marriage is blessed. Hope matters because it is attached to Jesus. Wishing blows in the wind. But hope is strong regardless of the circumstances."

That conversation has influenced my thinking ever since. It helped me understand where strength comes from—which is not from ourselves. Jesus is the connection between hope and strength. So when I encourage someone to be strong, it's not just empty words. I'm saying, "Put your hope in Jesus." If someone tells me I am strong, I acknowledge that what makes me strong is that I have hope in something—Someone—greater than myself: the One who has overcome the world. —Gwen Ford Faulkenberry

FAITH STEP: *Challenge yourself to use the word* hope *instead of* wish. *Every time you need strength today, remember the source of our hope—Jesus—and draw from Him.*

WEDNESDAY, NOVEMBER 16

I will be filled with joy because of you. I will sing praises to your name, O Most High. Psalm 9:2 (NLT)

WHEN PEOPLE LEARN THAT I live on a boat, they often ask where I get drinking water. I explain that the city supplies it and that we use a hose reserved for only that purpose to gain access to it. One end of the hose connects to a spigot on the dock. We insert the other end through a deck fitting, turn the spigot on, and presto! Water fills our two 150-gallon tanks in less than a half hour. The supply lasts for a couple of weeks or more, depending on how much we use.

A wall-mounted gauge tracks the water level in each tank, but I've learned to recognize the clue that tells me when they're nearing empty: the faucet makes a sputtering sound and water spurts rather than flows.

I've discovered a similarity of sorts between this aspect of boat life and my relationship with Jesus. Scripture promises that His presence fills me with joy, but that doesn't happen automatically. I need to connect with Him through disciplines such as praying, reading His Word, obeying His commands, and practicing gratitude. Consistent fellowship keeps my spiritual tank full.

If I disconnect from Jesus, my spiritual tank eventually runs dry. I feel impatient with my husband, fall into the comparison trap, become easily critical of others, and feel anxious for my kids' well-being. Joy no longer flows but rather spurts and sputters. These clues tell me I need to reconnect with Jesus. His supply of joy is endless, and it's always available to fill my tank. —GRACE FOX

FAITH STEP: *Drink a glass of water. Thank Jesus, the Living Water, for bringing fullness of joy (Psalm 16:11).*

THURSDAY, NOVEMBER 17

The Lord is not slow in keeping his promise, as some understand slowness. Instead he is patient with you, not wanting anyone to perish, but everyone to come to repentance. 2 Peter 3:9 *(NIV)*

I LIVE IN THE NORTHWEST, where heavy rains define autumn and winter. Every year, as the temperatures drop and the skies drip, I begin winterizing my garden. I follow the weather forecasts, watching for the final smattering of dry days. That's when I pick the last of my crop of tomatoes and line them up along my home's sunniest windowsills.

Then I wait. The sheer light filtering through the glass turns their green skins red. But it takes a lot of time and patience. Days, then weeks, can pass with no obvious change before the first few begin to show orange and red tints. Some seem to change color overnight, while others lag slowly behind. Deep into fall, most of the fruit has ripened, brightening our dinner plates.

Those tomatoes in the windowsill remind me of the different paths to Jesus. Some find Him early, as children. Others take longer, needing first to experience some of life's blessings and heartaches along the way. I was one of those late harvests.

Just as I don't know which of my tomatoes will ripen first or last, I also can't guess when some of my friends and loved ones will begin their transformation to become believers. My privilege is to watch, pray, and turn them toward the Light. He will take care of the rest.
—HEIDI GAUL

FAITH STEP: *Which of your friends can you bless today? Who can you help turn toward the Light? Make a list, and pray for each person's transformation according to God's perfect timing.*

FRIDAY, NOVEMBER 18

Let us strip off every weight that slows us down, especially the sin that so easily trips us up. And let us run with endurance the race God has set before us. Hebrews 12:1 (NLT)

I'M AN AVID JOGGER. MOST days, I run three to five miles. Running is vital to managing middle-aged spread, my mental health, and even my relationship with Jesus. I consider my morning jog to be my meditation, because my mind is quiet enough to hear from Jesus. I get so much inspiration while running that I stop often to record little notes for myself.

Running is a mental game. Some say that if you can run a 10K, you can run a full marathon. I'm not so sure about that, but I am sure that my mind plays a prominent role in how far, fast, and happily I run. If I allow myself to start thinking about how much more I have to go, how hot or cold it is, or what I want to do later, I'm doomed.

The words in Hebrews 12:1 encourage me to cast off anything that hinders me and to persevere to the very end of the race of faith. This requires mental and physical discipline—and through that, along with unwavering focus on Jesus who's cheering me on, I can finish the race. —ISABELLA CAMPOLATTARO

FAITH STEP: *What is hindering you in your race of faith? Ask Jesus to grant you insight and courage to cast it off, so you can run unhindered the race set before you!*

SATURDAY, NOVEMBER 19

Suppose a brother or a sister is without clothes and daily food. If one of you says to them, "Go in peace; keep warm and well fed," but does nothing about their physical needs, what good is it? James 2:16 (NIV)

LAST SATURDAY MORNING, KEVIN STOOD in the doorway of our bedroom with his cell phone in his hand. "I was going out to warm up the car when I got this text," he said. "I think you should see it." He snatched off his knit cap and took off his winter coat before handing me his phone.

"What time is it?" I mumbled, pushing cobwebs from my sleepy brain.

"Six thirty. Bible study starts at seven, but I think this is more important."

That woke me fast. Few things are more important to Kev than the weekly men's Bible study he attends. He's not a pastor or counselor or dad to anyone there. He's just one of the guys, learning along with the other guys how to best follow Jesus. That Bible study is his lifeline, the nourishment his soul craves, and his favorite activity of the week.

"Can you or Grandma come get me in Lyons, IN?" the text read. "My car caught fire. It's totaled. I need a ride home."

Our eldest granddaughter, who had been on her own for only four weeks. With a car, now ruined, that she'd had only four months. She was stranded two hours away, and her mom was at work and unable to get away.

"Of course we have to go," Kev said. "I'll text her back while you get dressed."

How proud I was to witness my husband give up his study of the Bible to live the Bible. I'm sure Jesus was proud too.
—JEANETTE LEVELLIE

FAITH STEP: *Ask Jesus for a way for you to show your faith by your actions.*

SUNDAY, NOVEMBER 20

Be strong and courageous. Do not be afraid; do not be discouraged, for the LORD your God will be with you wherever you go. Joshua 1:9 (NIV)

NO CARING FATHER WOULD SAY to a small child, "Get out there and learn how to ride your bike. And don't you come back inside until you can!"

Instead, good moms and dads instill courage by instructing, coaching, cheerleading, guiding, and affirming their children. "You can do it. I know you can. And I'm right here beside you."

That "here beside you" principle is the one cheering me on right now. So many of the courage or bravery or strengthening verses in the Bible have that reminder. When we read, "Be strong. Take courage," we're missing the most important part if we don't keep reading the following words, "for I am with you wherever you go" or "I am with you always." God the Father, Jesus the Son, and the Holy Spirit within me are the reason I can take courage no matter what I face, how much I tremble, or how uncertain the path ahead of me is. I'm not commanded, "Go out there and find yourself some courage, and don't come back in this house until you do!" I'm held by loving arms, watched over by loving eyes, and steadied by hands that will not falter.

There's a "because"—a reason—behind Jesus's encouragement to stand firm. *Because* He's with me, beside me, within me to make it possible. A. W. Tozer wrote, "The only safe place for a sheep is by the side of his shepherd, because the devil does not fear sheep; he just fears the Shepherd." —CYNTHIA RUCHTI

FAITH STEP: *Consider memorizing that A. W. Tozer quote, as well as Joshua 1:9. And watch for someone who needs those reminders today.*

MONDAY, NOVEMBER 21

So in Christ Jesus you are all children of God through faith.
Galatians 3:26 (NIV)

IVY, OUR CALICO, IS A handful. She comes from a long line of barn cats, and it shows in her behavior. She isn't like our other pets, who are prone to relaxing in a spot of sunlight. She doesn't even like to stay indoors, unless the weather makes it necessary. She's seven pounds of warrior huntress, ready to take on the unsuspecting rodents around our neighborhood.

But she's also ours. When we adopted this tiny rascal as a kitten, she became one of the family. We can't alter her genetics or rewrite her past, but we can brighten her future. We are committed to loving, feeding, and protecting her.

Before I met Jesus, my life was a lot like Ivy's, full of uncertainty. I had little to hope for. Now, when I face challenges, I know I'm not alone. The source of love itself has welcomed me into His family. Jesus says I no longer need to worry about what I'll eat or what I'll wear (Matthew 6:25; Luke 12:22). I am promised a future full of joy and wonder, far beyond anything I can imagine.

Am I still a rascal? Sometimes. It seems part of my nature. Am I forgiven? Always (1 John 1:9). That's what family does. —HEIDI GAUL

FAITH STEP: *At the top of a sheet of paper, write "Child of God," and at the bottom, draw a crown. In the middle, make a list of the qualities that make you who you are. Post the list where you can refer to it often and develop ways you can use those unique traits to honor Jesus.*

TUESDAY, NOVEMBER 22

Don't fall into the trap of being a coward—trust the LORD, and you will be safe. Proverbs 29:25 (CEV)

Peter and the other apostles answered, "We must obey God, not human authority!" Acts 5:29 (NCV)

STORIES OF CONTRABAND PLANTS SMUGGLED from one place to another intrigue me: heirloom roses brought west by pioneer women in covered wagons, tomato seeds hidden under postage stamps, seed potatoes smuggled in horses' feed bags, and garden seeds smuggled in waistbands or hollow canes. I admire the feisty courageous spirit that immigrants employed for these plants' survival.

Brave individuals have historically defied human authority to protect God's people from oppression, tyranny, and genocide. Moses's mother hid her baby boy in a basket along the banks of the Nile to save her son from being killed under Pharaoh's orders. Joseph and Mary smuggled their baby, Jesus, out of Bethlehem under the cover of darkness to save their son from infanticide under King Herod. Some brave believers helped Saul escape by lowering him in a basket through an opening in the city wall to protect him from being assassinated in Damascus.

When my mother-in-law was a girl growing up on a dairy farm in Holland, her family hid Jews during the holocaust. She remembers Nazi soldiers coming to their farm looking for Jews. She said her parents pretended the Jewish children were their own, while the Jewish parents hid under the hay in the barn. Such bravery!

I pray that, like these brave Christians before me, Jesus will give me the courage to always obey God by standing up for what's right in His eyes. —CASSANDRA TIERSMA

FAITH STEP: *Ask Jesus to help you to always trust Him and obey Him as your Authority. Thank Him for all the Christian martyrs that have risked their lives for the cause of Christ.*

WEDNESDAY, NOVEMBER 23

When he brings out his own sheep, he goes before them; and the sheep follow him, for they know his voice. John 10:4 (NKJV)

NEVER AGAIN WILL I DYE a twelve-year-old's—or anyone else's—hair purple.

When my granddaughter, Grace, asked if I'd dye her hair violet, I said, "Sure!" I'd been dying my own hair since I was thirty-five. That was—*ahem*—several decades ago. I could manage this tiny task. Ha.

An hour later, when I finally finished applying the purple dye into her scalp and down her thick locks, I sighed and looked around.

My sea green bathroom was now green and violet. The floor was dotted, the sink splattered, and worst of all, my hands were covered. Although the directions said to use gloves, I thought I was experienced enough to go without. Now I was a mess. And I was preaching the next day!

I had to do an online search for how to remove hair dye from skin. Dishwashing liquid and baking soda took most of it off. I used the remainder left under my fingernails as a sermon illustration.

"Always follow the directions," I said, and held up my Bible. I told the congregation that just as the makers of purple hair color knew what they were doing when they included gloves with their product, Jesus knows what will work best for our lives. All we have to do is read His instructions and follow them.

I could have avoided my purple mess—and many other messes in my lifetime—if I'd only practiced what I preached: Follow the directions. —JEANETTE LEVELLIE

FAITH STEP: *Place a drop of food color in both palms of your hands. Every time you look at the stains today, ask Jesus to help you follow His leading.*

THANKSGIVING DAY, THURSDAY, NOVEMBER 24

I will make every effort to see that after my departure you will always be able to remember these things. 2 Peter 1:15 *(NIV)*

THERE WAS A FESTIVE AIR in the small room filled with wrapping paper, ribbon, bows, and countless bags stuffed with gifts. Lively gospel music played in the background as five of us chattered away while we busily wrapped toys, clothing, and games to give away to families for my church's massive community holiday outreach.

I had decided to volunteer on this particular November afternoon to honor my father, who had passed away exactly a year ago on Thanksgiving Day. Dad loved to bless others, so there was no better way for me to spend the first anniversary of his Homegoing than by volunteering for this project.

Dad set an example of giving his time and talents to the church and its people. He loved the Lord and taught his children to do the same. My father delighted in spending time with his family, and we often heard him say, "Precious memories," whenever he recalled an occasion like Thanksgiving that made him smile. He wanted us to also remember those good times—and we do, even though he is no longer physically with us.

Peter told the first-century Christians that he, too, wanted them to remember all that he had taught them—his words of encouragement as well as his admonishments—especially the truths about Jesus. He also wanted them to stand firm in their faith. My dad, like Peter, desired the same for those he loved. And for that I will be eternally thankful. —BARBRANDA LUMPKINS WALLS

FAITH STEP: *Write down special memories and truths about Jesus for which you are thankful. Include them in your Thanksgiving prayers.*

FRIDAY, NOVEMBER 25

*My soul will find joy in the LORD and be joyful about
his salvation. Psalm 35:9 (GW)*

MY FRIEND ASKED IF I had been living under a rock. She'd just mentioned binge-watching a television show with her teenage daughter. My response had been "Who's Marie Kondo?" Later, a quick online search filled me in about the tidying expert known around the world through her bestselling books and popular show. In her own words, Marie's goal is to help people "transform their cluttered homes into spaces of serenity and inspiration." I felt encouraged by her short list of common-sense rules for keeping a house in order. Her approach recognizes the connection between our environment and our emotional condition. Marie urges her clients to evaluate whether to keep or discard an item by asking themselves if it sparks joy.

When you think about it, having a daily quiet time is a way to declutter the mind and keep it tidy. As I focus on God's Word and prayer, His Spirit realigns my priorities. I confess any sins nagging at my conscience and receive forgiveness. I turn over any burdens weighing me down into Jesus's capable hands. I submit my desires and personal agenda to His perfect will for my life. As I talk with Him about the day ahead, He gives me clarity of mind that helps me discern what most needs to get done. The more I learn about what needs to be discarded from my mind and my life, the more room I'll have for my Savior to fill with His joy and peace.
—DIANNE NEAL MATTHEWS

FAITH STEP: *Each time you notice a negative emotion invade your mind today, stop and tell Jesus one way that He sparks joy in your life.*

SATURDAY, NOVEMBER 26

We love him, because he first loved us. 1 John 4:19 (KJV)

WATCHING A NEWBORN GROW INTO a toddler has been such a lesson in wonder. The child goes from no skills to many. From an unformed personality to recognizable uniqueness. From grunts and gurgles to words and room-lighting smiles. From an involuntary tightening of her hand around my finger to intentionally leaning forward for a kiss. What wonder!

Not every grandparent has the privilege of grandkids who live nearby. I'm constantly grateful that my husband and I—Grandpa and Grammie—are given opportunities to watch our youngest grandchild grow as we care for her when her parents' work schedules overlap.

From the day I first held her in the hospital, every time I've had the opportunity, I've sung "Jesus Loves Me" softly in her ear. Whatever subliminal or imprinting messages a newborn can absorb, I wanted to make sure one of the first things she heard—and to this day hears when we're together—are the most important truths she needs to know: that Jesus loves her, that she can trust the Bible to tell her the truth, and that Jesus has His eye on her and her heart is in the palm of His loving Hand.

I don't care what preschool she gets into someday. It doesn't matter to me how the trajectory of her block-stacking and fine-motor skills predict what college she's best suited for, if college at all. But she needs to know—all children need to know—this immutable truth: Jesus loves them. It can change everything. It changed everything for me when I didn't just hear it with my ears but heard it with my heart. —CYNTHIA RUCHTI

FAITH STEP: *Sing that familiar children's chorus to yourself today. Bolster your courage with the reminder of His love for you.*

FIRST ADVENT SUNDAY, NOVEMBER 27

After Jesus was born in Bethlehem in Judea, during the time of King Herod, Magi from the east came to Jerusalem and asked, "Where is the one who has been born king of the Jews? We saw his star when it rose and have come to worship him." Matthew 2:1–2 (NIV)

LAST NIGHT MY HUSBAND AND I stood outside, bundled in our jackets. He slipped an arm around my shoulders as we took in the sky show, our breath forming tiny "puff clouds." Stars above twinkled and glistened like a blanket of crystal. Could I be gazing at the very star that portended Jesus's arrival? Conversation fell silent as we contemplated the sight.

Far away and long ago, a new star appeared in the sky that marked the birth of the King of kings. The wise men had heard the prophecies surrounding His birth, as told in Numbers 24:17 and Isaiah 60:3, and they heeded those words. They set out on a two-year mission, traveling only at night. It couldn't have been easy. Their hope for the future fueled the journey.

As the heavens dazzled my eyes, I reflected on the dreams caught up in that particular star and all it represented. In Revelation 22:16, Jesus tells us He is "the bright Morning Star" (NIV).

I am blessed. I don't need to cross deserts, craning my neck as I seek direction. I have Jesus guiding me all day, every day. His glory fills the celestial skies, even as His divine hope fills my heart.

—HEIDI GAUL

FAITH STEP: *Spend a few minutes tonight to enjoy the stars above and thank Jesus for the blessing of His special star.*

MONDAY, NOVEMBER 28

---

*He said, "Come." So Peter got out of the boat and walked
on the water and came to Jesus. Matthew 14:29 (ESV)*

THE TIPS OF MY SKIS hung over the ledge of a small cliff into a steep
chute. I watched my son ski over the edge and down the mountain.
I've done this before, I thought. Yet fear gripped me as my confidence diminished. All I needed to do was take a leap of faith and
push myself over that little ledge. I didn't *have* to do it, but I knew
I would be disappointed if I didn't. So, I took a deep breath and
pushed with my poles. My skis went over the ledge, and my body
followed. Immediately, my confidence increased, and I experienced
the joy of doing something I love.

Often, I desire confidence first and assume courage will follow.
But what if courage comes before confidence? Consider Peter, who
must have been terrified when Jesus asked him to come join Him
on the water. Peter couldn't have confidence because walking on
water had never been done. Yet he courageously took a leap of faith
and stepped out of the boat toward Jesus. Then Peter walked on
water! But when he looked at the wind and the storm, taking his
eyes off Jesus, he lost his confidence and began to sink. Peter cried
out and Jesus rescued him. Jesus is always willing to extend His
hand to help when we take courageous steps toward Him.

I want to always be brave and take a leap of faith and *then* experience confidence. If I mess up, it's okay—I'll just reach out for Jesus's
strong hand. —JEANNIE BLACKMER

FAITH STEP: *What's a courageous step you can take today toward something
Jesus wants you to do?*

TUESDAY, NOVEMBER 29

I am forgotten as though I were dead; I have become like broken pottery. Psalm 31:12 (NIV)

MY ELDERLY NEIGHBOR KEEPS A small china vase on the windowsill above her kitchen sink. It's obviously been broken and glued back together, as there's a tiny triangular gap from a missing piece.

Tucked inside the little vessel is a note justifying why she's kept the seemingly useless item all these years. Her explanation begins with these words: "This charming little pitcher is flawed but still worthy..." She says its graceful design makes her smile every time she sees it.

I identify with that charming little pitcher because I'm also flawed. David, the psalmist, wrote Psalm 31 at a low point in his life, a time of distress, grief, and affliction. He felt forgotten and discarded—like broken pottery—worthless in the eyes of friends and neighbors. I've been in a similar state during low times in my life when I didn't feel treasured.

But now when I consider the trinket pronounced "flawed but still worthy," I'm reminded of how Jesus looks upon me, with my own flaws and imperfections. I take comfort knowing that, even with flaws and imperfections, I'm still worthy in the eyes of Jesus. My neighbor couldn't bring herself to discard her lovely little treasure, however flawed. Likewise, Jesus doesn't discard me just because I'm flawed. He sees my flaws and still deems me worthy. He sees us all as His lovely treasure. —CASSANDRA TIERSMA

FAITH STEP: *Do you have a neighbor or a friend who may be feeling forgotten? Ask Jesus to reveal to you a simple way that you can reach out and affirm that neighbor of her worth in the eyes of Jesus.*

WEDNESDAY, NOVEMBER 30

In the same way, faith by itself, if it is not accompanied
by action, is dead. James 2:17 (NIV)

MY GRANDSON'S DOG, MISTER MIDNIGHT, is a high-spirited Maltipoo. A city dog who's comfortable in gentrified neighborhoods, he is a frequent visitor to doggie salons and pampering daycare spots where he romps with other canine pals.

Midnight had never been around open water until one day when the family visited friends with a lakeside home. He was so excited! Much to everyone's surprise, after a running start, Midnight fearlessly dove off the dock into the lake and started swimming like an Olympic champ. "Look at that guy go!" said my six-year-old grandson, Reed, squealing with delight. I wondered if Midnight knew he could stay afloat before he jumped.

Undoubtedly, the Lord had equipped Midnight to swim. And He has equipped me to do things I'm uncertain about. Unlike Midnight, I haven't always jumped at a calling when it came. As a college freshman, I was unsure that I could lead the university's gospel choir when classmates urged me to become its director. I was unsure about what type of wife and stepmom I'd be when I got married. And I wasn't sure if I would be a patient caregiver to my parents and father-in-law when dementia chipped away their mental abilities. However, Jesus was there to help me successfully navigate the waters of uncertainty so that in each case I would learn to swim and not sink.

Sometimes, like Midnight, I need to just dive right into the seemingly deep water and believe that the Lord will help me. But I won't know until I take a step of faith. —BARBRANDA LUMPKINS WALLS

FAITH STEP: *What is Jesus calling you to do that you feel unprepared or unworthy to do?*

THURSDAY, DECEMBER 1

For the Son of Man came to seek and to save the lost. Luke 19:10 (NIV)

DURING THE HOLIDAYS, I LIKE to watch the classic movie *It's a Wonderful Life*. In this Christmas favorite, all-around good-guy George Bailey is despondent after he runs out of options to save his family's small-town banking business. On the verge of committing suicide on Christmas Eve, George is saved by an angel named Clarence who comes to earth to show the dejected husband, father, and friend what his life—and the lives of others around him—would have been like if he had never been born.

That movie always makes me think about how different my life would be if certain people, such as my parents, husband, favorite teachers and best friends, hadn't been born. Also, how would someone else's life be different without my presence on earth?

Most of all, what would life be like if Jesus hadn't been born? Just the thought of living without the Savior is enough to give me pause. I'd have no hope and no assurance of a heavenly home. The world would be darker and lonelier. And I would be lost in all my sins. None of this sounds like a good place to be.

Thank God that He sent a little baby boy to save me and all of humankind from sin and darkness. Because of Jesus, I have a firm foundation to place my faith. I have a protector, provider, and redeemer. And He has paved the way for me and all believers to have a wonderful life, now and in eternity. —BARBRANDA LUMPKINS WALLS

FAITH STEP: *Meditate on Scripture passages that focus on why Jesus came into the world. How does His coming give you hope?*

FRIDAY, DECEMBER 2

---

*"Behold, the virgin shall be with child, and bear a Son, and
they shall call His name Immanuel," which is translated,
"God with us." Matthew 1:23 (NKJV)*

I LOVE THE WHOLE CHRISTMAS story in the Bible, but if I had to pick
a favorite Christmas verse, Matthew 1:23 would be it. There's just
nothing else that expresses what really happened—what Christmas
means—like "God with us."

We have a tradition in our family that illustrates the beauty of
this concept. Every Christmas Eve, the whole Triple F Ranch family
gathers at my house. We make cookies, turtles, Mexican food, and
mischief of one kind or another. The culminating event is a live
nativity play, which is cast and directed by all of the children. The
best-laid plans are always perfect until the play starts—and then
chaos ensues. Crowns fall off, angels fight for positions, baby Jesus
cries, and Joseph ends up smacking somebody with his staff. It is
always a comedy of errors—a complete zoo. Not unlike life.

Wasn't your spouse perfect before you got married? Your vacation
perfect before you took it? What about retirement? My kids were perfect before I had them. So was my job. In my head, church is perfect,
and so are friendships, and so am I. And then there is what happens
outside my head, in real life. But Jesus enters into the mess, the joy,
the heartache, the accidents, the headaches, the good choices, and
the bad. He is with us through it all. —GWEN FORD FAULKENBERRY

FAITH STEP: *As you decorate your house for Christmas, put baby Jesus somewhere prominent. Every time you see Him, remember the name "Immanuel": God
came to be with you.*

SATURDAY, DECEMBER 3

She gave this name to the LORD who spoke to her: "You are the God who sees me," for she said, "I have now seen the One who sees me."
Genesis 16:13 (NIV)

OUR CHURCH'S ANNUAL CHRISTMAS MUG Exchange is an intimate get-together, attended only by a few women. One Sunday after the annual event (which I had not attended), I asked a friend, "Did you attend the Mug Exchange?"

Nodding, she replied, "Yes, did *you?*"

Baffled, I couldn't comprehend how, if I'd participated in the small gathering, my presence would have gone unnoticed by her. I wanted to blurt, "Am I *that* unmemorable?!" But I said nothing.

That odd exchange perplexed me, until a few years later, when I unwittingly did the same thing to someone else! After a church Christmas choir concert, I asked someone if she had attended. I immediately realized my blunder when I remembered that she was a choir member, and I hadn't even noticed her onstage!

After that gaffe, Jesus reminded me of what I'd experienced a few years earlier. My friend had not intended to make me feel unnoticed, unseen, and unheard, just as it wasn't my intention to do the same thing to my fellow church member.

It's comforting to know that even though I can't always give others the recognition they desire, there's Someone who always sees us. Jesus never has to ask, "Were you there?" He sees all and hears all. To Jesus, I'm memorable, and so are you. —CASSANDRA TIERSMA

FAITH STEP: *Ask Jesus, "Who's someone that might be feeling unnoticed or forgotten?" Send an encouraging note that recognizes something positive and memorable that you've seen, heard, or noticed about her.*

SECOND ADVENT SUNDAY, DECEMBER 4

For to us a child is born, to us a son is given, and the government will be on his shoulders. And he will be called Wonderful Counselor, Mighty God, Everlasting Father, Prince of Peace. Isaiah 9:6 (NIV)

WE GATHER IN CHURCH TO sing "O Come, O Come, Emmanuel." The hope-filled lyrics welcome Jesus to the world. Like the Israelites long ago, we yearn for His presence.

As I join the others, I'm pulled in different directions. In my mind's eye, I see the sink piled with unwashed dishes and the living room strewn with boxes of Christmas decorations. Pandemonium has overtaken my house—a perfect match for the chaos cluttering my mind. Social engagements, shopping, wrapping…my stomach tightens as I consider the weeks ahead.

Yet my heart is drawn to the way Jesus entered humanity. In the midst of an overcrowded city, under the cover of darkness, He chose a quiet stable to provide his first bed. It didn't make sense to me. *Why Bethlehem, and why during the census? Couldn't He have chosen a better place, a calmer time?*

Then I understand. His divine peace isn't hidden in starry skies or country stables. It's not in the calming of the seas or the healing of the sick. It's in Him. He is peace itself—the Prince of Peace. And His peace lives in me. With Jesus, I can see past the disorder to the gift He gave us all. I smile as we reach the chorus. "Rejoice, rejoice, Emmanuel shall come to thee, O Israel."

God with me. God in me. He's come. And I rejoice. —HEIDI GAUL

FAITH STEP: *Close your eyes and reflect on Jesus. Let His peace cover and fill you. Pray thanks to the Prince of Peace.*

MONDAY, DECEMBER 5

On coming to the house, they saw the child with his mother Mary, and they bowed down and worshiped him. Then they opened their treasures and presented him with gifts of gold, frankincense and myrrh. Matthew 2:11 (NIV)

EVERY DECEMBER I SEE ARTICLES that mention the practice of "regifting," giving someone a gift that someone else has given you. When I thought about it, I realized that's what the wise men did. John 1:3 says that Jesus created all things, which means He created the gold in the earth and the trees that produced the frankincense and myrrh. These men were merely giving back to Jesus what He had created and then allowed them to possess. Traveling a long distance to offer such costly gifts to a child one or two years old from a poor family testified to the deity of Jesus and the fact that He had come not just for the Jewish people but for the whole world.

When the star led the wise men to the house in Bethlehem, they bowed down and worshipped before opening their treasures and presenting their gifts to Jesus. That shows me that one of the best ways I can honor and worship Jesus this Christmas is by offering Him gifts from my own treasures. I can "shop" from what He's entrusted to me and look for ways to present those gifts back to Him: material possessions, natural talents, skills I've learned, wisdom I've gained, as well as time and energy. Anything I've been given can be regifted to Jesus when I use it to love and serve others as He did. Why would I withhold any gift from the One who gave His all for me? —DIANNE NEAL MATTHEWS

FAITH STEP: *Spend some time thinking about the gifts Jesus has entrusted to you. Ask Him to show you ways to give those back to Him.*

TUESDAY, DECEMBER 6

You are all children of the light and children of the day. We do not belong to the night or to the darkness. 1 Thessalonians 5:5 *(NIV)*

I HAVE BEEN DOING A research project to help a writer friend of mine. She is working on a book about Christians who have been martyred in the last century. It is not lighthearted research. There are no funny stories to be found. Most of the people were targeted for their belief in Jesus, for their words of hope and their intolerance to injustice. Their lives were cut short because they refused to do anything other than follow in the footsteps of Jesus.

My research has been both disheartening and hopeful. Disheartening, because so many of our brothers and sisters in the Lord are persecuted. But hopeful, because they continue to recognize the light of Jesus's love at work in their lives. Even in the midst of brutality and chaos, these souls choose Jesus. Over and over and over again. Their lives convict and inspire me at the same time.

This research project has reminded me that Jesus has one purpose for my life: for me to shine the light of His love on those around me. Even when I'm struggling or scared or anxious. He doesn't leave me wrestling in the dark. He rescues me, flooding my heart with the bright hope of salvation. He wants me to share that amazing life-giving light with those who are around me.
—SUSANNA FOTH AUGHTMON

FAITH STEP: *Are you anchored in the hope of Jesus no matter what? Meditate on today's Scripture verse throughout the day. Ask Jesus to let the light of His love penetrate the darkness of the world around you.*

WEDNESDAY, DECEMBER 7

Of the increase of his government and of peace there will be no end. Isaiah 9:7 (ESV)

AS WE ENTER INTO THE season of peace that Christmas brings, I'm reminded of an overachieving peace lily that outgrew every pot I put it in and offered literal shade in a corner of our family room for longer than I can remember.

The peace lily was given in memory of my father. Years ago, the flowers and plants from my dad's funeral overwhelmed our family. After Mom took home the ones she could fit in her car and the foyer of our childhood home, my four siblings and I selected special arrangements or potted plants that held meaning for us. I selected the peace lily. The symbolism spoke of what it was like to have to say a temporary goodbye to a man who had lived his entire life with heaven on his mind and his soul at peace with God.

I attributed the lily's outrageous growth to the sunlight in the family room—or maybe because the plant was too large to ignore, it was watered regularly, unlike my smaller mostly dormant Christmas cactus. But a familiar Christmas season Bible verse adds more to the story. I think the lily was simply responding to its Prince of Peace namesake, about whom Isaiah tells us "of the increase of his government and of peace there will be no end." The plant kept growing because that's what Jesus's peace does. His peace has no end. —CYNTHIA RUCHTI

FAITH STEP: *How is the peace Jesus brings represented in your home? With a plant? A wall-hanging? Or the fragrance of peace you add to the scene?*

THURSDAY, DECEMBER 8

I am leaving you with a gift—peace of mind and heart. And the peace I give is a gift the world cannot give. So don't be troubled or afraid. John 14:27 (NLT)

JESUS TALKS ABOUT FEAR A lot because He knew we would face fear frequently. As a mother of three adventurous sons, I battle fear regularly. For example, one of my sons likes to hike 14ers (mountain peaks with an elevation higher than 14,000 feet) with his friends and watch the sunrise from the top. I know he and his friends are capable and careful, yet I often feel afraid as my mind wanders, imagining worst-case scenarios: a fall, a terrible lightning storm, or an encounter with a mountain lion and her cubs—which has happened.

My two other boys have their own thrill-seeking activities: rock climbing, bowhunting, skiing, mountain biking, and more. As I allow my mind to dwell on the dangers of the activities my sons do for fun, I physically feel fear. My heart races, my hands get sweaty, and my breathing becomes shallow.

Thankfully, I've learned to stop allowing my fearful thoughts to run rampant. Now I replace these thoughts with the truth, the promises Jesus gives. One of the greatest gifts He gives is peace. When I'm afraid, I close my eyes and imagine unwrapping a present. Inside is a gift the world cannot give—peace. My body relaxes and my mind stops racing as I accept the peace Jesus offers. I'm doing my best to not live afraid, and I can only do this because of Jesus and the gift He gives that the world cannot give—a peace that surpasses my understanding. —JEANNIE BLACKMER

FAITH STEP: *Today give yourself the gift of peace that Jesus offers. Write down John 14:27, put it in a box, and wrap it. Unwrap it when needed.*

FRIDAY, DECEMBER 9

These things I have spoken to you, that in Me you may have peace.
In the world you will have tribulation; but be of good cheer,
I have overcome the world. John 16:33 (NKJV)

MY MOTHER HAS BEEN IN my thoughts because this year she would have celebrated her hundredth birthday. She was Norwegian, and both her parents had emigrated to Minnesota from the "old country." Her father, a commercial fisherman, drowned when she was two, leaving her mother to raise six children alone. Mom's life was not easy, but she made the best of it. She depended on Jesus to see her through, always remaining positive.

That is, until she became afflicted with tinnitus, the perception of noise or ringing in the ears. In Mom's case, tinnitus was a symptom of her age-related hearing loss, and it drove her crazy. At first, her tinnitus took the form of loud, thunderous booms that awakened her in the night. Then came the incessant ringing—sometimes louder, sometimes softer—but always there. For the first time, I saw Mom tormented by her circumstances.

Then one day, out of the blue, Mom began to hear music in her ears. Google informed me that Mom had musical tinnitus, a rare form of the condition. She liked being special! Later she told me, "I've been in my prayer closet talking this over with Jesus, and we've decided to enjoy the music." From then on, she did. Sometimes she'd say, "Oh, they're playing 'Where or When,' Dad's and my song." Around Christmas, Mom's music switched to carols. With Jesus's help, Mom made the best of her situation. —PAT BUTLER DYSON

FAITH STEP: *In times of tribulation, ask Jesus to show you how to make the best of things.*

SATURDAY, DECEMBER 10

She brought forth her firstborn Son, and wrapped Him in swaddling cloths, and laid Him in a manger, because there was no room for them in the inn.
Luke 2:7 (NKJV)

I LIVE IN A DIVIDED household. My husband, Hal, always wants a real tree for Christmas. I am fond of artificial evergreens for their convenience. After more than twenty years of marriage, Hal has won the annual tree standoffs.

One recent Christmas, I felt overwhelmed by responsibilities and expectations. The big day was a week away, and we didn't have a tree. I told Hal to forget about finding one. We didn't need it. Hal thought otherwise and said, "I'll get us a tree."

A few days later, I walked into our living room and found that Hal had made good on his promise. There in the corner was a miniature ceramic Christmas tree sitting on top of some boxes that were draped with a tablecloth. This homemade display was wrapped in a single string of colored lights. I called it our Charlie Brown tree—reminiscent of the sapling the *Peanuts* character chose for a holiday celebration—and it made me smile.

Our humble little tree was special, even without all the usual flashy lights, ornaments, and ribbon. It reminded me of Jesus, who also had humble beginnings. Born in a stable surrounded by animals and hay, the Savior of the world entered with no fanfare or bright lights, except for the star that guided the wise men to the manger.

I hope our Charlie Brown tree will be a new tradition, reminding me to focus more on Jesus and less on the holiday hoopla.
—BARBRANDA LUMPKINS WALLS

FAITH STEP: *What can you decrease so that Jesus will increase in your life this holiday season?*

THIRD ADVENT SUNDAY, DECEMBER 11

*An angel of the Lord appeared to them, and the glory of the Lord shone
around them, and they were terrified. But the angel said to them,
"Do not be afraid. I bring you good news that will cause great joy for
all the people. Luke 2:9–10 (NIV)*

I LOOKED AT THE MISHMASH of scraggly people and felt a familiar tug inside. Removing a bill from my wallet, I rolled down the car window. One man hurried closer to claim it before the traffic light changed. As his fingers touched mine, I fought the urge to pull back, but instead of filth, I sensed only a gentle touch. We exchanged a few words.

The homeless—society's lowest rung—live outside day and night, garnering neither trust nor respect. They were outcasts, just like the shepherds tending flocks during Jesus's time. Yet God chose them to receive the first announcement of Jesus's birth. The joy they experienced at that honor must have been immeasurable. And as soon as they'd gathered their wits, they hurried to Bethlehem to find the Lamb of God and share the news with everyone they encountered.

I looked once more in the man's eyes. Gratitude, hope, and happiness spanned the space between us. A moment later, traffic started moving. As I drove off, he called out, "God bless you." I smiled. Blessed indeed! The Good Shepherd had shown me the pleasure of giving a gift—and respect—to someone He loves, somebody not so different from the shepherds of old. The joy was mine. —HEIDI GAUL

FAITH STEP: *Ask Jesus for guidance for ways you can help the homeless community. Whether your gift is food, fellowship, money, or time, reassure these individuals of their worth.*

MONDAY, DECEMBER 12

"And they will call him Immanuel" (which means "God with us.")
Matthew 1:23 (NIV)

IN THIS OLD HOUSE WHERE we live, any renovation project reveals layers of living within these walls. We find treasures in the old insulation when we take down a wall or cut a hole for a larger window. When we replace an outlet, we discover layers of wallpaper underneath all the layers of paint.

I rarely look into my Bible without discovering—or rediscovering—more and more layers. In preparation for Christmas, I've been looking at a promise, which is mentioned two times in Isaiah, that a woman would conceive and bear a son whose name would be called Immanuel (or Emmanuel or Emanuel).

It appears again in the Bible when Matthew 1 quotes one of these Isaiah references. The angel uses that name—Immanuel—to assure Mary's betrothed husband, Joseph, that the baby she carries is truly the Son of God, "God with us."

God often inspired the biblical writers to repeat a theme or concept hundreds of times. "Be strong." "Take courage." "Fret not." But the Greek and Hebrew words for Immanuel are used only three times in the Bible. After the angel's pronouncement to Joseph in a dream, there's no record that anyone walking the earth at the time of Christ called Him by that name. Commentators propose various theories, but I wonder if Jesus as "God with us" is such a life-altering concept that it stands on its own merit. God, the *I Am*. Jesus, the *I Am with You*. —CYNTHIA RUCHTI

FAITH STEP: *As you make your way through this Christmas season, use the pronouncement of Jesus as "God with us," or "I Am with you," to propel you to a deeper understanding of His nearness.*

TUESDAY, DECEMBER 13

Jesus said to her, "Martha, Martha, you are worried and troubled about many things. Only a few things are important, even just one. Mary has chosen the good thing. It will not be taken away from her."
Luke 10:41–42 (NLV)

I'M A MARTHA. I ADMIT it. And never is my "Martha-ness" more apparent than on Christmas morning. If Jesus were here, He'd admonish me, but I can't seem to help myself. I'm up at dawn, rattling pans, getting ready for my family to come for brunch. Sixteen kids and adults descend on us, and they come hungry. I can prepare some food ahead, like banana bread and a breakfast casserole, but cinnamon rolls, sausage biscuits, and blueberry muffins have to be baked at the last minute to make sure they're hot.

Our family loves to give humorous gifts. Year after year, the leopard-print footie pajamas appear. Someone gets an embarrassing framed picture of himself, an ancient flip phone, or fish slippers. Hilarity reigns! Last year I missed out on much of the fun, as I often do, because I was busily making sure everyone had coffee or fresh orange juice or a warm cinnamon roll. I didn't even witness my granddaughter Ana's ecstatic reaction when she opened the designer tennis shoes I'd given her.

By midafternoon, I'd finished cleaning the kitchen, having refused help from anyone. *Jesus, I'm just mad,* I told Him. *Why couldn't I be more like Mary, recognizing what was truly important rather than striving to be a good hostess?* I thought I heard Him whisper, *It's not too late.*

Next Christmas will be different. I'll let people help themselves, and I'll be part of the fun. —PAT BUTLER DYSON

FAITH STEP: *On Christmas Day and throughout the year, ask Jesus to help you determine what is really important.*

WEDNESDAY, DECEMBER 14

Then Simeon blessed them and said to Mary, his mother: "This child is destined to cause the falling and rising of many in Israel, and to be a sign that will be spoken against, so that the thoughts of many hearts will be revealed. And a sword will pierce your own soul too." Luke 2:34–35 (NIV)

CHRISTMAS IS A BEAUTIFUL STORY about how God came to earth as a baby and dwelt among us. We love hearing about the shepherds, angels, and wise men following the star. It's magical. But there are elements we don't hear much about, even though these parts of the story are just as true and, I think, just as important.

Because I've been a mother, imagining Mary's experience has been poignant for me. The line from today's verse—about Simeon telling Mary that her heart will be pierced—doesn't fit the warm fuzzy Christmas narrative. Instead, it highlights the other side of the story, foreshadowing what is to come. In this, we see at least two things: on a grand scale, that Jesus's purpose was to die from the beginning, and on a personal level, that mothering is hard.

The moments when each of my children were born were the happiest moments of my life. But by becoming a mother I also made myself vulnerable to a lot of pain—the pain I'd feel when other people would hurt my children and even the pain I'd feel if I were to lose them. Simeon's words remind me of the core message of Christmas: God understands the human experience, and in Jesus, He came to redeem it all. —GWEN FORD FAULKENBERRY

FAITH STEP: *Read the entire chapter of Luke 2 and ask the Lord to give you fresh eyes. What other things that highlight the humanity of Jesus jump out at you?*

THURSDAY, DECEMBER 15

*Let us lay aside every weight, and the sin which so easily ensnares
us, and let us run with endurance the race that is set before us, looking unto
Jesus, the author and finisher of our faith. Hebrews 12:1–2 (NKJV)*

SOMETIMES I HEAR PEOPLE MARVEL at how they can look back over
their life and see God's hand working out every circumstance for the
best. Yes, I can recall specific answers to prayer. And I can pinpoint
incidents that can be explained only by divine intervention. But to
make a blanket statement like that? Even though I understand God's
sovereignty, it's hard for me to say that I saw God working out everything for the best. Too many events in my past seem haphazard—
they just don't make sense. But the Christmas story gives me hope.

The story of Jesus's early years seems a little disjointed: the trip to
Bethlehem so close to Mary's due date; the sudden overnight flight
to Egypt to escape Herod's murderous rage; and settling down in
Nazareth, a city with a bad reputation. These chaotic details actually fulfilled ancient prophecies about Messiah's birth. That seemingly random visit from the wise men and their costly gifts probably
financed the family's stay in Egypt. From our vantage point in history, it's easier to see how all the pieces fit together perfectly.

Taken separately, some passages in the Bible seem not to make
sense. But all the pages of the Bible put together as a whole tell
the greatest story of all time, with Jesus as its centerpiece. As I see
Him as the center of my life and the author and finisher of my
faith, I can trust that eventually all the details that don't make sense
now will add up to a beautiful story, started and finished by Him.
—DIANNE NEAL MATTHEWS

FAITH STEP: *Think about events in your past that puzzle you. Tell Jesus you
trust Him to put all the pieces together and finish writing your life story.*

FRIDAY, DECEMBER 16

On coming to the house, they saw the child with his mother Mary, and they bowed down and worshiped him. Then they opened their treasures and presented him with gifts of gold, frankincense and myrrh. Matthew 2:11 (NIV)

BEFORE MY KIDS MARRIED, I assumed that someday, when they were on their own, they'd want to celebrate Christmas Day together at our home. They had grown up opening presents early Christmas morning and then enjoying a brunch of bacon and pancakes served with ice cream and fruit toppings. Following brunch, we played table games as the aroma of a turkey roast filled the kitchen. We always invited guests—the more the merrier. Who wouldn't want to continue that tradition? My assumptions proved wrong within months of my first child's wedding.

My kids have tried to establish their own traditions, while balancing time with both sides of the family. This has become more challenging as everyone's circumstances have changed over time. It's now apparent that, barring a Christmas miracle, we'll never spend December 25th together again. We've compromised by gathering at one of their homes a couple of weekends prior.

At first, I felt disappointed. Maybe even a bit cheated. But working through my emotions led me to an "aha" moment: I'd placed more importance on celebrating family festivities on a specific calendar day than on celebrating the Christ child.

Determining to worship Jesus rather than the traditions surrounding His birth has helped me release my expectations. Even though my immediate family can't be together on Christmas Day, we are together in spirit, worshipping Jesus and thanking Him for the gift of hope He gives to all who place their faith in Him. —GRACE FOX

FAITH STEP: *Light a candle. Reflect on the beauty of Jesus, whose birth we celebrate this season.*

SATURDAY, DECEMBER 17

*Do not seek revenge or bear a grudge against anyone among your people,
but love your neighbor as yourself. I am the LORD. Leviticus 19:18 (NIV)*

EVERY YEAR, I BAKE SCORES of Christmas cookies for friends and
neighbors. They've come to expect them! This year I agonized over
one customary recipient. Should I take cookies to my next-door
neighbors?

On prior holidays, our neighbors had brought us their traditional Indian Christmas dessert, and I'd given them my homemade
Christmas cookies. We were cordial, if not close. That was before the
falling-out we'd had over a tall cypress tree the neighbors had planted
that blocked our property's view. My husband, Jeff, and our neighbor had exchanged angry words. Now we didn't speak.

I felt certain Jesus would want me to bake and deliver those cookies. But what if our neighbors were insulted and snubbed me? I
didn't want to feel foolish. So I made cookies for dozens of people
but held off on that neighbor's batch.

A devotion I'd read recently reminded me of the greatest gift of
all—Jesus—and urged me to explore the dimensions of His love.
Love. He's all about love!

I went to the kitchen, baked five dozen Christmas cookies and
walked next door to deliver my gift. The housekeeper answered the
door, and I went back home, not knowing how the cookies would
be received but assured I'd done what Jesus expected of me. That
night the doorbell rang, and there stood our neighbors, bearing a
dish of warm, fragrant gulab jamun and saying, Merry Christmas!
Now it truly was. —PAT BUTLER DYSON

FAITH STEP: *Honor Jesus's birth by letting go of a grudge or a hurt you have
been nursing.*

FOURTH ADVENT SUNDAY, DECEMBER 18

We know and rely on the love God has for us. God is love. Whoever lives in love lives in God, and God in them. 1 John 4:16 (NIV)

MY FAMILY IS GATHERED AROUND the table for a holiday dinner. My husband's eyes, full of mischief, follow me while I serve the food. At the opposite end of the table, my son-in-law smiles, his face alight as he glances at my daughter. I lock eyes with my only child, our mutual love crossing the table and welling in my heart. We bow our heads, giving thanks to God for the food and our blessed Savior. And we rejoice in the warmth of this circle of love.

Looking at my family makes me think of another family—Mary, Joseph, and the precious baby Jesus. Great love was shared through their obedience, and many different types of love were demonstrated. I learn so much from their story. Mary obeyed God's request and was gifted with the priceless love known by only mothers. Joseph cared so deeply for his fiancée that he set aside the respectability of his previous life to wed her. Together they forgave those that condemned them and loved beyond the pain. And as they raised Jesus into adulthood, they knew the perfect love of our Lord intimately.

The words used to describe the bond Jesus's family shared define my closest relationships: *rejoicing, laughter, pain, forgiveness, trust, patience, loyalty, eternity.* I'm blessed to see Him in so many people in so many ways. I live in love. —HEIDI GAUL

FAITH STEP: *List various ways God taught love through Jesus's family. Find new ways to share love with your dearest family and friends.*

MONDAY, DECEMBER 19

*Neither the world above nor the world below—there is nothing in all creation
that will ever be able to separate us from the love of God which is ours
through Christ Jesus our Lord. Romans 8:39 (GNT)*

I'M A "MESSY-ANIC" (MESSY, ABSENTMINDED, Normal-ish, Imperfect,
Creative) person. I coined that acronym because cluttery, scatterbrained, nonconforming, and flawed creative just sounded too
embarrassing! But I admit…my house is messy. I can't function
without to-do lists, calendars, planners, reminders, timers, and a
clock (or two) in every room. I'm a work in progress, never quite
measuring up to my own ideal or best intentions. Nevertheless, the
Holy Spirit continually inspires me with a surplus of creative ideas,
more than enough to enact in one lifetime.

Can you relate to any of this? Are you, in some way or another,
a fellow messy-anic person? If so, you're in good company. Because
Jesus has a heart for messy, flawed people. When He walked the
earth, Jesus hung out with imperfect people with blemished reputa-
tions. People who'd blown it a time or two. He welcomed, healed,
forgave, and loved those who were considered defective or inferior.

I used to believe my messy-anic traits disqualified me from answering God's calling on my life. But once I fully understood that Jesus
loves to use imperfect people to do His will, I no longer let those
messy-anic traits hold me back. I love how Jesus embraces not only
the clean and tidy folks, but also the incorrigibly messy-anic ones as
well! —CASSANDRA TIERSMA

FAITH STEP: *No matter how messy, scattered, imperfect, or flawed you may
sometimes feel, remember: There is no mess, flaw, or imperfection that can
separate you from the love of Jesus. Spend some time in prayer, talking to Jesus
about your messy-anic self. Thank Him for loving you anyway.*

TUESDAY, DECEMBER 20

You will be enriched in every way so that you can be generous on every occasion, and through us your generosity will result in thanksgiving to God. 2 Corinthians 9:11 (NIV)

DURING A SMALL-GROUP MEETING WITH couples from our church, we witnessed a miracle. As we sat in the host couple's home, the husband, who had been unemployed for eight months, shared how he felt peace because he trusted God would provide. While he was speaking, the doorbell rang. His wife went to see who it was. When she returned, she had tears in her eyes. She had answered the door and found an envelope on the doorstep with a big sign that said, "God bless!" She opened the envelope, and inside were lots and lots of one-hundred-dollar bills. We were all astonished! We praised God together and gave thanks for His much-needed provision at just the right time.

Jesus encouraged generous giving. He praised the courageous widow who gave all she had (Mark 12:41–44), and the Bible says, "God loves a cheerful giver." (2 Corinthians 9:7, NIV). Jesus gave without limits until He finally gave His life. The experience in our friend's home not only reminded me to be a generous giver but to know that generosity has a ripple effect of thanksgiving on those who receive. All of us praised God for how He had provided miraculously and exactly at the moment our friend was talking about his trust in God's provision. Generosity creates great joy and thanksgiving in the lives of those it touches. Experiencing this encourages me to be boldly bighearted in my own giving. —JEANNIE BLACKMER

FAITH STEP: *Plan a surprise anonymous gift today for someone you know is in need, and trust Jesus will use your gift for His glory.*

WEDNESDAY, DECEMBER 21

We do not lose heart. Though outwardly we are wasting away,
yet inwardly we are being renewed day by day. 2 Corinthians 4:16 (NIV)

FOR YEARS, WHEN UNPACKING CHRISTMAS decorations, my husband, David, and I talked about replacing our ancient artificial tree. We'd remember how, late one season long ago, we'd been blessed to find one still available. We laughed at the way the branches resembled not only pines but firs as well, with needles of every length and style represented. I love the absurd, so of course, I'm attached to this tree.

But this year, we held back from any conversation about a new tree. It seemed disloyal, as if we were rejecting an old friend. It was maybe as old as we are, in "artificial tree" years. We looked past the lone branch that can't be connected at all anymore, past the frayed threads struggling to hold the tips in place. Instead, we placed extra ornaments in the bare spots and showcased the good sections.

Jesus was born, died, and rose again to erase my sins and give me new life. He did this so that every year, every week, and every day, I might wake up new, clean, and pure in His sight. Through Him I can enjoy life fully, despite my frayed bits and missing pieces. Jesus hides my flaws and decorates my days, filling them with His endless love. He does the same for each of us.

I'm privileged to play a small part in Jesus's never-ending Christmas story, one full of hope, peace, and love. I stand tall, beautiful, and complete, just as I am. I am unique and irreplaceable. —HEIDI GAUL

FAITH STEP: *Consider the care you took decorating your tree, enhancing its beauty. Disregard your weaknesses. Instead focus on your strengths to showcase Jesus's glory.*

THURSDAY, DECEMBER 22

---

*Don't be afraid, little flock, for your Father has been pleased
to give you the kingdom. Luke 12:32 (NIV)*

I SHOPPED THE MALL, SPURRED by the excitement and joy of the
Christmas season. Moving from store to store, I searched for the
perfect gifts to delight my loved ones. Elves, penguins, and reindeer
decor greeted me, and the scent of peppermint filled the air. Beside
the escalator, a trio dressed in Victorian-style clothes sang carols.

Then I approached Christmas Land, where a line of little ones waited
to present Santa Claus their wish lists. On an oversized chair sat the old
saint himself. His red suit, stocking cap, and long white beard brought
back warm childhood memories of the requests I had made and the
encouragement he had offered. And there was a candy cane to boot!

But the toddler on Santa's lap wasn't gazing into those kind,
bespectacled eyes. Her hands were balled into fists, and she wailed
loudly. I thought, *She's afraid. She doesn't know he wants to help her
and make her happy. This could be a wonderful experience if only she
would trust him.*

Like a package dropped down the chimney, landing smack on my
head, it hit me—for so long Jesus had invited me into the safety and
warmth of His love, but I had instead scrambled off His lap, crying
and unwilling to trust Him.

When a different child hopped onto Santa's lap, his eyes glittering
with hope, I saw a reflection of my current relationship with Jesus. I
now trust Him with the desires of my heart and accept the blessings
He's chosen for me—yesterday, today, and always. —HEIDI GAUL

FAITH STEP: *Watch children interacting with Santa. Are they fussy or happy as
they share their dreams with Him? Pray that you'd have the innocent trust of a
child and accept the gift of being in Jesus's kingdom.*

FRIDAY, DECEMBER 23

On coming to the house, they saw the child with his mother Mary, and they bowed down and worshiped him. Then they opened their treasures and presented him with gifts of gold, frankincense and myrrh. Matthew 2:11 (NIV)

I'VE SPENT THIS MORNING WRAPPING presents. The sofa was blanketed in items awaiting my attention, and the dining table stood awash in paper and ribbon. It was a scene of happy chaos: cookies in the oven, a scented candle burning on the hearth, and Christmas music playing in the background.

As I prepared gifts for loved ones, I recalled some of my family's earliest Christmases. Simple gifts seemed to please my daughter most, such as a box of brightly colored feathers, a stack of felt, or popsicle sticks.

Why did those inexpensive presents bring my child such joy when just a foot away lay an expensive popular doll? Perhaps because those simple gifts required her to think, act, and create—to make her world a better place. Something I desire to do as I follow Jesus.

After almost all the wrapping had been completed, one small empty box remained. I wrapped it and placed it alongside the others under the tree. This gift is special, though, because it's for Jesus. It may seem empty, but as I covered it in festive paper, I contemplated how it's really not. This container is filled with all the plans I have for the coming year that I hope will bring Jesus glory—actions I can take, people I can help, and ways I can make His world a better place.

This symbolic gift won't ever need to be opened. Jesus knows my heart, my intentions, and my love for Him. It's for me to remember...and to keep giving. —HEIDI GAUL

FAITH STEP: *What can you offer Jesus this year? Create your own gift for Jesus...and remember.*

CHRISTMAS EVE, SATURDAY, DECEMBER 24

Love is patient, love is kind. It does not envy, it does not boast, it is not proud. It does not dishonor others, it is not self-seeking, it is not easily angered, it keeps no record of wrongs. Love does not delight in evil but rejoices with the truth. It always protects, always trusts, always hopes, always perseveres. 1 Corinthians 13:4–7 (NIV)

OUR FAMILY SHARES HOLIDAYS, SPENDING Christmas Eve at my home and Christmas Day at my daughter and son-in-law's. On Christmas Eve, after our meal, we open gifts and then end the evening with a candlelight church service. I always look forward to our celebration of Jesus's birth.

But tonight, I sit on the couch and reflect. At some point, each of us has encountered trials, whether through infidelity, abuse, jealousy, pride, lying, anger, or unforgiveness. We've stumbled our way to living, not just reading, the words of 1 Corinthians 13. We're human. It's been a long road, one that we've walked each step with Jesus at our side.

Contemplating on Jesus, Mary, and Joseph, I don't see trials and egos at play. In complete submission to God, Mary endured shame by bearing the honor and sacred burden of Jesus. Joseph accepted dishonor by wedding Mary, though it put an end to his respectability. Jesus's earthly parents were special—selfless and obedient. They understood what love truly entails, both the hard and the easy.

This quiet night is full of hope and love. I thank God for the sacred gift of His Son. And as I await tomorrow, when I'll bask in the blessings of my faith, all my thanks go to the tiny baby Jesus asleep, abed in the straw. —HEIDI GAUL

FAITH STEP: *Meditate on 1 Corinthians 13. Insert Jesus's name and then yours. Give thanks.*

CHRISTMAS DAY, SUNDAY, DECEMBER 25

. . . and she gave birth to her firstborn, a son. She wrapped him in cloths and placed him in a manger, because there was no guest room available for them. Luke 2:7 (NIV)

CHRISTMAS MORNING CAME TOO QUICKLY. I rose early, planning to spend a few minutes alone with the Lord. I poured a cup of coffee and struggled to reflect on Him, but my thoughts raced here and there. Praying calmed me, and my eyes settled on our nativity. Jesus's first bed was a feeding trough, surrounded by livestock. I wondered, *Was He born in a stable or a cave?* Did it matter? Not at all. What mattered was that He came to those who were His own, but they did not receive Him (John 1:11).

But as I stared at the manger, tears welled in my eyes. The humbleness of the space, the lack of even the simplest of comforts—and the complete vulnerability of that tiny baby resting in the straw. I ached to pick Him up. Reaching for the porcelain figurine, I grasped it in one hand. It was as if my eyes were opened to His holiness.

I returned the figurine to its spot and finished my coffee. In the bustle of this season, only one gift matters—Jesus. His love and forgiveness are ready, waiting in the form of an infant asleep in a stable. On this special day, I hold Baby Jesus close in my heart.
—HEIDI GAUL

FAITH STEP: *Steal a few moments this morning to meditate on Baby Jesus. Cradle His tiny image in your heart throughout the day and give thanks.*

MONDAY, DECEMBER 26

I will give them a crown to replace their ashes, and the oil of gladness to replace their sorrow, and clothes of praise to replace their spirit of sadness. Isaiah 61:3 (NCV)

MY HUSBAND GAVE ME A great dress for Christmas—a long-sleeve tent dress in an eye-catching, bright-red African print. It even has pockets and can double as a long jacket! I receive lots of compliments when I wear it. I love the dress because it's comfortable and beautiful and inspires happy feelings.

Wouldn't it be wonderful to have garments in your wardrobe that you could put on whenever you feel down in the dumps and not up to doing life? I know I would. What would be even better? Not just clothes that would make me feel and look good, lifting my spirits, but garments that would inspire me to praise Jesus no matter what.

The prophet Isaiah told the Israelites that the Lord would once again give them joy, gladness, and a spirit of praise to replace their sadness, when they were held captive in Babylon. There are times when I feel that I'm held captive—by fear, burdens, anger, sorrow, or frustration. It is during those moments that I have to remind myself to seek comfort, strength, and courage through praying to and connecting with Jesus, the supplier of all my needs. That's when I ask the Lord to help me dig deep to replace negativity with praise and to trust Him to see me through.

I know I have a garment of praise in my spiritual closet. I just have to put it on. —BARBRANDA LUMPKINS WALLS

FAITH STEP: *Feeling low? How can you put on a garment of praise to replace your weak spirit? Take a praise break with one of your favorite Christian songs.*

TUESDAY, DECEMBER 27

Who, being in very nature God, did not consider equality with God something to be used to his own advantage; rather, he made himself nothing by taking the very nature of a servant, being made in human likeness. And being found in appearance as a man, he humbled himself by becoming obedient to death—even death on a cross! Philippians 2:6–8 (NIV)

I LOVE A GOOD BARGAIN, especially after a holiday. And especially if that holiday is Christmas. My husband, Kevin, and I will peruse the clearance aisles, looking for presents we can give next Christmas, new gift bags, and 75-percent-off dark chocolate. Yes!

When it comes to shoes, however, I always shop for the best brands. Having a steel plate in one foot and knees that act ornery in cold weather, I'm willing to pay high prices. Even if I have to save up for months, the cost is worth the comfort.

Oh, how I love Jesus for the immeasurable price He paid to buy my freedom from sin: His own life. His position in heaven. Even the sweet fellowship of His Father. When He cried from the cross, "My God, my God, why have you forsaken me?" (Matthew 27:46), the veil of the temple ripped in two, welcoming me—and every lost soul—into God's throne room.

Jesus paid full price for our friendship with the Father. Ours is no clearance-aisle Christianity. No discounted deliverance. Because we are worth everything to God, He gave us the most expensive gift ever: His very own Son, the center of His heart. —JEANETTE LEVELLIE

FAITH STEP: *Give an after-Christmas gift to Jesus today. Whether it's a beloved possession given to a needy friend or some valuable time, thank God in a tangible way for His most expensive gift to you.*

WEDNESDAY, DECEMBER 28

Set your mind on things that are above, not on things that are on earth.
Colossians 3:2 (ESV)

AFTER CHRISTMAS, MY HUSBAND, ZANE, and I decided to do a five-day detox because of all the unhealthy foods we indulged in during the holidays. I found a plan that included various protein powders, with a complete shopping list and day-to-day menu to follow. *Easy,* I thought.

But it was anything but easy. Most of the day, my thoughts were consumed with what I wasn't allowed to eat or with how hungry I felt or with imaginations of all of the delicious foods I would be able to eat after the detox was over. In fact, I was so focused on what I could *not* eat that it was a challenge to think about anything else. I was experiencing what some people call a "scarcity mentality." My thought life centered on what I lacked rather than on my abundant blessings. I realized that an attitude of lack frequently extended into my everyday life, beyond just food. In Dallas Willard's book *Life Without Lack,* he wrote, "What we place our minds on brings that reality into our lives. If we place our minds on God, the reality of God comes into our lives."

The food detox was difficult, but I'm grateful I did it because it caused me to really look at my thought life. It urged me to make a constant effort to turn my thoughts to Jesus, especially when I find myself dwelling on what I think I lack. Thankfully, as I set my mind on Jesus, I have everything I need. —JEANNIE BLACKMER

FAITH STEP: *What's occupying your thoughts? Meditate on Colossians 3:2 and ask Jesus to help you keep your thoughts set on Him.*

THURSDAY, DECEMBER 29

*Immediately Jesus reached out his hand and caught him. "You of little
faith," he said, "why did you doubt?" Matthew 14:31 (NIV)*

IN THE PAST YEARS, MY neck and back have seized in crippling pain
multiple times. My doctor noticed a pattern: it happened each time
I faced significant stress. It hit when the delayed move-in date to
our new house caused issues with switching our kids' school district.
When our van died between Christmas and New Year's, shocking us
with an unexpected repair bill. And when my dad suffered two life-
threatening strokes. Rushing to him meant dropping everything at
home and driving more than fourteen hours through the Rockies
in winter.

I'd prayed about these concerns when they came, and I
acknowledged Jesus's invitation to cast my burdens on Him. But
knotted muscles indicated that I was still carrying the burdens.
Subconsciously, I was afraid that Jesus wouldn't work out the details
of our move, provide for repairs, and care for my family and me
while I traveled and cared for my dad.

"Why did you doubt?" Jesus asked after Peter jumped from
the boat into the wild waves and then began to sink. Peter didn't
answer, but I suspect fear was the culprit. Fear of the waves. Fear of
his ability to stay atop them. Fear of Jesus's ability to save him from
drowning.

Nowadays when I'm under stress and my neck and back develop
acute pain, I ask myself, *Am I doubting Jesus? If so, in what way, and
why?* The answer's always revealing. —GRACE FOX

FAITH STEP: *Are you carrying a burden too heavy for you to bear? Cup your
hands as though holding the burden and offer it to Jesus. He will carry it for you.*

FRIDAY, DECEMBER 30

The Spirit you received does not make you slaves, so that you live in fear again; rather, the Spirit you received brought about your adoption to sonship. And by him we cry, "Abba, Father." The Spirit himself testifies with our spirit that we are God's children. Romans 8:15–16 (NIV)

MY HUSBAND, KEVIN, TAUGHT ME several techniques for memorizing Scripture. Kev has memorized thirteen entire books of the Bible. While I haven't done that, I did learn Romans 8. (It took me months!) This chapter of Scripture is one of my favorites.

A few mornings ago, while preparing for work, I recited this uplifting chapter to myself. I came to verse 15, where the apostle Paul tells us that the Spirit gives us the right to call God "Abba."

Abba is the Aramaic word for "Daddy." This name denotes an intimate relationship filled with trust and love. It's the same word Jesus used in the Garden of Gethsemane a few hours before His death. He said, "Abba, Father... everything is possible for you. Take this cup from me. Yet not what I will, but what you will" (Mark 14:36, NIV).

Since I knew this chapter by rote, I'd always breezed through the words and babbled them without thinking—until that day when worries about my family members smothered my joy. As I recited, the anguish in my heart rose up and I cried out, "Abba, Father!" I threw myself on God's mercy. A sweet, supernatural peace filled my heart.

Kevin, at work in his den down the hall, heard my cry. He said, "Honey, are you all right? It sounded like you were in pain."

"I'm okay now," I said. "Just talking to Abba."—JEANETTE LEVELLIE

FAITH STEP: *If you're wrestling with a worry, imitate Jesus's example and cry out to God as your Daddy, asking Him to rescue you.*

New Year's Eve, Saturday, December 31

*I know the plans I have in mind for you, declares the L*ORD*; they are plans for peace, not disaster, to give you a future filled with hope.*
Jeremiah 29:11 (CEB)

TODAY IS THE PERFECT TIME to look ahead and think about what I want to accomplish in the upcoming year: new goals and dreams, healthier habits, new activities. I pull the old calendar that's full off the wall to make room for the new empty calendar. Today is also a good time to clear space in my heart and mind to make room for the new ways God wants to work in my life.

First, I take inventory of what I might need to let go. Do I need to kick my habit of worry to make room for more prayer time with Jesus? Am I completely ready to release my regret over past mistakes to clear space for the joy of abiding in His love and forgiveness? Can I replace the fears that hold me back with greater courage and boldness in serving Him?

No matter how insignificant I feel, Jesus has plans for my new year. *Big plans.* Maybe not big in the world's eyes, like winning a lottery. Rather His plans—serving Jesus in new ways, understanding His Word more deeply, knowing Jesus more intimately—are big because they have eternal value. As I celebrate the eve of a new year, I trust in His exciting hope-filled plans for me. —DIANNE NEAL MATTHEWS

FAITH STEP: *Today ask Jesus to help you make two lists: "Out with the Old" and "In with the New." On your new calendar, jot down a word or phrase for each month related to something Jesus wants to build in your life.*

ABOUT THE AUTHORS

SUSANNA FOTH AUGHTMON is an author and humor writer in Idaho. She is the mother of three fantastic teenage boys, Jack, Will, and Addison. Susanna is also wife to Scott, a pastor and writer who makes her laugh every day. Susanna's books include *Hope Sings* and *Queen of the Universe*. She loves to use Scripture and personal stories as a way of embracing God's grace and truth every day. Susanna often connects with her readers and fellow Christ followers through her blog, Confessions of a Tired Supergirl, her Facebook page, and speaking engagements.

JEANNIE BLACKMER is an author who lives in Boulder, Colorado. Her most recent books include *Talking to Jesus: A Fresh Perspective on Prayer* and *MomSense: A Common Sense Guide to Confident Mothering*. She's been a freelance writer for more than thirty years and has worked in the publishing industry with a variety of authors on more than twenty-five books. She's also written numerous articles for print and online magazines and blogs. She's passionate about using written words to encourage women in their relationships with Jesus. She loves chocolate (probably too much), scuba diving, beekeeping, a good inspirational story, her family, and being outside as much as possible. She and her husband, Zane, have three adult sons. Find out more about Jeannie on her website at www.jeannieblackmer.com.

PAT BUTLER DYSON lives and writes from her home in Beaumont, on the steamy, hurricane-prone Gulf Coast of Texas. A freelance writer, Pat has written for Guideposts publications for twenty-five years. A former English and special-education teacher, she is also a contributor to the website www.prayersideas.org. For over ten years, Pat has experienced the joy of volunteering at OASIS, a respite program for people with Alzheimer's disease. Pat and her husband, Jeff, celebrating their thirty-ninth anniversary, are the proud parents of five children and grandparents of six. Jeff, a family hardware store owner and business instructor at Lamar University, shares Pat's love of the outdoors, biking, and visiting their little place at the beach in Galveston. In between writing, cycling, and entertaining grandchildren, Pat bakes dozens of cookies, sampling a few but mostly giving them away. This summer, Pat and Jeff are planning a hiking trip to Yosemite, trading the beach for the mountains. Pat feels privileged, once again, to share devotions featuring slices of her life with the readers of *Mornings with Jesus.*

ISABELLA CAMPOLATTARO (formerly Yosuico) a loves encouraging others with both her everyday and epic life experiences, even while she's preaching to herself. Isabella is a recovering perfectionist who longs for people to be their authentic selves, confident they're different by divine design and fully loved as they are—a truth she only recently grasped herself. She has been contributing to *Mornings with Jesus* since 2018 and is included in several other Guideposts books. Her Bible study *Embracing Life: Letting God Determine Your Destiny* is aimed at helping women navigate challenging life events. With an MS in public relations and management, Isabella is a longtime communications consultant. She and her two boys, Pierce and Isaac, live on Florida's lush Suncoast where she enjoys Jesus, travel, cooking, writing, reading, running, arts and culture, random adventures, deep conversation, the beach, music, and singing. Connect with Isabella at isabellacampolattaro.com, Instagram, Twitter, or Facebook.

GWEN FORD FAULKENBERRY is a mother of four who teaches English at Arkansas Tech University. She lives on a cattle ranch in the mountains of Ozark, Arkansas. Gwen likes to bake sourdough bread, play the piano, and travel. She loves Jesus, her family, and expensive chocolate. Gwen has contributed to *Mornings with Jesus* every year since its inception. She is also the author of numerous novels and devotional books and chronicles her imperfectly beautiful life at www.gwenfordfaulkenberry.com.

GRACE FOX lives on a 48-foot sailboat moored at a marina near Vancouver, British Columbia. She and her husband Gene have shared this teeny space for four years, and they're still best friends! They'll celebrate their fortieth wedding anniversary in February. Grace has been a career global worker for twenty-nine years. In 2007, she and Gene became codirectors of International Messengers Canada, an evangelical mission serving in more than twenty-eight countries. She trains church leaders in the Middle East, and she and Gene lead short-term mission teams to Eastern Europe annually. Grace is the author of ten books. Her latest, *Finding Hope in Crisis*, was released in 2021. She's also a devotional blogger and member of the writing team for First 5, the Bible study app produced by Proverbs 31 Ministries. Grace enjoys speaking at women's events internationally, walking, practicing hospitality on her boat-home, and spending time with her family—three grown kids and eleven grandchildren. Connect with her at www.gracefox.com and www.fb.com/gracefox.author. Learn more about her resources at www.gracefox.com/books.

HEIDI GAUL and her husband share a historic home with their furry family in Oregon's beautiful Willamette Valley. Heidi loves good food, good friends, and good books. When she's not busy with those passions, you'll probably find her hiking, gardening, or planning her next trip. Winner of the 2015 Cascade Award for devotionals, her work can be found in Guideposts' *Every Day with Jesus* and past years of *Mornings with Jesus*, and *Short and Sweet Takes the Fifth* devotionals for *The Upper Room*. Ten *Chicken Soup for the Soul* anthologies carry her stories. She enjoys leading workshops, mentoring fellow wordsmiths at writers' conferences, and speaking to groups about discerning God's direction for our lives. Represented by Jim Hart of Hartline Literary Agency, her current project is *Broken Dreams and Detours: When God's Will Doesn't Match Your Plans*. She'd love to hear from you. Connect with her at www.HeidiGaul.com and www .Facebook.com/HeidiGaulAuthor.

SHARON HINCK loves spending mornings—and all day— with Jesus. When she isn't writing devotions, she pens "stories for the hero in all of us." These are novels of imaginative faith journeys full of adventure and inspiration. Her new series is The Dancing Realms. She enjoys hiking, gardening, choir, teaching an MFA writing class, and speaking to various groups. Her heart is full of people dear to her: her husband, four grown children, three grandchildren, mom and stepdad, and many friends who give her powerful examples of following Jesus each day. She loves visitors at her website sharonhinck.com

PAMELA TOUSSAINT HOWARD is a native New Yorker who currently lives and works in Atlanta, Georgia. After graduating from Fordham University with a degree in communications, Pamela followed in her dad's journalistic footsteps and became a women's magazine editor, then a trade newspaper reporter, and has now written or coauthored eight books with major publishers. Pamela also held the position of media spokesperson with the American Red Cross of Greater New York, and later served as one of their Top 100 health and safety trainers. She currently cohosts a program on "Church Around the Corner" which airs on WGNM-TV and on Facebook Live. Pamela enjoys life with her husband, Andrew, their teenaged son, Andrew Jr., and their calico, Emmy.

JEANETTE LEVELLIE lives in Paris, Illinois, with her pastor husband, Kevin. If you were to peek through the window of their home, you'd be sure to hear "Help me, Jesus!" several times a day. This is Jen's favorite prayer, and she applies it to everything from keeping her temper in check to taming her fiery red hair. Apart from writing for Guideposts publications and a variety of magazines, Jeanette is the author of six inspirational/humor books, including *Hello, Beautiful: Finally Love Yourself Just as You Are,* an interactive devotional for women who need to see themselves through God's eyes. Jeanette is a prolific speaker and recently became an ordained minister. She loves to share her life message of the bottomless grace of Jesus along with her heartfull of humor. Jen proudly wears the hats of wife, mother, grandmother, and #1 spoiler of cats. Her favorite food is kettle corn, which she loves to eat while watching reruns of *Perry Mason* or *Monk* with Kevin. Jeanette would love to connect with you on Facebook, Instagram, and her website, *Hope Splashes,* at www.jeanettelevellie.com.

DIANNE NEAL MATTHEWS started daydreaming about being a writer at age five when she picked up her first chunky pencil and lined tablet. Her fantasy became a reality when she finally attended a writers' conference in her mid-forties. Since then she has written, cowritten, and contributed to nineteen books. Her daily devotionals include *The One Year Women of the Bible* and *Designed for Devotion: A 365-Day Journey from Genesis to Revelation* (a Selah Award winner). Dianne has also published hundreds of articles, guest blog posts, newspaper features, stories for compilation books, and one poem. Since 2012, her favorite writing project each year has been penning a new batch of devotions for *Mornings with Jesus.* She and her husband, Richard, have been married since 1974 and currently live in southwest Louisiana. When she's not writing, Dianne enjoys volunteering at her church, helping with ladies' Bible studies, trying new recipes, knitting—and most of all, FaceTiming with her children and grandchildren who live too far away. She loves to connect with readers through her Facebook author page or website (DianneNealMatthews.com).

CYNTHIA RUCHTI started her career in a chemistry lab, wrote and produced a scripted radio broadcast (slice of life scenes and devotional thoughts) for Christian radio, has written close to three dozen books, and serves as a literary agent, helping other people get their stories out to a reading world. In every endeavor, she's done the only thing she knows to do—say yes to Jesus. His quests are always unexpected, but the adventure is never a disappointment. Her books have garnered many industry awards, but her greatest joy is connecting with readers who have been touched, moved, or inspired by the words she's been given to share. The *Mornings with Jesus* readers are a true treasure for her, providing welcomed responses and the gift of their prayers. Cynthia and her husband live in the heart of Wisconsin, close to their three children and six grandchildren. You can connect with Cynthia at cynthiaruchti.com or hemmedinhope.com.

CASSANDRA TIERSMA is a self-confessed messy-a.n.i.c. (messy, absentminded, normal-ish, imperfect, creative) woman. She is also an author, poet, and professional journalist whose articles, photography, and poetry have been published in multiple newspapers. Her book, *Come In, Lord, Please Excuse the Mess!*, is a guide for spiritual healing and recovery for messy-a.n.i.c. women who struggle with clutter bondage. Blessed with a sense of humor, Cassandra's not afraid to be a fool for Christ, whether writing and performing comedic monologues and song parodies, teaching kids' dance classes, or singing and playing her antique autoharp. With a history as a performance artist, writer, speaker, workshop presenter, and ministry leader, it is Cassandra's mission to bless and encourage women in their faith, so that they can become the full expression of who God created them to be. Cassandra lives with her husband, John, in a small mountain town with the "Best Water On Earth," in the frontier territory of the mythical fifty-first state of Jefferson, where she serves as women's ministry director at the historic little stone chapel that is their church home. Cassandra loves to hear from her readers. You can connect with her by sending an email to Cassandra@CassandraTiersma.com.

BARBRANDA LUMPKINS WALLS is a writer and editor in northern Virginia, where she fights traffic and gets inspiration daily for connecting God's Word to everyday life. Barbranda is the lead essayist for the photography book *Soul Sanctuary: Images of the African American Worship Experience* and serves as the editor for her church's annual Lenten devotional. The former newspaper reporter and magazine editor has written for a number of national publications, including *Guideposts*, *Cooking Light*, and *Washingtonian*. Barbranda and her husband, Hal, enjoy spending time with family, especially their adult son and daughter, son-in-law, and beloved grandson. Connect with her on Twitter @Barbrandaw and Instagram at barbl427.

Scripture Reference Index

Topical Index

A NOTE FROM THE EDITORS

WE HOPE YOU ENJOYED *Mornings with Jesus 2022*, published by the Books and Inspirational Media Division of Guideposts, a nonprofit organization that touches millions of lives every day through products and services that inspire, encourage, help you grow in your faith, and celebrate God's love.

Thank you for making a difference with your purchase of this book, which helps fund our many outreach programs to military personnel, prisons, hospitals, nursing homes, and educational institutions.

We also create many useful and uplifting online resources. Visit Guideposts.org to read true stories of hope and inspiration, access OurPrayer network, sign up for free newsletters, download free e-books, join our Facebook community, and follow our stimulating blogs.

You may purchase the 2023 edition of *Mornings with Jesus* anytime after July 2022. To order, visit Guideposts.org/Shop, call (1-800) 932-2145, or write to Guideposts, PO Box 5815, Harlan, Iowa 51593.